Wounded Dogs
and
Werewolves

Out of a Life of Wreckage

John Agustín Rubio

WESTBOW
PRESS
A DIVISION OF THOMAS NELSON

WestBow Press books may be ordered through booksellers or by contacting:

WestBow Press
A Division of Thomas Nelson
1663 Liberty Drive
Bloomington, IN 47403
www.westbowpress.com
1-(866) 928-1240

ISBN: 978-1-4497-1852-7 (sc)
ISBN: 978-1-4497-1851-0 (hc)
ISBN: 978-1-4497-1853-4 (e)

Library of Congress Control Number: 2011930632

Printed in the United States of America

WestBow Press rev. date: 6/16/2011

ALTHOUGH MY FATHER DIED YOUNG, IT is not like I have ever been or will ever be without him. I am without what I needed that he might have given me had he lived. This work is dedicated to him.

There are certain events that can gash the spirit of a man while yet in the boy and leave him bleeding. And there are certain men who can reach it and will try.

They are a prism through which the events of life pass, casting off the colors of a loving God.

We need to see them. I need to see them. And so I write for you as well.

j.a.r.

Acknowledgements

I'd like to thank Claudia Fahrenthold for her patient attention to detail and loving generosity with her time, Carrie Hartman for her help with the cover, Stephen Curtis, and Jared Feria for his kind words and encouragement. And I owe a special thanks to Pastor Forrest Pershall (Arizona) for being willing and waiting for his assignments when I became one, and to Pastor Ron Griggs (Oregon) whose faith was big enough for both of us. There are others who helped me during this writing who probably aren't even aware of it, and if you suspect that you are among them you probably are. Thank you.

Forward

I FIRST MET JOHN IN THE spring of '07. He attended a men's weekend I was co-leading. He attended a second the following year. My first impression of John was that he was a kind and intelligent man, someone unafraid to peel back the layers of his life, despite how exposed or wounded they may appear to the listener. I could tell he had been through a lot of heartache and pain, but was the kind of man who was really good at inspiring others to hold onto hope despite their circumstances.

Henri Nouwen, when asked to write about Thomas Merton's book, *Life and Holiness*, said, "This is not a book about doctrines or dogmas, but about life in Christ." Nouwen wrote that line nearly fifteen years ago, and yet I can't think of a more fitting description of *Wounded Dogs and Werewolves*. Isn't a life in Christ really about freedom and isn't freedom what we all seek? Yet, so often people lose their way on the path to freedom and don't know where to turn.

The book you are holding does not include a top ten list of secrets to a life of freedom. There is no trace of formulaic thinking here. So why should you read this book? For one simple reason—through the telling of his story, John shows us that freedom is more of a journey than a destination. And the path John takes will certainly be recognizable to the reader willing to trek with him. Weaving humor with tragedy and sorrow with ending joy, John blazes a trail of gut-level honesty and uncertainty that will resonate with readers ready to dig deep into their own humanness and find that small glimmering shred of hope.

The level of candid vulnerability introduced to us through open-minded Christian writers like Donald Miller and Susan Isaacs could be equated to stepping into the shallow end of a pool. For those readers, however, who are ready for deeper waters, John's book will lead the way. He'll even give you a few arm floaties just in case you forget how to doggie paddle.

In the pages that follow, John shares his path to freedom: drunken stupors, heart attacks, prostitute binges, near-drowning accidents, and, most importantly, overwhelming grace and paradigm-shattering forgiveness. The kind of forgiveness we both undeservedly get and should, in return, unselfishly give away.

Jared Feria
Director: In His Fullness, Inc.
Gainesvile, 2011

Introduction

In the year 2004 I attended a conference in Wilmington, Delaware that included speakers on the subject of deliverance and spiritual healing. I was there because I had gotten to the point where I could not go on living the way I had been living the previous thirty-something years.

In the year 1980 I became a Christian and lived the enthusiastic evangelical life of a new child in Christ…that lasted about two years. Then, while still considering myself a Christian, I fell back into my old ways and habits and lived a life pretty completely given over to sin. Life for me during that time was mostly a thrashing about, having what we all considered to be "fun"; reckless affections, drunken episodes lasting days on end, careless and oblivious to the pain I was causing myself and others at the time – and certainly unaware of the pain I was storing up for myself for the future. Looking back I recognize that those years were not just eaten by the locusts, they were fed to them.

By 2004 the spark of the same Holy Spirit that had traveled so far to come and get me all those years earlier in 1980 could not stand anymore, nor could I. But I had no idea what to do. Because I had become part of an on-line Christian support group I came to hear about the conference in Delaware and so planned to attend and did.

In the months leading up to the conference I felt a strong desire to write a book about what it was like to struggle with sin. I mean deep strongholds of sin not just simple trips and falls. Even at the time I was sensing the urge to write about the subject I had no idea of the actual enormity of it in my life, or the depth of it in my soul. I had no premonition that there was before me the kind of desperate spiritual grief to bear that I would come to know. I was like a child oblivious, pleasantly thinking how clever I was to write a book about rowboats as I paddled my way into a hurricane.

One morning at the conference I was in my hotel room at the mirror shaving…all was right with the world, and I was now a new man, a new good man, and I was planning to write a book for God because after all, I was a new man. So I was thinking to Him. You know how sometimes we carry little conversations on with God in our head? I am reminded of toddlers who have just learned to talk and so carry on pleasant little conversations with themselves whether or not anyone else is listening and who would most likely be offended if they discovered someone who was.

I was thinking, *So God, how should I structure this book about struggling with sin? Should I start from a theological perspective and research scripture first, and then discuss it in present day? Should I come up with some catalogue of sins that seem to be frequent in our culture these days and do individual treatments for each? Or maybe I should put it all in the context of some story….* I was really very arrogant, now that I look back on that morning while I was shaving away so pleased with myself.

I believe that God speaks to each of us in a variety of ways. For each of us, however, He seems to use a specific method more frequently than others. Because it matches our temperament, I suppose. Some people He reaches by placing them in the peace and beauty of nature. Others He places in a worship situation where they can connect. For me, He puts thoughts in my head that I know are not mine. Thoughts that I am certain are not mine. And so it was that morning.

"I want you to write about *your* sin."

Once in a while I can recognize when He is the one putting the thought in my head because I am instantly gripped and horrified by it.

I am pretty sure I dropped my toothbrush in the sink as I staggered back, shaving cream still clinging to my ear lobes and nose, but I may have swallowed it whole. I walked away from the sink area like someone had punched me dizzy, toward the window walking away from God to shut down the conversation. Blaring in my head were the words:

"No Way!!! Not one teeny tiny smidgeon of the beginnings in a trillion years of your imagination of a way!"

And as it happened, the conversation did then shut down. At least two weeks went by during which I prayed daily about the subject with the clear sense that He simply was not going to negotiate.

In the six years since that day I have done three things I never thought I would ever have the courage to do, and agreeing to write this book the way I believe He wants it written constitutes the fourth. I have come to believe that life takes courage, and to choose to follow the will of God all in is the most intense way to live, sometimes demanding the greatest degree of it.

I attended a healing retreat in Florida. I was told beforehand to give it over to God and allow Him to heal what He chooses to heal. I had hopes for a specific healing, but He had other things in mind. Among them was the message that after five years of being stuck on this thing it was time to set my fears aside, sit down, and write the book.

But I urge you not to think that the book is written as a confession. My sins have been confessed to Him and to others and have been forgiven. Nor is this book a catharsis for me to purge the effects of the past. I believe that catharses are extremely overrated, generally speaking, and when they do sincerely occur they are much more spontaneous and nowhere nearly as tedious to construct as a book.

This book has a purpose, and that purpose has nothing to do with me. It just happens that in order for it to make sense it has to begin from the truth, and since I am writing it the truth has to be mine. Otherwise it will be nothing more than idle attempts at intellectuality on a page. I knew before I even wrote the dedication that if I did not have the courage to tell the story before I write anything further, He was not interested in me writing anything at all. And it is true that in every event that I have ever displayed the courage I was certain I didn't have, I hadn't had it. He had given it to me then and would again.

I will limit the personal historical editorial to only that which is necessary to continue so as to make sure that the book has what it needs but is not self-serving. I will not hold back those events of which I am ashamed. They are critical, but they are not the subjects of the book.

It has been said that I have an extraordinary long-term memory. My short-term memory is among the worst I have ever encountered, however. I can't remember what I have for breakfast on any given day, or the events of two days ago at any point at all. But I can remember the exact wording of conversations from forty-five years ago. When I would make such claims members of my family would scoff. My mom once said, "John has such a good memory he remembers things that didn't even happen." Then I proved it to my parents by reminding them of exact words spoken many years earlier, after which I once heard her warn someone, "Watch what you say around him; he never forgets anything."

But there are things that go so far back that there may be parts that I cannot be absolutely sure occurred the way I remember them. I will be careful to clarify the difference between what I remember with certainty and what I remember with some measure of doubt.

There have been people that God has placed in my path that have gotten me to the point where I could even face events in my life and their effect, let alone speak or write about them. And I have been taught more about faith and the fullness of life in Christ in the last three years than I ever would have estimated there to be to know. And I suspect that I scarcely know a fraction of it.

I had the great good fortune to be introduced to a ministry called Ellel at that conference in Wilmington, Delaware. That began what is now a strong interest in spiritual healing, and I have attended one of their addictions training classes (Florida, 2008) and a deliverance retreat (Florida, 2009).

I was on a course to recovery and searching. I came to learn about a program called "In His Fullness" and I attended a weekend event held by them. During that weekend I was led out of my rote defenses, gently but concertedly. And into a clarity about my own state of authenticity, or lack thereof.

And through a series of random connections I ended up at a church in Chandler (Arizona), where a group of guys met on Saturday mornings led by a man to whom I will forever be indebted. These men listened to me confess what I so deeply feared anyone knowing and responded with genuine Christian brotherhood. In them I saw Christ and felt that I had a place among men for the first time in life.

And ultimately I found a home in a church in the Yucatan where I now live. My pastor there (now in Oregon) led me through a deliverance of a specific kind, fully predicated on forgiveness. He didn't then know the full nature of my wounding and it didn't matter. He knew me as a child of God and heir to a love we can spend a lifetime desperately seeking yet never understand. Later, he and a dear brother spent four hours in prayer with me at my insistent pleading, and after forty years I took my first step outside the prison cell that had been my home since childhood.

Through all of this I began to understand the relationship between strongholds of sin, lives spent in delusion and pain, spiritual wounding, and the narrow path to healing. How even though I didn't know it, I was always being drawn blind and backwards into grace.

That is the subject of this book.

John A. Rubio

PART ONE

A WOUNDED DOG WILL BITE YOU. A werewolf will bite you too but for very different reasons. They resemble each other even though they differ in purpose, so you may not recognize one from the other. If you get too close to either, however, you are likely to get hurt and not likely to ever know why.

Spring, 2011

My good friend,

It is hard to make sense of it, I know.

I sometimes wonder what makes us think that making sense of it is even worth doing. Would things change? Would they get easier? Truth is there's nothing easy about it and nothing changes the past.

It would even be a waste of time for me to tell you that I know what you're going through. If you were honest with yourself you would know you wouldn't believe it and hearing it would only be annoying. It doesn't matter anyway because I don't know what you're going through. But I know what I did.

As I sit down to write this, I have gone over it with myself more times than I can count. Not sure if the way I decided to proceed is the best way, but it is the way I landed on, I guess.

You've been a good friend. I've really enjoyed the walks we have taken when we have had the talks about all this, and there is so much I wish I could do for you. I want to explain what I understand now that I didn't understand before. There's an old saying that the years reveal what in the days we can't see...and I know now that it is true. I'd like to think that there might be something you can use, or something that will spare you a little bit of it that won't cost you what it has cost me.

That's my hope, anyway.

And there is something in the stories that I want you to know....

1. Things Up to April Fool's Day

I WAS THE FOURTH KID BORN to a man we all grew up thinking was Mexican American, and my mom's family was all from Eastern Europe originally, but she was raised in south central Texas where they met. Whether or not he was actually Mexican or "purely Spanish" seems to be something about which there remains some differences of recollection. But we learned very recently, like in the last six months or so, that his Mexican parents didn't have any Mexican in them. They were Cuban. So it strikes me as kind of ironic that I have so many memories of him trying to make sure that we grew up proud of being Mexican. My mom's parents were Austro-Hungarian back when it was Czechoslovakia.

Everything that I know of him, and all that I remember indicates that he was a brilliant man with an extraordinary sense of humor, a keen and motivating sense of integrity, who was devoted to his family and had an almost perfectly basketball-shaped stomach. He had a laugh that broke in and out of a falsetto that was uniquely his, although his sister, my aunt Leonor, had a similar laugh. If someone could laugh with a Mexican, Cuban, or purely Spanish accent, he did. His face was always rough with stubble when he spent a few minutes with each of us after we were in bed, saying a few words here and there and kissing us good night. He loved us more than the sun shone on the day, and we knew it.

My mom's still with us, so I can describe her in the present first and then put her in context as needed when I speak about events all those years ago. I have always used a handy image to describe my mom to others who have heard of her but have never met her. I describe her as a mix between Lady Bird Johnson and Annie Oakley.

She has the subtle gentility that is unique to South Texas and almost gone from the planet, mixed with an attitude. She is the type that you might imagine in some '60s Western comedy flick, shooting her pistol to unlock a door while her cohort in crime is handing her the key.

She has always trusted herself to such an extent that she never really had to consider anything she ever said or did. She just said or did it. I see this trait now as confidence, even if sometimes the situation may not have called for quite so much confidence. But I do love that about her—that strength. And my sisters seemed to have gotten it, even if maybe a little more measured.

I am still convinced that, although they had children together, they had a family for different reasons: he had children because he needed little pliable minds with which to amuse himself, and she had children because she was married to him. Now, mom has confessed that she did want children—she just didn't want so many. Considering that she married a purely Spanish Catholic Mexican Cuban man, who did not believe in birth control and lived in an age before abortions were legal and long after selling children into slavery was on option, she could have thought through things a little better.

I once asked Mom how many children she had wanted, and she told me that she really only wanted two. Then, in her inimitable fashion, she told me which ones.

My very early childhood was probably pretty typical. Mom was loving, dutiful, and of almost biblical ability to provide; She could feed the multitude with a few cans of things and a bag of macaroni. Dad was as the wrath of God, but kissed us tenderly as we settled off to sleep each night. As for my three older sisters, I might likely have wrapped my own umbilical cord around my neck in the womb opting for stillbirth over the little play-laboratory into which I would be born, had I any premonition.

In thinking out how I would organize the early stories for you I decided to group them according to the central characters. Therefore, what follows is a brief catalogue of early memories presented in three groups: those related to my father, those to my mother, and those to my sisters.

As I've told you before, my dad was generally very good-natured, loving, playful, and extremely clever. I have already speculated that his primary purpose for having us was to have gullible minds for his own entertainment, and he sure got what he was hoping for. He was very convincing. He had us convinced that he was omniscient and that every word that came forth from his mouth was true. Even when we couldn't believe what he was telling us because it just didn't seem possible, he would just play the wild card—magic.

He once told us that the trees in Sugarland, Texas, talk. When we would drive through Sugarland, we would roll down the windows and shout out at the trees, hoping to engage them in a conversation. I don't recall what explanation we fixed in our heads as to why they did not call back to us, but the fact that he was teasing us was not among the options we considered. As we grew older, on no specific date, without any real closure, and without explanation, we stopped calling out to the trees in Sugarland. His omniscience and assumed truthfulness was left intact. What's really weird is that, about a year ago, I had the occasion to drive through Sugarland again, and I have to admit that, as I was going by, I couldn't help but look out the window at the trees, particularly this big old oak that looked suspiciously familiar.

My mom would fry up a big batch of chicken for dinner back in the day when the grocery stores only stocked whole "fryers" instead of individually packaged parts. Mom would buy them and chop them up herself into a variety of chicken pieces, and we would all eat whatever piece we wanted. The problem was that no one ever wanted the wings. They were too small, maybe a bit too delicate to really sink your teeth into. In any event, they usually were just left and went to waste, or one of us would grudgingly eat them, complaining the whole while. Dad had a solution.

My dad knew that, more than anything in the world, I wanted to be able to fly. As a young boy, like so many, I strained every bit of imagination I had to figure out how I might accomplish flight. My experiments usually involved jumping off platforms of a variety of heights. I suppose many children go through a similar quest at some age, and then eventually abandon it. Well, my dad very officiously announced to me that he could help me in my ambition for flight. He happened to know that if you eat enough chicken wings, sooner or later you would be able to fly. How soon, he explained, depended on how many you ate.

From that point on, anytime we had fried chicken, it was understood that I would get the wings. I craved them, demanded them, and asserted my right to them. It was imperative that I not only *have* the wings, but that I have *all* of them. My sisters never asked me why I suddenly decided that chicken wings were my favorite, or at least not that I can remember. But he had covered this base beforehand by telling me that their magical effect was a secret. He tied up all the loose ends by making sure I understood that, if everyone knew about the flying properties of the wings, everyone would want them, and then no one would ever get enough to be able to fly. His logic was flawless, and I was the secret beneficiary of his magnanimous plan.

The charade ended when I injured my wrist jumping from the roof, convinced that I had eaten enough wings. I lost interest in flight and in chicken wings, but looking back, I never wondered whether I had been "had," and I never even considered that it was all a big ruse. If anything, I'm sure I just concluded that whatever the amount of chicken wings that you needed to eat in order to fly, my parents simply couldn't afford that many. Or maybe it was the frequency with which they had to be eaten. Every day? Every day, three times a day? It didn't matter. It wasn't going to happen.

On another occasion, I was in his lap while he was driving the car. He had a habit of turning on the turn signal with the little finger on his left hand, which I could never see. All I saw was the green arrow starting to flash in the direction he would subsequently turn. It seemed to me that the car *knew* where he was going to turn. I asked him about it. He corrected me that the car was not anticipating the turn, but rather advising him of it, indicating the turn he would need to make. I was mystified. When I asked him how that was possible he told me that, when I got older and went to buy a car, I should talk to it, get to know it, so my car would someday help me out in like fashion. I knew that a horse whose rider fell off would eventually make his way back. I think Roy Rogers' shows taught me that, so it did make some sense, or at least it didn't seem too far-fetched.

I was fascinated. One morning, while everyone was inside, I went out to the driveway to investigate. My first question concerned where you might actually talk to the car so that it could hear you. It certainly wasn't obvious. I looked all around until I noticed a small object inside the grille that looked strikingly like an ear (the horn). I sat down "Indian style" and decided to have a chat. I began by asking the car how long it had known my dad. It occurred to me that dad never told me that the car would talk back or ever say anything. So I concluded that it wouldn't, never mind that I couldn't find anything even remotely resembling a mouth. After all, the ear was hard enough to find, so the car's silence in response to my chatter became perfectly acceptable. Besides, horses didn't talk either.

I had a wonderful time telling his car all about myself and what it was like living in the house with everyone else. I almost sensed a camaraderie with the car, as if it had become a friend if albeit a silent one. But then I worried that his car might like me better than my dad and might start pointing us in directions with me in mind rather than my father. We would end up constantly going to the convenience store for candy bars or to the swim club. And just how would I explain that?

Well, my mom came outside and noticed me sitting at the car talking into the grille and asked me what I was doing. When I explained it she stormed off leaving me to wonder what I said. Later that day they had an argument and I do remember her screaming at him that he was ruining my mind.

Another of the ruses for his enjoyment involved the transformers on the tops of telephone poles. I asked him what they were, once. I think I was seven years old. You have to remember that this was the early sixties, the season of the Cuban missile crisis. We were aware that the parents were often discussing what to do in the event of a bombing. Our neighbor at the end of the street even started construction on a bomb shelter in his back yard. That kind of thing rattles even the most unsophisticated minds. At our Catholic school we were taught to get under our desks when the sirens went off blaring the news that bombs were about to start falling out of the sky. The fact that our house lay in the flight path to Hobby Airport and we would often lie on our backs and look at the planes roar overhead so close you could almost see the rivets and could easily imagine little panels in their bottom sides that could open up and let loose any manner of bombs didn't help. Just like we would lie on our backs and "play dead" when helicopters flew overhead thinking we could lure them to land in order to save us. I digress…

Well, when I asked him what those gray steel cylinders were stuck to the tops of telephone poles, he in a very matter-of-fact tone responded, "bombs." Somewhat horrified I pleaded, asking why in the world there would be bombs stuck to poles throughout the neighborhood, one set of them in our very own backyard not thirty feet from my dog's house. He, with feigned patience, explained that the Government was very intolerant of uprisings and so had fashioned bombs to poles throughout all the neighborhoods. Any neighborhood that rose up in revolt would cause the government to throw the switch and the bombs would go off crushing the revolution.

I was mortified. I naturally concluded that our neighbor who was installing a bomb shelter had some inside information about our neighbors that we didn't, and I'm sure I spent a little bit of time wondering why we weren't building a shelter too. I think my dad's calm about the whole neighborhood blowing up thing ultimately helped me, a little. If he wasn't panicked about it, why should I be? But deep inside I still was, a little.

One morning I was outside playing in the front yard. I think this was not long after Christmas because my friend across the street's older brother had a new BB gun that he got for Christmas. Well, he looked around and didn't see any birds to shoot at, no frogs, and no dog that didn't belong to someone that would get him trouble. So he decided to shoot at the transformers to hear the ping and test his aim, I suppose.

Visions of the entire neighborhood exploding filled my imagination and even though he was at least two years older than me and a good twenty pounds heavier, maybe three inches taller, I threw any concern for myself to the wind and took off running toward him to tackle him and save the neighborhood. Evidently he did not know what he was doing or realize the true peril in which he was placing himself and very conceivably hundreds of other innocent lives. I hit him in a full-on body tackle and we both tumbled to the grass, his BB gun flying out of his arms. It was at that point that he proceeded to beat the crap out of me. I went home crying, bruised and a little bloodied, but excited about the parade they would most likely hold for me in a day or two. I couldn't wait to tell my parents about how I had saved the neighborhood. I was a hero. I was THE hero.

I don't remember an argument between my folks that night, but I'd bet there was one.

Every boy should have at least one thing he remembers his father telling him the way a father does when he is giving advice. Something that is supposed to set the stage for him to someday be a man himself. A profundity that he can carry with him all his life reminding him that yes, he did have a father, and that father was a good man who wanted his son to be a good man too.

My dad sat me down once; I think I was about nine. I peg this memory at that age by the house in which the conversation occurred. Because of the house where it happened I could not have been younger than nine or older than twelve (when he died). He was trying to teach me not to steal or lie having been shaken into concern about this by my proclivity for shoplifting at that young age. He said "Remember what I am about to tell you; you will need it for later. When you get older and decide you might want to sell your integrity, make sure you get a high price, because you can only sell it once."

Some people have visual memory, some conceptual. My memory is auditory. I remember what I hear almost as though I just re-listen to it. It is not the content I fix in my brain, but the sound of the words. I later attach the meaning. I am convinced that he knew or understood that and did not dilute or simplify his words. At nine years of age, he spoke to me as though I were eighteen. And I am grateful for that because I recognize it now as a respect that he showed me in contrast to everything after the change. And I can now go back and fetch it across the decades of his absence, when memories of his contempt toward me carry the day.

But my single earliest and most cherished memory of my father occurred sometime prior to me being four years old. Dad was devoted to classical music and had a nice collection of records, some of which would be quite valuable if we still had them. Looking back I can tell that he was attempting to impart to me a number of his interests at a very young age. I'm sure there must be something almost tribal about that between fathers and their very young sons.

One day when I was very young, he sat me on his lap in a chair next to the stereo he had concocted out of an expensive turntable but not built into a cabinet. It sat on soup cans. Before he put on the record we were going to listen to he explained very carefully that there was a story in the music. After we had listened to the entire thing he would expect me to be able to tell him what the story was.

So we listened to Tchaikovsky's First Concerto, B Flat Minor. I couldn't have been older than three years old but I remember it clearly. I remember trying with everything I had to figure out the story. I listened so intently because I was afraid I wouldn't understand the music that I was hearing before it moved on…that I wouldn't catch the part that was passing before it went on to some other part. But I hadn't ever caught it, and the music always moved on. At the end when I told him I wasn't sure what the story was ("Is it about deer?") he would tell me that it was okay, we would listen again another day. He knew what he was doing and I did not.

I never got the story, but sometimes I catch myself wanting him to know that I'm still listening.

Sometimes I speculate that it was my early and intense exposure to classical music that lead to an almost hyper-emotionality as a child and an adult. That sensitivity that he may have helped create would haunt us both, if at different times. His purpose was probably to give me an appreciation for classical music, like he had. And maybe to give me a deeper appreciation for all things that are beautiful; things that speak to the more graceful aspects of human nature. But it may have gone too far. It may have made me too sensitive. A boy of four cannot always see the line where he crosses over from being sensitive to feminine.

I know that like any boy my age the single thing in the world that I most wanted to do was to please my father. By the age of four I was playing Beethoven on the piano by ear.

I wish I could forget all else but these two memories of the man: the first concerto, and integrity. They are enough to prove that beneath the years that followed there was a noble, gentle, loving man that any boy could worship.

All these many years later I sometimes still wonder what got to him before I did.

But there are other memories...like weeds.

One was on my birthday. As closely as I can remember he came home from work and he and my mom had a huge argument. This was not uncommon, but this particular argument was about the fact that he had forgotten that it was my birthday. My mom was furious with him and he was equally prepared for a fight. They were in the kitchen and I was in the living room wanting it to stop. I can remember (or imagine) that I would gladly accept his slip of memory if she would just not argue with him about it. It would have been easier to accept that he forgot my birthday than deal with what my birthday was causing in the kitchen. And when he was done defending himself against her, I expected he would just pass it on down to me. There didn't seem to be any way he was going to be pleased with me, afterwards.

He ordered me into the car and drove me to the toy store. I remember even the drive, being worried that I did not know how to make this situation okay. Once in the store he ordered me to pick out a toy, but I didn't want to. I wanted to go home and get out of his proximity but he insisted that we not leave until I had a toy. I reluctantly picked out a sailboat hoping it was not too expensive. It was a little plastic toy sloop. When we got home he got out of the car and headed straight for the door. I followed immediately after him and in the more pathetic corner of my delusion assumed we would set up the sloop together and see if it would sail. Three paces behind him and walking fast to keep up I called out the question if we were going to put it together now.

He walked away from me without so much as a glance back, not even noticing that I had stopped following. His duty was done. Getting mom off his back had cost him four bucks at the toy store and a twenty-minute drive, there and back. Don't ever think children don't know when they've been bought off. They know. I never even took it out of the box.

I'll have more to say about him later, but let's move on to my mom.

As I mentioned earlier, my mom was a miracle worker in how she provided for us. My parents were struggling financially, with four children in my early childhood, and eventually six. But we were never hungry. No matter what else happened, she was always able to prepare a meal for us regardless of what was left in the kitchen.

But there were signs that having four children clamoring at her all the time was taking its toll. One day I remember that in the morning she had a pronouncement for us. She officially banned the use of the term "mom" as well as "mommy," "mother" or any known derivative, synonym, or word used the way you would address someone with whom you have a maternal relationship. She was resolute.

I remember us (my sisters and I) looking at each other somewhat befuddled. We weren't sure exactly what to call her. We knew if we called her by her first name ("Esther") we, except the middle sister of course, would have to face the wrath of dad when he got home. Addressing either of our parents by their first name was not dissimilar to uttering "Bloody Mary" in the mirror as you were spinning circles three times. You just couldn't be sure what would happen, but you knew it wouldn't be good. "Hey lady" was also ruled out.

We thought that maybe "Mrs. Dad" might work. But it seemed so formal. In our early childhood we learned that the terms with which we could address our mother that were comfortable, accurate, and strategically safe were few. But we were missing the point. It was not about which word to use to address her; it was about whether or not to address her at all, of course. It wouldn't matter if we took a shot with "Your Most Gracious and Exalted Highness." She just needed a vacation.

Another memory involves summer when we were off from school and constantly underfoot. She banned us from the house. She decided that by 8:00 a.m. we were to "go play." When we protested that we didn't know where to go to play, she just replied with "Out. But don't come back until your father gets home." It didn't really feel like exile any more than it felt like exodus from captivity, maybe a little of both. It was a mixed thing. "Out" became the world where we were supposed to be, as distinct from "Inside" which was her world, where we were not supposed to be. She never gave us any more specificity than that.

Usually we went to the swimming club down the way from our home, but I have a different story about that.

One of the most memorable events of my childhood that involved the entire family is the night the parents decided to go out and leave us at home with my eldest sister as the babysitter. At that age, her matriarchal bent had already begun to show, but her judgment abilities…well, they had not. We decided to play "Roller Skating Rink."

Our den floor was pegged oak. The comparison to the wooden floors at the Roller Skating Rink was unmistakable to us that evening, particularly since my mom had spent the entire day on her hands and knees waxing it. We moved all the furniture we could to other rooms and pushed the rest back against the walls. We rolled up the rag tied rug and carried it away. Then we put on our *outdoor* metal-keyed overshoe skates and proceeded to skate circles on the hardwood floor, not only scratching it but actually cutting grooves into it. Before long there was even a visible trail in the circle we were skating. We liked it.

The folks came home unexpectedly early as we were in mid-skate and I remember (or imagine) looking over my shoulder as they walked in, and coasting, not sure whether to keep skating or brace myself for being in real trouble. Had I a minute to think, I probably would have just kept skating right through the kitchen, out the back door, and either over to the police station to turn myself in or on down to Mexico to live life on the run. My sisters could fend for themselves. I guess my mom remained self-collected long enough to utter "Oh Ed…" and stagger back into his arms hiding her face from the destruction. While holding her limp body in his arms he calmly instructed us, "We're leaving. I'm coming back in five minutes and I am going to kill every one of you."

I remember wondering exactly how he was going to do it. And I remember in my very early youth feeling the self-pity and sense of poignant tragedy that perhaps only a martyr really knows. Innocent (it wasn't even my idea) but condemned.

There is also the story of how I called the police on her (my mom). There was a child in our neighborhood that was battered and ended up in the hospital. These were the days when those things were rarely even noticed, let alone acted upon. So it was a big thing in our neighborhood and all the kids were collected together so that we could be made aware of the problem. The police came to our neighborhood and explained to us what "battered child" syndrome actually was. We were taught the concept and had a new term to use if we ever had the need to tell someone: "child beater." It was a truly unique and new perspective on what we had heretofore understood as normal parental behavior. At four, I remember thinking, *hmmm…now this is information I can use.*

And it wasn't long before I had the occasion to use it. I don't remember what I did but whatever it was it must have hit a nerve. My mom turned into the cartoon character that starts whirling like a little tornado, kicking up dust and sending things flying in all directions. It was time for me to exit stage left. I ran and I ended up crouching in her bedroom corner where the phone was. I knew it wouldn't be long before she got there and I knew what would happen when she did, so I decided to be proactive. Thinking on my toes, I dialed "o" for operator (this was before the days of 911) and then asked to talk to the police. I was crying and telling them that my mother was a "child beater" (whatever that was). She stormed into the room, and upon realizing what I was up to and hearing what I said started shouting, "You want to see a child beater? I'll show you a child beater!"

I whimpered into the phone "She's beating me..." as I gradually pulled it away from myself for effect. I meant to suggest that she was dragging me away from the phone and so to communicate a sense of urgency. But it was ultimately just little more than premature, as it turned out, because then she hung up the phone and actually did drag me away from it. Astonished that the police did not break down the bedroom door at that very moment, I decided to sit on the front sidewalk and wait for them, relishing the events that would certainly transpire on their arrival. It did not occur to me that they would need more information than "John" to figure out who and where I was. She told the story for years. She brought it out when she would try to explain to others what an ordeal it had been raising six.

The one story I remember that really did have a sense of tragedy to it involved my mom getting hurt. She used to walk me to school in the morning when I was in kindergarten. One morning we headed out to go to kindergarten and we crossed the street to the neighbor's house. There had been a broken water main at their house that was leaking water across the sidewalk for some weeks. A slow but steady leak that had resulted in a patch of green slick, almost like algae growing right on the sidewalk.

As we walked along the sidewalk and got to that spot my mom slipped and fell straight to the concrete. She was hurt and had difficulty getting up. I could tell she was in pain but I was completely helpless to do anything about it. I will never forget the sense of powerless desperation that I experienced, and the angst. It would be something I would eventually experience again for her, later.

In everything she worked hard to make a good home for us, from the African violets to the Girl Scout duties she took so seriously.

Which gets me to the discussion about my three older sisters....

My three older sisters each had very distinct personalities. It was almost as if the qualities that my mom has always had sort of split up between the three girls and you could observe them apart from each other. In the oldest was the sense of maternal responsibility and, well, unbridled authority. In the middle sister, ingenuity. And in the youngest (at the time) a sense of almost divine purpose. So just for emphasis, let me summarize thus: unbridled authority, ingenuity, and divine purpose. The three of them were close in age and so as a group had some additional qualities (or characteristics) that my mom didn't really bestow on them, or at least not intentionally: seniority, girl-bonding disease, and a general disregard for all life that happened to be male (other than my father, that is). Into this mix I was born.

I am pretty sure that when the girls discovered that the new baby was a boy it meant something very different to them than if they were told it was another little sister. It did not mean that their little club had a new member to indoctrinate into their order of things; it meant that their little laboratory was finally "going live."

I was not one of them; I was a helpless alien given into their playhouse and made available for their curiosity. They would need to be big girls and take care of me. While mom was striking rocks with her staff, going about divining meals for the whole family from little more than saltine crackers, I was left absolutely helpless with them.

As I alluded to earlier, the oldest sister, Cindy, was a matriarch when she was seven years old, near as I could discern. She may well have emerged from the womb with matriarchal instincts fully intact but she was six years old when I was born and it took me a year to catch on, so I didn't really become aware of it until about the age of one. There are numerous memories of her exerting this authority but I will select one in particular.

This sister had convinced me that in order to be healthy it would be necessary to swallow one tablespoon of salt per day. As she prepared my tablespoon I asked her if they (the girls) were going to take theirs and she assured me that they already had. At about five years old I was fed a full tablespoon of salt for the exclusive purpose of my sisters' entertainment. This was my first exposure to their most successful tactic. They would collude on their experiments before they conducted them on me. I was already used to believing things like talking trees and benevolent cars that pointed out the way home, bombs on telephone poles and chicken wings with magical powers; and these all came from one source. Three people asserting the same thing could convince me that I was Daffy Duck, with or without the feathers. But this particular ruse – the salt thing - did have a pay-off for me. To this day I do not like salt.

Because she was the oldest she was also often our parents' proxy. A role commonly referred to as "babysitter" but one that she interpreted as being beyond just sitting with babies. She considered it governance. If I knew what reincarnation was at that age and bought into it, perhaps I would be tempted to suspect that she was Catherine the Great and maybe even questioned what happened in her life as Kate the Great that could have taken her from the courts of Russia to a three bedroom ranch style on Grape Street in Houston, Texas. But we were not being taught reincarnation. We were Catholics. We were being taught about sin. And we cleverly incorporated the word into a nickname for her that rhymed with her name. We were young little Catholics and we were catching on. We didn't really fully understand what sin was at that time but we knew it was bad, and we knew it rhymed with her name and that was enough.

The second oldest sister, Claudia, was and is the genius of the family. I was truly frightened by her. The oldest would slap me from time to time but this one introduced me to the workings of a gifted mind, whose motives could not really be known.

She had the ability to make my dad believe anything. Truly. What was most profoundly disturbing was that she could throw you a glance that made it clear to you that she knew she could. And she knew that you knew it. She had him believing that she was absolutely incapable of anything less than the angelic. It was ironic that the youngest of my older sisters actually was angelic, or saw herself as a future saint. My oldest sister was a strange combination of martyr when the folks were around, and self-appointed empress for life when they were not. My middle sister, however, was genius. And she had dad wrapped around her little finger.

I once wrote that I sensed that she could sneak into my room repeatedly stabbing me with a butcher knife and as I lay there dying he would barge into the room immediately noticing her holding the bloody knife up high, ready for the next blow, and exclaim, "Who did this!?"

The first story that I always think to tell was that of the Saturday morning TV show incident. Each Saturday morning we would get to choose what we wanted to watch. The selection rotated every Saturday and we got to pick our shows on our day. But we were not allowed to argue over it lest we wake up our parents, and that was absolutely forbidden. We could wither and die of the withdrawal from our favorite cartoon, but we could not wake the parents.

One Saturday it was my turn and I wanted to watch Augie Doggie, my favorite stuffed animal's namesake. The middle sister, however, did not. Without any apparent consideration of the consequences and with the comportment of an official approaching the bell to harken the end of a competition, she rose, approached the TV, and changed the channel. I protested as loud as I could without waking the parents, insisting that it was "my Saturday" over and over. I had no allies in the other two, but even at that young age I knew it was ridiculous to assume that I might. Nothing in my yet known life indicated that any one of them would ever abandon their pact to come to my assistance on anything, let alone the selection of cartoons. And nine times never against the genius who seemed to have such influence over dad.

I am not sure if it was the smug assuredness with which she considered the matter concluded, or the fatigue of always being odd-man out against the three of them. But something snapped. A cable that usually held back actions of the kind that you normally get in a lot of trouble for came spinning off its pulley and as my sister walked away from the TV I noticed a screwdriver cart-wheeling through the air toward her that seconds earlier had been in my hand.

I missed her, but not the aquarium.

To my horror the screwdriver shattered the aquarium glass on impact and all the contents came pouring out onto the hard oak floors. My mom's prized breeding guppies were flopping around on the floor and as they were gasping for breath in their dying throes I saw *my* life pass before my eyes. But did any of the three sisters jump in to help me try to save their little guppy lives?

No.

They were far too occupied following Claudia into the parents' bedroom to deliver the shocking news about how John just went berserk and started throwing things, and of course, it was for no reason, and no one knows why he did it, and all the guppies are dying on the floor now. The guppies were indeed doomed, and so, they would have it, was I. Missing "Augie Doggie" that morning paled by comparison.

But there is with her, as with all of them really, a memory that stands out of context. At times alone, they sometimes seemed to have had a kindness that they reserved for me that collectively they never seemed to remember or admit. But it was always there. I remember it.

We would all walk to school at Holy Ghost and I was often terrified to go to school. I don't know why. But one day I just couldn't cope and because I couldn't stop crying, the nuns allowed me to go see my sister, the middle one. I remember standing next to her in her chair in the middle of class, and she was so embarrassed. All I had to talk about was the big pickles you could buy for a nickel at lunch, because I was certain that I could not explain why I was there. But things in my life often brought me back to her. No matter what, she has always been a safe port whenever I have found myself in a storm.

The youngest of the older sisters, Chris, was the most unassuming and seemingly harmless of the three. She even seemed fraternal with me at times. With her it was more a matter of separating her from the other two, in order to form some kind of sibling bond. Sometimes we even had things in common. But then, there is the flip off the high dive story….

When we were children we belonged to a swim club in the neighborhood, the one I mentioned we were banished to during the day in the summertime.

It was nothing fancy, only a pool and a snack club. But it was walking distance from home and somewhere to head off to when we were kicked out of the house on summer mornings. I remember it well. I remember the white shell parking lot that always hurt my feet when I forgot my sandals.

I think I was six when this sister and I entered into a bet that if one of us did a flip off the high dive, the other had to do one too. Well, she apparently demonstrated her ability to form alliances for purposes of deception without the other two sisters, when she needed to. She engaged her friends in a plot to convince me that she had indeed done a flip off the high dive and they had all seen it. Faced with the incontrovertible testimony that she had done the flip I had no option but to do one myself.

Very reluctantly I climbed to the top of the high dive and walked to the edge. After agonizing at the end of the board by the mere sight of the deep blue deep end, I held my nose, closed my eyes, tucked my head and fell forward.

I'm really not sure how many flips my six-year-old body actually did before it slammed into the water, but I think that the lifeguard who fished me out of the water probably knew. I do know that it was at least one full one or maybe two full ones, and then some fraction of another one. Because no flip could be created to have you land the way I did as a matter of design.

I do remember there being significant pain involved. The lifeguard did fish me out of the water, and I don't really remember but I bet he was muttering something about me being a stupid crazy little jerk. But when the pain wore off, it occurred to me that the whole deception thing should backfire. In a rational, reasonable world where justice prevailed the bet would still stand, even if she never had done a flip and had lied to me about it. Having done a flip or two and some fraction thereof would mean that I HAD done one. So now, she had to satisfy her end of the bet. After all, MY flip(s) off the high dive had been witnessed by the lifeguards and the official emergency safety staff employed precisely for just such an event – and they can't be conned. Chris' had only been a matter of the testimony agreed upon by a few eight-year-olds. No other reliable witnesses could be produced.

It was with that instance along with some others that I learned that the world was not a rational, reasonable world where justice prevailed. At least the world I occupied wasn't.

The last story I will tell involves the swim club and my sisters collectively.

The membership allowed for children to get something to eat or drink from the snack bar and rather than pay for it then, sign a piece of paper for it – a chit. At the end of the month the chits would be collected and mailed to the home of the club members (my parents) along with a bill. Routinely the number of chits that arrived at the end of the month with my signature would always outnumber the average of the other three. And I always got a lecture. Each time I tried to remember buying more stuff than my sisters, but I couldn't ever remember doing that. It seemed like something was wrong, to me. And even though I suggested to my parents that something must be wrong, they just said that I needed to stop being a pig.

They never believed me. Instead they assumed that I was just a lying glutton in need of more discipline.

Until the month when every single chit in the mail had my signature. Not a single chit from any of the girls was included for the entire month. I had apparently been eating four hotdogs, innumerable ice creams and sodas, as well as chips, every day and amazingly had not put on any weight. As it happened, my sisters' abilities to coordinate things with each other did not match their ability to forge my six-year-old signature.

They didn't consider the chance that if ALL the chits came back with my name on them, even the middle sister's freakish effect on my father's ability to reason wouldn't help them. They would be caught, and that would mean that they would get in trouble and I wouldn't, and that my parents would realize that I was telling the truth all along and they weren't.

And the trees in Sugarland talk.

I was not vindicated. My sisters were not even chastised let alone punished. If memory serves all that happened was that we were put on strict budgets and the chits had to match our budgets or we got in trouble. Big deal. I accidentally had some guppy collateral damage over an Augie Doggie dispute and you'd think the next stop for me was twenty-five to life. My sisters committed forgery, a federal offense in some circumstances. No problem.

Such was life as a boy with three older sisters. It may have been unfair at times but it was not unhappy. Everything was an adventure in discovery. The bayou that ran next to our house was all the hunting ground a boy could hope for, filled with minnows, crawdads, and even the odd rumor of quicksand where once a heavy machinery operator mowing the side of the ditch fell into and he really died.

I remember that once my friends and I wondered aloud *where must minnows come from?* Having no reasonable explanation otherwise, we concluded that they come from rain. So rather than go to the considerable effort to catch them in the bayou, like we usually did, we thought it would be easier to just collect rain water and let them hatch. So we gathered every pot and pan, every bucket and pail, and collected rainwater at the next opportunity. Full of rain, we set them all in the garage and waited for the minnows to appear. When they didn't, we weren't discouraged nor did we abandon our theory; we just revised it. We concluded that they must only come from rain in muddy bottom places and contented ourselves to go back to hunting them like before, when we didn't understand the world as well.

One of the greatest gifts my parents gave us when we were young children was a truly magic Christmas. Although struggling financially, they never failed to lavish presents on us so that when we woke in the middle of the night the Christmas lights filled the house with every color. The tree filled the room with the scent of pine, and we were overcome with the sight of gift upon gift, stacked and scattered. It was grandeur of the sort that spins a child's senses dizzy. Each Christmas Eve one of our neighbors would gather the children in the neighborhood for cookies and Christmas carols and the folks would always let us open one of our presents that night before we went over to their house. One sister always pointed out that amazingly, they always managed to pick out the ones for each of us to open that turned out to be new pajamas, and we would then wear them to the caroling party that night. And it seemed like every Christmas Eve walking home from the party the girls would all claim to see Santa Claus flying across the sky, but I never could.

Life was discovery and there were rules. Mom and dad were in control and we knew it. Every child needs rules because they tell him that the world is ordered, and an ordered world is safe.

I need to mention that everything that I'm writing to you I remember with a pretty significant level of certainty that they happened exactly as I describe. I do need to tell you some things about events that I do not remember completely. I remember parts with absolute certainty, and other parts with a little doubt, and still other parts not at all. I sometimes wonder if over the years my imagination has added details where my memory doesn't have them.

It doesn't really seem to make sense that in the act of remembering things we would inadvertently add details that did not occur. It would seem much more intuitive to suppose that we would forget some details while remembering others, but at least the ones we remember we can be pretty confident are true. But I am not sure it always works that way. If there is a benefit to having additional details that were not part of the original events, I am not sure I can guess what it is. But this whole discussion on what actually definitely happened and what might be some sort of exaggeration caused in my mind over the decades is really important before I get into some of the stories I need to tell you now.

In recent times the scientists who study memory have suggested that each time we remember an event, the act of remembering itself changes the memory. If this is true, it is possible to take a past event and in the ensuing years remembering it can turn it into a memory of something much worse than the original event, or inversely, something not so bad.

I find this idea intriguing because it suggests that an event remembered with an ever-increasing sense of horror or tragedy associated with it must have to have been remembered alongside something else horrible and tragic. Otherwise the added memory would make it better, not worse. I mean, if your brain wanted to add things to memories for reasons you aren't even aware of, why would it add things that are more horrible than the original event rather than better? Why, for instance, would our mind seem to block some memories altogether because they are too painful or scary for us to face, but then go around making other memories that are not so bad worse? Unless whatever happened really was as horrible as you remember it, even if the details can't be proved. And if that is so, the accuracy of the memory becomes academic. It is the horror that matters.

I know what I am saying might seem confusing and I am not sure if I am saying it clearly. So it might make better sense if I mention what was in an article I read. In it the writer indicated that some scientists are saying that the brain revises memory so that we remember events as being more horrible than they actually were. I wonder if this is true because it doesn't seem logical that a brain would actually block some memories altogether because the events were too traumatic, but then take other events that weren't so bad and make them worse. I know these ideas (revisionist memory) are in their infancy and the scientists are studying it, but a lot about it just doesn't make sense.

But regardless, for what follows there are sections I remember that I am absolutely sure of, some parts I can't remember at all, and some parts that I can't even myself explain how they could have happened. I will describe first the details of which I have no doubt.

When I was seven years old I was being baby-sat by a young man much older than me; I will call him John. There are more guys that I am going to tell you about and I call them John too, so to keep it straight let's call him "Quarters John."

Why I was alone being baby-sat and not with my sisters I do not know, but everyone was gone except for the baby sitter and me. We were sitting on the couch watching TV; he was wearing tan casual slacks – what we call "Dockers" now – and I was in my pajamas. I do not recall what program was on but I do know we were watching TV. At some point he asked me if I would like to play a game and I answered that I would.

He said it was "The Quarters Game" and it was very simple. I only had to put my hand in his pocket and figure out how many quarters he had in his pants. I remember that even as he described the game to me, well before playing it, I sensed that something was wrong. The game was wrong somehow. I remember being afraid but not really knowing why.

I inserted my hand into his pocket and with his assistance wrapped my hand around what was his erect penis. At that age I did not even know that they did that kind of thing (got bigger like that), but I remember the exact second that I realized what was in my hand, and that it was not quarters. I remember the confusion about what was going on and wondering if he was hurt or something. And being unable to understand what it was he was enjoying or why, and being afraid. I was very afraid. It was all wrong somehow and I knew it.

But this is the point where the events of which I am certain stop. The rest of the memories are speculative and there is what the psychologists and I years later came to refer to as the "missing hour" in which I do not remember anything. Sounds like an alien abduction, huh?

My next memory is of myself naked (or partially naked) under the bushes in front of our house, hiding. I remember being terrified, in physical pain; and I remember the smell of bacon. Years later when I was in therapy I remembered the smell of bacon associated with being in the bushes and I told the therapist that it seemed odd that I would associate bacon with the memory. I found out that gardenia leaves smell like bacon when they are dead and dried. I asked my mom about it and she confirmed that there were gardenia bushes in the front of the house, by the dining room window.

Everything between the "quarters" game and the bushes smelling like bacon I do not remember at all, and after several attempts to figure it out, I think the amount of time was half an hour to an hour, but I really do not know.

When I was a freshman in college and had my first break I underwent treatment at the Texas Research Institute of Mental Sciences. I was there for depression. There were a number of sessions where I was hypnotized trying to remember the missing hour. I am not sure why.

I know that the memory of the event involved a point at which I was under the bushes hiding, sometime after the "quarters" game, but nothing in between. We (the therapist and I) had come to think that it was a fairly traumatic event for a number of reasons. First, it would explain why I was hiding, and even why I could not remember it. And it would make sense of a lot of other things as well.

To this day I do not remember the missing hour, and I only remember the bushes with a little confusion. If I could imagine any reason why my brain would add that to the other memory when it didn't actually happen, I might doubt that it did. I suspect that I know what happened, but I don't like thinking that I could be right. And it is all too far into the gray to be sure. It doesn't matter anymore, anyway.

I believe that that night opened the door for further sexual abuse when a friend's older brother who I will also call John began playing games with the two of us that involved all of us being naked. We knew it was wrong and we knew that we would get into trouble if we told. John assured us that he would "beat us up" and that no one would believe us anyway. I recall with certainty at least one event of these games that occurred at their house. I believe that it went on for quite some time (about a year) but I am not certain of that, either.

My friend and I eventually did tell the parents but John was right; they did not believe us and we were blamed as willing participants. We were treated with disgust by the adults, and I was ordered never to go down to that end of the street again. If there was ever any punishment that resulted from this for John I am not aware of it. And the consequences I would come to know were far worse than the abuse itself. Sometimes I wonder how it all played out for my friend. I never saw him again.

Eventually we moved away from that neighborhood.

These events were fleeting, one of them a matter of minutes. In a life that spans more than fifty years as I write this to you, they seem like bad press, decades stale. No hospitalization, no ambulances or sirens of any sort. In fact, little occurred beyond those events except for perhaps some very uncomfortable and accusatory conversations between the parents, and a few new rules. Innocence is not necessarily loud when it is shattered.

But in the developing mind and emotions that I was operating with there was a huge and complex system of interconnected gears, each interlacing with the other at only one point. Each driving others in their cycles one to the next and to the next and back again. Some small, some large. And each gear moved in sync with the others so that all moved together in unison and balance... cycles upon cycles, rotations against rotations, each driven by the rhythm and motion of the others. And in those events there was a slip.

I am convinced that my father knew well what happened to me, but I have no proof of that. I have no distinct memory of any conversation when he addressed the events in a way that would anchor his awareness in my memory. There were no arrests, no punishments…nothing external to research. My sisters now have heard the stories and they find them hard to believe. Knowing my father, they reason, why would he not have gone crazy and killed the guy? It is something he would have done.

I do have a memory of him grabbing his sixteen-gauge shotgun and tearing off down the street to kill the guy. But I asked my mom about it and she said it never happened. So I have to think my brain added it at some point. Maybe my brain wasn't trying to make things worse after all. Maybe I needed to have a memory like my dad grabbing a gun over it added in there.

But my dad's behavior toward me took on a different characteristic, and of that I am absolutely certain whether there are any guns or shared memories by the others or not. That part was not added; it was real.

I know that the prohibition against going down to the end of the street and playing at the house of the older brother was real. My sister remembers that too, but she never knew why we couldn't play at that house, although we were allowed to play at the one next door, until she heard this story. It started adding up.

As for my dad, I know he knew. Why he did not try to kill someone, I don't know. But I know he knew what happened. Later, I came to believe that he probably didn't try to kill anyone because he thought I was okay with it. Like they were games I wanted to play.

Prior to the gardenia bed it was Tchaikovsky and stories, but after that it was very different. It was like *I* was different and affections were not possible anymore. Now there was a much larger objective…no longer the gradual teachings and learning – the delights and fascinations of a father with his son. It was all no longer new. And whether I was a victim or a willing participant didn't matter. I was damaged goods. And I had no idea why or what, exactly, I had done.

He no longer corrected me with patience; he ridiculed me. He no longer had patience for me at all. Introduced into the strong emotions of love and need that I had for him was a new frontrunner – fear. The others would fade. Then I would just vaguely remember them and wonder what it must be like for other boys. For other sons of other fathers.

He once threw me out of a softball game in front of all my friends imitating a girl crying, "boo hoo hoo" and accusing me of running like a girl. His words were not laced with affection, or even humor. They had the pitch and tonality of disgust. And my ears were keen to it, having once been coached with such gentle care and patience, lovingly taught how to listen. I was listening for the story in everything by then.

I will never forget walking home from that game utterly destroyed. The difference was made permanent in that moment. I would never be back in the game.

He once backhanded me. Sent me spinning into a wall, because I was so excited to tell him that I had completed the puzzle in the paper and could send it in and maybe win an encyclopedia. But I was interrupting his conversation with a friend. It was so sudden that I didn't even realize what was happening until I was crumpled on the floor, looking up at him dictate "First you stand there, then when I recognize you, you can say 'excuse me' and say whatever it is you want. But do not ever interrupt me again." I couldn't imagine that there would ever again be anything I would want to say to him worth the risk. And there never was.

In the years following the molestation he really didn't ever show me affection at all anymore. My little brother was old enough to start following me around and wanting to spend time with me, so my father's concerns fell not to me but to how I was influencing him. It was as if I was no longer his son as much as his other son's older brother.

In those days I bonded not to my father but to the piano. I spent long hours when other kids were out throwing the football or shooting hoops sitting at the piano deciphering Bach or Chopin. I could sense every emotion in every piece of music written as though it were my own. I found solace there. I found security, safety. But he would not be part of it. Boys don't play the piano. Girls play the piano. Boys play soccer.

At nine years old I was transposing twenty-page Bach organ recitals into piano music and playing them from memory, and hiding it from my father because he did not approve. This from the man that sat me on his lap to listen to Tchaikovsky's First when I was not yet four years old. I was not allowed to play the piano for a variety of reasons...it interfered with the TV, it interfered with homework time, or he just didn't like listening to it.

But it came to define me. At the piano I was no longer the girly boy whose father didn't like him; I was a musician who understood it and could perform it. I fought off his opinion that it was beneath contempt. I kept it from becoming mine because I needed the piano. I needed it badly, and I stupidly kept getting better at playing it.

The more I played, the more I studied, the closer I identified with the composers, and the further I retreated into their world and away from my own. My emotions found their way into the pieces of music and could be spilled out there where I did not have to figure them out. Where I did not have to understand them, and could bear their pain if not their explanation. But as for the piano, all was femininity, and I knew it. I could sense it.

Not until sitting down to write all of this to you did I ever realize that my playing the piano was more than a retreat. All these many years I have been operating with the certainty that the piano saved me by giving me a safe place to hide at the same time that it was absorbing the emotions from me. These decades I have never questioned that it was ever more than that.

But it was more. Without knowing it I was not spending those countless hours just playing the piano. I was furiously working out the story in the music, hoping he would come back.

I was trying to win him back.

Often, in the small hours of a Sunday morning he would come upstairs drunk and wake me up so that I could go downstairs and play the piano for his party friends, in the candlelight and stink of bourbon and cigarettes. And he never seemed to remember doing it. I sometimes wondered if he should apologize to me, but he never did.

Hidden in those dimly lit hours was the growing sense that I no longer feared him. And I became convinced that he was gone beyond gone, and would never come back. I confess that I started to feel yet another emotion not typically meant for sons to have toward their fathers. Hatred.

His demeanor toward my sisters was quite different. He was playful, affectionate and always supportive. My dad was a natural practical joker and nothing pleased him more than to successfully pull a prank on someone and then laugh about it every time he could call it to mind. Back in the mid-sixties the movie "The Birds" (Alfred Hitchcock) was popular. One night one of my sisters (we don't all seem to remember it being the same sister) was babysitting at the neighbor's house two doors down. She had put the children to bed and was watching the movie (dad checked on that by calling her to make sure she was). When the movie was over he called again, only this time instead of speaking to her he took his duck call and started making duck noises into the phone. She must have screamed, thrown the phone and fled, because he then calmly said, "Children, we have to go check on your sister." And we went across the cul-de-sac to see if she was okay, where we found her hiding underneath the bed in one of the bedrooms.

When a men's accountability group that used to meet at my house got together it was always fascinating to me to hear about the other guys' relationships with their dads. How different they all were.

My father did engage me in a sort of one-to-one relationship after I was seven at times, but as I mentioned earlier, it almost always centered on my little brother. He would speak to me with a serious tone about my responsibility toward my younger brother because I had an example to set. My brother was four years younger than me and very impressionable. So the things I did or didn't do, the things in which I had an interest or none whatsoever, became important because of the example they set for my little brother. Had I not had a little brother he might have been able to ignore me altogether, the odd birthday and late night piano-playing thing notwithstanding.

We (my brother and I) were once caught shoplifting, along with two other boys from our neighborhood. The punishment was pretty severe and involved a lecture, a spanking, and my brother was excused to go to our room. Then my dad focused on me. There were some more harsh words; I think he told me that I made him sick to his stomach. And then he threatened me with *real* consequences (whatever they would be) if it ever happened again. The cardinal sin was not the shoplifting. That was just a petty crime and I was just a thief. The real disgusting sin was how I was setting a bad example for my little brother. I was guilty of my shoplifting AND his.

It was like the only time that my brother would be punished rather than me was if I was in a foreign country at the time his offense occurred. And even with that, the chances were good I'd get blamed anyway because my dad had already begun to attribute anything bad he did to my influence.

In fairness I would have to say that there were times when he tried to be fatherly, do fatherly things with me. Why, I wouldn't know.

I have a photograph of my father and myself on a small pier at the base of a cabin yard in Matagorda Bay. We had been duck hunting (or rather, he had been duck hunting and I was brought along to sit in the blind) and we were both squatting on our ankles with four mallards dead on the dock in front of me. Lifting and holding one of the mallards by the neck, I have a giant smile and my dad had the expression of a fireplace portrait. George Washington crossing the Potomac.

My smile was much too large to be convincing. And as I look at the photo today I see a desperate boy trying to please his captor and in my father the look of obligation but absolutely nothing more. He does not have his arm around me; he has his hand on the small of my back as though there were no other comfortable place to put it but he had to get it out of the way. He had to make it look as though we were close. But he isn't smiling.

The photo is painful to look at now, because over time more can be seen in the expressions on our faces. Or less. It bothers me that I don't have a photo where the expressions really are what they look like; the pride is really pride, and the happiness is not a show for the cameraman.

Much later in life I worked as a therapist in a residential treatment center in Hawaii. I had eight guys on my caseload and I would do two group sessions every day and usually two "one-on-one" sessions. These guys all had horror stories related to their fathers and at least one that I know of was wrenching to hear. His father attempted to kill him not once, but twice when he was only ten years old, forcing him to flee and live on the streets. I confess that I cannot imagine surviving that kind of thing. I cannot imagine dealing with that...my experiences seem so minor by comparison.

But they have one thing in common. They both present a situation in which a young boy comes to understand that his father is the enemy.

After we moved away from the neighborhood where the abuse occurred, we moved into a neighborhood across town that was predominantly Catholic. It even had a wall around it with a sidewalk through the wall so the kids could walk to the Catholic Church where the school was. The households in our neighborhood were all "good Catholic" families, which means six or more children. There was even an outlier family not far who had fourteen.

In the summertime, our pine cone wars were the stuff of a Cecile B. Demille flick. You might be too young to remember those, but he was a guy who made films in the early days, with thousands of extras for the battle scenes.

The school we attended was a small Catholic school with grades one through eight and a total of about three hundred students for all. Two of the teachers there were aunts of mine, and the rest were a mix of "lay" teachers and nuns. I think just my cousins, kids in the neighborhood, my brother and sisters and I alone made up most of the enrollment.

But it was a wonderful school to go to...because it was safe, it was fun, and the nuns were always a good source of fascination. We were an island of naiveté in a sea of public school kids who actually smoked cigarettes. They would wait for their public school bus at the end of our Catholic neighborhood sidewalk and call us "mackerel snappers" and "minnow munchers" (because in those days Catholics ate fish on Fridays) as we passed them in our bright and tidy uniforms. I thought they probably robbed banks on the weekends.

I had two good friends, Mike and Kevin. Mike was my best buddy. And Mary was the girl I had my very first real crush on. She was the first girl in the school to ever get swats. A legend in her own time – I'll tell her story in a bit.

In those days it was still legal for the nuns to administer corporal punishment (swats) and there was even a nun at the school who had once been a lady's pro baseball player and could lift you off the freakin' floor. Mike and I were competitive in everything we did. He was the better athlete by far, but I could run faster. I ran barefoot.

The principal was a very wise and street-smart nun, whose cheek flesh overlapped her white starched face-hood thing (from her habit) that was bolted so tight onto her head we could not tell whether or not she actually *was* bald under there. She had a quirky sense of justice that induced her to ask us how many swats we thought we deserved when we were caught doing something bad. If we answered "three" which was the unwritten rule maximum, she had pity on our poor pitiful soul and gave us only one. If we answered "one," she responded in stern reproach and informed us that our lack of remorse indicated that we deserved three.

The problem for us was not that we didn't fully understand this, but that we could not predict it. You never knew whether or not you would actually get away with one if you said you deserved three, or three if you said you deserved one – so when asked, we always answered "two." I'm sure that if she figured out that strategy of ours she would have considered it equally indicative of our lack of remorse and would award three as a result. Or maybe she would just get frustrated that we might be gaming the swat decision deal she had going on and given us fifty. Who could say? Given enough years, the average number of swats any child would ever receive for any wrongdoing would surely migrate to the maximum, in this give-and-take strategy situation between nuns and us unrepentant children. Such is the nature of Catholic school, I guess.

One day Mike challenged me to a foot race, but it was raining so we had to run down the main corridor of the school, about fifty yards. Running in the hallways was strictly forbidden, but that didn't really matter. The building was shaped like a long shallow "U" with the two ends only about thirty or so feet, but the middle hallway about two hundred feet long. At one end of the corridor were the first grade classrooms. That's were the race was to start. At the other end of the long corridor were the offices of the principal and her secretary. There was a ninety-degree turn and the corridor continued on for another thirty feet or so to the right. Along that branch were the doors of the principal and the secretary, with the secretary's door on the left. So after we took off running from the first-grade area along the main hallway we were actually running *toward* the secretary's office door, with the principal's door about ten feet to the right of it after the turn.

Because I was faster barefoot, I took off my shoes. The floor was highly polished terrazzo. "Ready, set, go" and we took off running. I was beating Mike by about five feet (as I usually did outside) but as we were coming to the end of the hall where the principal's office was I began to sense that I could not make the turn in my socks unless I slowed down. But if I slowed down, Mike would overtake me. I had no idea if he was beginning to question his ability to make the turn or not, but he wasn't slowing down so neither was I. By the time I realized that I could not make the turn it was too late. Not only could I not make the turn but I couldn't stop...or even slow down. I slammed into the secretary's door at full speed sending a "boom" resonating off the terrazzo floors and block walls all the way back to the first grade. I bounced off the door in time to see Mike's feet slip out from under him as he made the turn. He slid right past the principal's office just as she was opening her door to see what had exploded. Sliding past her on his back he looked up, held up two fingers and said, "I'll take two, Sister." That was cool. I almost thought she would give us both a pass just because Mike was so quick-witted.

Eating candy during school hours was absolutely forbidden. We could eat anything we wanted at lunch whether it was nutritious or not, evidenced by the food they sold at school. But during class hours candy was serious contraband. Well, clever as we were, we latched onto one of Mary's brilliant schemes and discovered cinnamon oil. We learned that we could dip our pencils in it over night and then suck on our pencils during class. It was as good as having hard candy, and the teachers wouldn't know. Within days every grocery store for a three-mile radius was out of cinnamon oil.

It didn't take long for the nuns to trace the overwhelming smell of the oil to our pencil tips and ban it all. They were pretty annoyed and may well have banned pencils themselves, just to make things tough on us. But I guess they didn't want to grade papers written in Crayon. If we were found to have a pencil, or any long stick-type item, any fingers, articles of clothing, paperclips, rubber bands or anything normally purchased at the drug store in the school supply department dipped in cinnamon oil, it was confiscated and we were sent to the principal's office. While cinnamon oil was impossible to see, you could smell it under water. And those nuns and teachers turned into blood- hounds.

One day the smell of cinnamon oil was very strong in the classroom but they couldn't find the actual object that had been dipped in it. The nuns were convinced that it was *somewhere* but didn't know where, and that meant that they didn't know who had it. So they lined us all up against the wall (boys in one line, girls in the other). As an aside, we could never understand why the nuns always kept separating the boys and the girls. I mean, I never once thought about spontaneously grabbing one of the girls and having sex while in the hallways of sixth grade no matter how fetching the little plaid skirts might have been, and I am quite sure that neither did any of my buddies.

The nuns made perfectly sure of that by demanding that the skirts were long enough to touch the floor, when the girls kneeled, anyway. Who knows how many unwanted pregnancies would have occurred had they relaxed *that* little bit of decorum.

Well, Mike was allergic to cinnamon oil. It made his skin blotch in big red patches. As the principal moved down the line of boys asking each one "Did you have any cinnamon oil?" I was standing stiff against the wall next to Mike, whose face looked like an allied strategy map of Europe during World War II. When he was asked the question he answered "No, Sister" and I "busted out" laughing. Mike turned to me and said, "Damn it, John!" adding to the sin of cinnamon oil the sin of profanity. I was just glad he didn't put a "God" in front of that; after all, he was my best friend and although I didn't like losing to him, I certainly didn't want to see him crucified. We all could only speculate what sort of wrath would result if we took the name of the Lord in vain, but we were absolutely sure that three would not have been enough.

One other story about Mike and then I'll move on. We had a lay teacher for reading class who was a sweet lady from Chicago, or maybe Ohio, who tried her best to be stern with us but who just couldn't really pull it off. She was short and pretty round. In fact, she had the shape of a snowman, usually upholstered in tweed.

She had a thing for M&M's and used to eat them during reading class. Now mind you, as candy was serious contraband for students, it was not tolerated for teachers either. After all, how would it look? So our reading teacher used to pour her M&M's in the pencil tray of her desk and while we were reading, she would also read. But from time to time her book would gradually lower from a reading height to just flush with the edge of the desk. After the M&M retrieval mission was complete, it would then gradually rise to the eating coordinates or, rather, putting the M&M's in your mouth coordinates. It remained there, we would speculate, just long enough for any outward appearances of chewing to be over and then begin its gradual descent back in the retrieval stage of the overall operation. Looking back it would seem a little hard to believe that she thought we would not question a copy of <u>Les Miserable</u> behaving like the big ball up and down at Times Square during New Year's Eve. But there you have it.

Well, Mike and I had an idea. We were joking before class one day about the idea of putting bugs in her M&M drawer because she never appeared to look down during these reading sessions. She didn't really need to. We thought it would be great fun to see her pop a June bug in her mouth along with the blues and yellows, and wondered if she would gag, scream, and run from the classroom, or if she would just keep reading as if she had chanced on a stale one. It didn't take long for the joking exchange to morph into an actual plan.

June bugs were too big. We would need a smaller bug. "Roly-poly's," pill bugs. Perfect. Maybe a little small but that meant that she wouldn't detect them in a group of real M&M's; after all, she never looked at them. From the pencil tray to the mouth they went, completely unquestioned. But we could do better if we painted them to match the M&M's, then even if she did see them she might mistake them for oddball defects the M&M factory didn't catch, just as chocolaty good even if maybe a little smaller than the others.

That afternoon we gathered about twenty of them, carefully picking out the largest ones and hoping that maybe that day she would have the peanut variety which were rounder and more like a large pill bug rolled up. We touched each one until it rolled into a ball and then we painted it with tempera colors to match the M&M's, reasoning that the paint would keep them rolled up long enough to make it to her mouth. They were a work of art. We quickly threw the colorful bugs into her M&M tray just before she walked into the classroom.

But like so many brilliant schemes, this one contained a tragic flaw. While the bugs did indeed resemble a peanut M&M remarkably well, as it happened the tempera paint was not strong enough to hold them into their rolled-up state. Once the bugs realized that they were not in the hands of a couple of sixth graders being painted, they were free to unroll and go about their day as usual, finding themselves in a colorful tray of M&M's and painted all festive like Mardi Gras or something. Mike and I did not know that they were unrolling as the whole room was reading, and we sat full of anticipation as we waited for her to chew on one of them.

But it never happened.

On one of her grab expeditions as her fingers nestled in the pile, one of them began to crawl up her finger. I can only imagine what she must have thought as she noticed a bright yellow M&M clinging to her pointer. No deception perpetrated on the innocent goes unpunished in the halls of Catholic schools (not even those perpetrated by teachers) and perhaps the demons normally consigned to the torments of the damned had been unleashed in her candy to teach her a good lesson. <u>Les Miserable</u> was launched skyward as she screamed "oh my god oh my god oh my GOD," if memory serves, and ran from the room. Most of our classmates looked at each other completely puzzled, as if there was something really shocking in that book and maybe they just need to get a copy themselves, check it out. Mike and I just looked at each other in frustrated disgust, cheated. We *wanted* to see her eat one. And trust me, our deception did <u>not</u> go unpunished. What was curious was that they never even initiated an investigation as to who was responsible; they just knew. It had all the earmarks. But after that Mike and I knew that whenever we planned something, we also had to figure out how to make it look like someone else had done it. They were on to us.

Now for the Mary story.

Later, we had another teacher for reading class. No, we did not drive the other one insane. It was because we were in eighth grade by then. She was an elderly lady, thin as a rail, and had an expression etched into her face over the years that seemed to express a permanent state of abject boredom. She also had a disdain for children that was palpable. We knew that she didn't like us, but we really didn't mind. We just assumed that she didn't like anybody. But she also seemed to deeply distrust us, for what reason we surely didn't know.

She even arranged her reading class with her desk at the back of the classroom, facing forward in the same direction as our desks faced with her looking at the back of our heads. It was very effective because we could never see where she was looking. Sometimes we would try to gradually turn our heads very slowly so as to see if we could get a glimpse without her noticing, but upon doing so our eyes were always met by her condemning stare. Or other times we would sort of hold our books so as to allow us to look *under* our arm and turn our head at the same time, but that didn't work either. We would find her meeting our stare with the expression that seemed to demand, "Do you really think I am that stupid, you little twerp? I have children like you for breakfast."

Well, as I said earlier, candy was forbidden. Actually, we were not allowed to have anything to eat outside of the cafeteria or the play yard just outside the cafeteria building. But one day Mary decided to bring to reading class (our first class after lunch) a crisp red apple that she decided not to eat at lunch. I noticed her carrying it but didn't really think anything of it.

After a while when the class was completely quiet because everyone (including the teacher, who, of course we could not see) was deep in our reading, we heard someone from the edge of class chomp into an apple "CRUNCHOMP !!!" - and then heard and saw a bright red apple tumbling along the floor across the classroom, with a bite almost the size of a third of it taken out.

Mary had waited until just the right moment, bit into the apple in what could only be described as a bodacious mouthful crunch, then immediately tossed the apple across the floor burying her face in her book so as not to be detected as she chewed. Brilliant.

I knew it had to be Mary because I recognized the apple. But I am quite sure the teacher would never have known it was Mary had she not been ratted out by the kids sitting next to her, the goody-two-shoes type that iron their socks and spin off suicidal at the threat of an A- on their book reports.

Mary was immediately ordered to Sister Mary's office. I'm not sure exactly how we learned that she had received swats. Just the sheer shock of the news blew us away and I know I can't remember how we found out. This was big, I mean really big. No *girl* had ever been given swats before…no girl had ever stepped far enough out of line for it to ever be considered. We had come to conclude that a girl would have to do something truly unspeakable to receive swats and no girl like that ever existed! Mike and I were in awe, and I was in love. It was school history and we were living in the moment of it.

We did find one way of annoying that particular teacher that was unaffected by the way the furniture was arranged.

She was the teacher who gave us spelling tests. We had a piece of paper, she would call out a word, and we would write it down. Now because sometimes two words can sound exactly the same but be spelled differently, if we had a doubt about the word we could ask a question to clarify it. For example, if she called out "principal" but we thought that maybe she meant "principle," we were permitted to ask, "Is that 'principle' as in finance?"

Some of us were better spellers than others. So latching on to this provision we started asking questions on words that we thought Mary might not get, or I might not get. For example, "Is that 'psychiatrist' as in 'potato'?" She would become enraged.

There are lots of other stories from my memories of that little Catholic school. Today it is a highly-regarded learning institution and there is a waiting list of students hoping to get in. I have been told that there are no longer nuns there, and I had the chance to return to the town I grew up in and visit the campus grounds not long ago. The convent is gone as is the pear tree we once denuded of every single one of its pears even though they weren't even ripe. It is now a vacant lot waiting to be sold to have a house built on it, I presume. There is a new church building that is really very beautiful. As I drove past the school and church, I allowed myself a full measure of poignancy remembering a period and place in time precious to me and gone.

I wondered if the children there still push the boundaries of authority, knowing full well that they are loved in spite of anything they do. I wondered if any of them had figured out how to work the hot chocolate machine in the teacher's lounge and were brave enough to sneak in to get some. Were any of them still throwing each other's books out the window immediately before class as the teachers were just getting started? I wondered what the ultimate penalty could possibly be…what did the children have to fear, binding them together in the fraternity of mischief. Or was it that the laws now in place to protect them had actually stolen from them the certainty but safety of consequence and blurred the boundaries? Were they all little adults now not in grade school but in some collegiate prep where mischief really is criminal and childhood itself is managed as with the gravity of a more sinister world? Was it all too serious now?

On April 1, 1968 I came home from that school where my brother, sisters, cousins, friends and I attended, where my aunts taught, and the principal played ping-pong with my father. It was Wednesday afternoon and I was in the pasture riding Joe, our neighbor's horse, along with some friends. One of my sisters came to the fence and told me to get off Joe and come home right away, something bad had happened.

When I got back to the house I was told that dad had had a heart attack and was in the hospital. My sisters were in hysterics, crying and shouting questions and answers to each other that I can't remember. I kept saying that heart attacks were common and that he was in the hospital already so everything would be fine, not to worry. I think I really believed it. But they didn't. They just kept screaming and crying.

We lived in a large two-story home and the front two bedrooms had windows that overlooked the front lawn and cul-de-sac on which the house was situated. I stood in the window holding the curtain aside waiting for my mom or my dad's car to pull up to the house, home from the hospital. I knew it would be any minute and he would be home, perhaps with a cane and a bag full of prescription bottles and she, the dutiful wife, would be clinging to his arm walking him up to the front gate. He would be fragile, but home.

After a time, I do not recall how long, I did see a car approach the yard followed by two others. They all parked along the yard and eventually the door closest to the yard of the front car opened. Then a foot appeared and planted itself on the concrete. My dad's partner "Goldie" was already around the back of the car and ready to assist at the opened door. He lifted my mom out of the car.

It would be more accurate to say that what emerged from that car was what was left of her...and that wasn't much. She could not bear her own weight and so couldn't walk. Goldie half carried her as the two approached the front gate arm in arm, my mom seeming to cling to him more than to try to get herself to the door. My sisters had been screaming that he was dead before the cars had arrived but I was sure that they were wrong – it just couldn't happen. In that moment looking down out the window, however, without being told, I knew.

My father was dead.

2. Pond John

THE DAYS FOLLOWING THAT AFTERNOON WERE a blur. A mix of scenes and conversations, strangers speaking words of encouragement as foreigners from a foreign land attempting to speak a language they didn't know. There was so much food all throughout the house it made me wonder who was being fed.

The family in the house next to us had a boy about my age and we had become very close friends as soon as we moved to the new neighborhood. We were usually inseparable after school, but since he went to the public schools I didn't see much of him during the day. More about him later. But the day after my father's death, before the funeral, we went fishing at a pond near the new house he had moved into. As we stood on the bank of that pond not saying a word just going through the motions, a choking pain kept lifting in my throat upward and I was straining with everything I had against confusion. What was there to say? I didn't know, and neither did he. So we stood there as if catching a fish was why we were there. But that day no word was ever spoken, neither of us laughed about anything, not even once. It is impossible to accurately describe what that was like.

The morning of the funeral broke sunny and cool. April in Houston can be very beautiful and it was a perfect day. The sky was brilliant blue. At one point of the morning, having put on our good clothes, we were to leave the house, walk down the long front sidewalk, and get into a limousine, lead a train of cars to the church, and eventually to the cemetery. There were still large crowds at the house and we had each been in our own little glass bubbles being stared at by the mix of people we knew and those we didn't.

Occasionally we would glance at each other, meeting eyes, and exchange that split second of shared terror and desperate confusion.

I very vividly remember that there were a lot of people in the front yard waiting for us to come out and get into our cars, so that they could then go get into theirs. They were there to show us support and to be available to comfort us if need. There were a lot of them. Instinctively they did not stand on the sidewalk but rather on either side of it, sparing it for us. But the effect was to turn our walk toward the limo into a gauntlet.

As I walked down that sidewalk, immersed in confusion and pain, I noticed the faces of my buddies staring at me. And in their faces I did not see empathy or concern. I did not see affection or a yearning to help me…I saw fear. I saw confused searching looks as those from an overwhelming curiosity to see whether I had somehow changed…was there a mark. I saw in their eyes a hint of panic that maybe what I had was contagious. I couldn't look back at them because I couldn't answer them. I accepted that they now saw me as different. I had to. I was.

I don't remember much of the time immediately following the funeral except snippets of conversation and the scenes in which they occurred. I remember overhearing some gentleman who I did not recognize talking to my youngest sister. This sister was only six when dad died, and she would come to survive many more trials than most people I know. She has always risen to every one of them with a grace and strength that would amaze you. And she did even then.

I am quite sure she didn't know who he was either. But he wanted to try to help her. He said, "Don't worry: I'll be your father." She looked at him patiently but with a slight curiosity showing. It was as if she didn't know why he was saying it. Maybe he didn't know. Maybe he hadn't found out, whoever he was. And she quietly answered, "I have a father, but he's dead." I will never forget it.

So many events spoke to that. They spoke to the fact that no one witnessing the grief of another can understand it, no matter how well-intentioned or kind their efforts. When we make offers of empathy that assume our understanding of another's grief, we sometimes inadvertently belittle it. And the person is left more alone than before.

I have lost two people in my immediate family, my father and that younger brother. And I can tell you that what you can do for a person in grief is to think of what needs to be done (do the dishes, run errands, pick the kids up from school, etc.) and just do it, without even mentioning it other than to let someone near know what is going on. When you are in this situation, and you surely will be someday if you haven't been already, don't offer; just do it. If you offer they will say, "no" because they are too overwhelmed to understand, too bombarded with pain to be able to bridle their thoughts toward the mundane. All you will have done is consigned for yourself the satisfaction of the offer to do something but the freedom to do nothing.

The most important thing, however, is to be willing to sit with them, quietly, and listen. Listen to them as if the two of you are in a prison cell alone, appreciating that one of you is. One of you is shackled to a pain that they will never escape, while you are free to come and go as you please. So hear that pain. Offer affection, not advice. Let them talk to themselves in your presence. Cry with them, but never for them. A person who suffers the loss of another they love knows not just death but life, probably better than you do. So spare your pity for someone else.

Okay, enough of the lecture.

My mom, who was in deep shock, struggled with what to do to ease the experience for us, but she really didn't know what to do. She held at least one group talk wherein she asserted that we were a family and that we would survive the events as a family if we stick together. It seemed like it helped; it at least gave me some hope. I was aware that we (the children) were not experiencing the tragedy the same as my mom, but I couldn't quite figure out the difference exactly. I knew that she was very alone. She was alone in a way that I could do nothing about.

My sisters were playing out their grief as though the man who died was a different man than the father I knew. And different each, one to the next. And none of us had anything close to an understanding of the man whose absence my mom now grieved. How could we?

I would hear her later speaking to us but probably talking to herself. She suggested that dad had died because he wanted to. Now you may recoil a little to think of that, but I don't. You see, she was desperately trying to make sense of it. The randomness of the event could not possibly be paired with the gravity, in any way. I think she suggested that he could not bear to see us grow up and leave him as we eventually would, and so death was a better way. He would never be able to stand being without us as we matured and left to pursue our own lives, so it would be simpler to just die. Much later, as an adult, I understood that what she was saying was an effort to communicate to us that he loved us so we would not be angry at him the way she probably was. And I think she may have been trying to convince herself that he did not die out of indifference toward her.

I can appreciate now as an adult that in addition to the catastrophic blow that was the loss of the love of her life, the stunned grief and fear, there had to have been anger. He left her alone to face the rest of life with six children, no life insurance, and no means to support the family. He had bailed on the plan.

But secretly I knew the truth at twelve years old. I knew that he did not want to die because he could not face our leaving home eventually. He did want to die, yes, that part I bought. But it was because he wanted to get away from me. My mom was correct on his strategy but as regards his motive, mistaken.

What settled on me was the sense that five years of scorn and disapproval if not open animosity had fully fledged. I was wholly abandoned. Nothing, in a child's mind, can seal the certainty of their worthlessness more effectively.

The years following my dad's death were the years in which I became more and more certain that something about me was not right. I was different, and the damage done was not getting better. It was getting worse. It was settling in, working its way down to the deeper reaches. It was insinuating itself into every cell, every thought, every experience. I was becoming more and more profoundly isolated, from the inside out.

My first memory of the emotion of it was simple and very clear. I was standing in the bedroom to the left at the top of the stairs. I was looking into the closet after having hung up some clothes. Suddenly as I was looking at the clothes hanging on the rack, a wave of emotion came over me. Or maybe it was a thought; I'm not sure. I almost instantaneously knew that I was never going to be *right*. It wasn't so much the not being right that disassembled me as much as it was the *never*. Nothing I, or anyone, could ever do was going to fix it. Nothing I, or anyone, could ever do was going to make me normal. And the worst part about it was that none of it could be seen. It was not just an abject hell but it was a completely private hell. I knew in that moment that even if I could describe it to someone -- and I knew I couldn't – they could not even understand it, let alone make it change. And if they really understood what was going on inside of me now, they would reject me just like my father had when he discovered what had happened. I didn't fear abandonment, because you do not truly fear that of which you are certain. You just ache in the sickness of it.

I wouldn't say, as some might, that that was when I truly began to grieve. I would say that that is the point at which I stopped grieving. That was the moment I began to live life in the aftermath.

At about that time, a new and very strange emotion grew up in the day-to-day interaction I had with my friends, particularly my school buddies. Looking back I would have to call it a jealousy. First I was jealous of them because they seemed to be living life with no problems. Their life had no changes in it. I was jealous of every word of affection given them by their fathers. I was jealous of what they did together with their fathers – but it was more – I was becoming jealous of who they *were*.

Most of the time I really couldn't identify what I was feeling, but I definitely knew that I was having strange and painful emotions. Nothing was the same; nothing was innocent; everything was the subject of an intense analysis that could only be performed in isolation. Everything had to be understood. The desperate need to understand each and every nuance in my boyhood friendships was the only defense against the new and awkward difficulty I was having with them. If I could understand each word and why it was said, each meaning that was really the hidden meaning because nothing was just at face value anymore; if I could just understand it all it would go back to the way it was before. I didn't have any clue that the desperate need to understand was *keeping* it from being the way it was before. I was caught in a hopeless cycle of attempting to fix everything using the very instrument of its current destruction – my brain. And outside the walls of this brutal slashing torrent, no one could see a glimpse of it. They did not know it was happening.

In these early days, it was my friendship with Mike that was the first to crack. His was the first friendship that needed me to be the same as before to be held together. But I couldn't reason through it. I couldn't *think* the situation away, and there was no way to be just myself anymore. There was no self. Reason is a poor maker of intimacy, and innocence often its first casualty.

Mike was always good at baseball and I would go to his games where I witnessed his father lavish praise and affection on him. I was twelve years old and seeing that sent a stab of pain into me that I had no idea I could even experience. I would never be like him, I would never be normal, I would never know a father like the one he took for granted. Funny that to this day, baseball caps have been almost a symbol of my inadequacy. They are not simple things to me. They're not innocent if I wear them, only if someone else does. If I wear them they are pretense.

I remember once a bunch of us guys in the locker room were getting ready for some formal function at the Catholic school I attended. This was seventh grade. All the guys were in the bathroom getting dressed out of our uniforms and into more formal clothes. I stood and watched all the guys putting their ties on. They all knew how to tie them. It only took a few minutes before a growing panic started seizing me. I did not know the first thing about tying ties, but they ALL did. How long would it be before they noticed that I was standing there, scared that they would notice? How do you fake tying a tie? I think I was about to leave or run, but where would I go? What excuse could I possibly have for this? How could I joke this away?

Mike must have noticed me looking scared and confused and came and tied my tie for me as he was facing me. For whatever reason completely incomprehensible to me, no one even mentioned it. No joke was made; no snide remarks were tossed my way. It is as if I had just been plucked from the edge of a cliff and no one even noticed that I had been shuddering there at the precipice, in cold fear.

On some deep emotional level I became attached to Mike in a way that had never happened before. A new feeling was part of me that I had never experienced before and it was one that terrified me and set me on the stage of my own scorn.

I have to interject a story here that might help explain this.

When I was growing up I was given my first BB gun at about the age of nine. Before the BB gun I had a bow and arrow set, and I used to shoot target with it as often as I could. Robin Hood was my hero.

After we left the neighborhood where the abuse occurred, we moved to an area that was still being developed. There were pine forests and large pastures immediately adjacent to our home…one of them being where I would ride the neighbor's horse. The boys in the neighborhood (some of us) would take our bows into the forests and hunt squirrel and sometimes rabbit. Rabbit were much harder to hit and required quite a bit of strategy and understanding of how they behaved. To hunt rabbit was not childish stuff; it was the skill of a true hunter.

When I was old enough to have a BB gun it became an essential component of summer. The first day of summer two things happened; we took off our shoes and we stocked up on BB's because we *always* had our BB guns with us. Always.

I got to be a really good shot and once even, on a dare, hit a horsefly on the wall of a two-car garage from the opposite wall…solidifying for perpetuity my reputation as a dead-eye shot.

Well, there were lots of times that Mike and I would take our guns into the forest to shoot birds, or snakes, or really big bugs if we found them. If there wasn't anything like that to shoot we would invariably decide to have a "war" and shoot each other. One day (this was before dad died) we were deep in the woods and there were no birds, no snakes, and no bugs. We were walking side by side and Mike said, "Let's have a war…" I had the kind of BB gun that you could keep cocked and the BB would not roll out – some of them if the gun was cocked you had to keep the barrel pointing upward or the BB would roll out. So my gun was cocked and ready to shoot draped over my arm pointing toward the ground as I walked next to Mike. I said, "Okay," shot him in the foot, and peeled off running.

Even though these BB guns were really just toys, if you got hit by one from about twelve inches away, you would know it.

Mike jumped up, dropped his gun, grabbed his foot and yelled, "Shit, you butt hole!!" (There were no nuns around). I knew that as I ran to a safe distance that he would shoot to sting and the war was on, whether I tired of it or not. He would not quit until I had a corresponding red welt of my own.

The point is that, before, I had no fear of Mike and I saw nothing in him that caused me to notice something lacking in me. We were equals. As much as I loved our adventures and our competitions, as much as I cared for my buddy, I didn't need him.

But I think the day that he tied my tie that all changed.

His friendship became painful to me in a way that he could not have understood and of which he was completely unaware. His life was coursing its way full and complete, and he would have no capacity to understand the difference. I no longer just mindlessly enjoyed the pranks we pulled at school, or the competitions we fell into as a matter of casual routine. I no longer just counted on some kill time with Mike now and again; I wanted to *be* him. I ached with each observance that he was different. I wept bitterly in the silence of nights that passed unnoticed and without significance to everyone else.

Mike went on to a private Catholic high school, as did all of my buddies from grade school. I wanted desperately to go as well, but we couldn't afford it. And I never saw him again. A few years ago at my brother's funeral I asked my Aunt – one of the teachers from that Catholic school – if she knew of his whereabouts. I had decided that I wanted to reconnect with him after all these years. She told me that he had died of cancer, she thought.

It was not long after the tie incident with Mike that my friend that didn't go to the Catholic school, Pond John, and I discovered alcohol. He had become more like a brother to me when dad died than a friend, really. I say this to mean that he spent so much time with me away from school and lived so close, that our friendship had much more of an assumption of connectedness than the others. We never invited each other to do anything together, we just always did.

He and I broke into his father's liquor cabinet and proceeded to get drunk in his upstairs bedroom...I believe it was bourbon. His older brother caught us and tried to discipline us in some silly unauthorized way. But as the saying goes, the cat was out of the bag. It was not long at all before I would be what is now referred to as "pathologically alcoholic." But I'll talk more about this later.

Also by that age I was seriously devoted to the piano. The amount of time I would spend at the piano daily would be measured in hours per day, not minutes. And I began composing in earnest. My technique at the piano had matured considerably and I could easily transition in and out of chord signatures as though my sense of harmony had become innate. The piano was no longer an external hunk of wood at which I sat. It was a horse I rode, a bear with which I would wrestle, a favorite dog with which I would run, no destination in mind, slowing only for fatigue.

It was not so much that I knew the piano but that the piano seemed to know me. My isolation included the piano; no one and nothing else. It bled from me the emotions I could not stand to hold. Often I would not really be thinking about anything in particular, but when I sat down to play, my feelings would come out in the music. I know this sounds strange and I know you may think this is crazy, but it really was as if I wasn't playing the piano but rather having a conversation with it. And it always calmed me.

The music that had the greatest satisfaction for me was Chopin, although I was also drawn to Beethoven and Rachmaninoff. Interestingly, even though later my teacher would insist that I work the compositions of Debussy, I never had any interest in him. What piqued my enjoyment of the music of Chopin and Beethoven was what I knew about their lives.

Chopin and Beethoven were definitely people who suffered. I knew that because I had read everything I could get my hands on about them. Their music became a window into their lives and a point at which you could see their frustrations, angers, and the full spectrum of their angst, for lack of a better word. You could hear it; you could hear beyond it.

Playing the Etude in E by Chopin was kin to experiencing his devastation over Georges Sand; the adagio from the Sonata Pathetique (C Minor) was a profound mystery. How could Beethoven produce "passionate sorrow" as the name he gave it is translated? And how could passionate sorrow be so simple, so sweet? To play it was to search. To move in it was to use Chopin's angst and Beethoven's sorrows and, with them, to paint over my own.

When I started composing my own works, in earnest, I began to accept better. I didn't understand anything any better than before, and I definitely did not necessarily *feel* any better than before. But I could get up and walk away from the piano, just as easily as I could go to it. And I had become fluent. What I mean by this is that the piano, and playing it, had become a container of sorts. I could store everything there, and then leave to go to bed to wake up and face the next day. But I wasn't comfortable anywhere other than at the piano. Knowing that the piano was there made it easier for me to set things aside and not think about them during the day when I was away from the piano. I could think about them when I came back to the piano, so in a sense it helped me to accept.

Entering my freshman year of high school at that time was terrifying, in its own right. I went from that very small Catholic school where I knew everyone and had two aunts who taught, to a huge public school of over three thousand students. And these were not just any students; these were the same kids we had to pass at the bus stop wearing our little Catholic school uniforms; the ones who called us "minnow munchers" and "mackerel snappers." In those days being raised Catholic at a Catholic school, being an altar boy and such was not just a different education. It wasn't even just a different lifestyle; it was a different culture altogether. Public school kids were not just Protestants or such to us; they were a flat-out different race of human being. We were from different planets.

I was a nerd even by Catholic school standards, but public school was way out of my league. I was reading Poe and Dickens at the age of ten, along with my Catholic school colleagues. In public school I learned, to my astonishment, that there were people who could not read a cereal box.

But the most debilitating legacy of my prior years was the abject naiveté that defined all of us, really. As late as the eighth grade I was convinced that anyone who cussed and smoked cigarettes probably robbed banks on Saturday nights. And although there were the occasional students admitted to St. Cecilia's who had pretty foul words in their vocabulary, they generally didn't last long. For example, on one occasion I heard my buddy Mike drop the "f" bomb almost loud enough for Sister Mary to hear it. I broke into a cold sweat fearing for his life. If Sister Mary didn't catch it I felt sure Jesus would, and was expecting something really terrible to happen, if not immediately, eventually.

So I entered public school where cuss words were not only common, they were hurled at teachers even, and with no apparent consequences. I gradually began to understand that I was among a group of people for whom academic achievement probably didn't feature as a very important objective. And I saw them smoking! While I may have been a bit nerdy at St. Cecilia's, at least I fit in. At the new school I may as well have been at a maximum-security prison where only the most hardened are warehoused...but for the 3:15 bell.

I was miserable.

Our home life was stable, but awkward at best. My mom had remarried. Her new husband was a bit overwhelmed with the new big family and, looking back, woefully ill-equipped. It was readily apparent that he had not worked out in his own mind whether he was a father, a stepfather, an acquaintance, or a friend. And to be honest, we didn't like him. To us he was simply a strange, overweight, somewhat simple man. When he did try to administer discipline (maybe thinking it was his husbandly duty) it came off laughable; in large part because of his north Texas accent combined with his fifty word vocabulary and his unmistakable profile – that of a pig on hind feet. His efforts at punishment consisted mainly of platitudes that just didn't hit home. Like "I can't make you do nothin', but I can sure make you regret it if you don't." I used to hear that and wonder what he thought he could possibly do that would give me something *more* to regret than his marriage to my mom.

I remember that once I angered him so much that he decided to give me a "whuppin" and loudly announced that he was going to do just that. I responded that he would have to catch me first. I kicked off my shoes and took off, easily gaining enough distance to laugh as I was running, without fear of him closing the gap. I was a lot smaller than him, but a lot faster. Since I really had no idea what exactly he meant by a "whuppin" I thought the chase a better option. Besides, I reasoned, if he did try to catch me -- if he kept up the chase – he might just throw a clot and die right in his little upright pig tracks, and the matter of my misdeed along with many other matters would be settled. He never caught me. I never got a "whuppin" and I don't remember how the situation resolved. But I've heard it said that the soul of diplomacy is offering your opponent a graceful out. And I assume that one of us did the other.

My sisters, my brother and I quickly retreated into our own private worlds, wrestling with our own problems, and not really reaching out to each other or including each other in our own private corner of the new situation we were all working out for ourselves. And then my mom announced that we were selling the house and moving to Dallas.

His family was in Dallas. His mother who made "Coke Salad" had the exact same vocabulary, and she looked a lot like an older version of him in a wig and lipstick. Moving to Dallas would enable us all to be closer to her and to his son from a previous marriage that ate nothing but hamburgers and would not allow anyone to see his bare feet.

I had never been to Dallas before. But more unsettling, I had never before imagined that we would ever leave the house we were living in. It was bad enough for my mom's new husband to be living there too, but to leave it was unthinkable in the true sense of the word. My imagination did not give me the means to envision it. It was too unreal. But what we did understand was that we were leaving because of him, mama Coke Salad, and junior.

Mom tearfully explained to us that she could not continue to pay for the house and it is true that she had been left penniless by my dad's death with no way to care for us. Six children, four more than she ever really wanted, and left alone to raise us at a very young age. Besides, she would plead, the house had too many memories. She wanted to sell it so badly that she priced it to sell quickly, and it in fact did sell to the very first person to see it not more than hours after it was put on the market. We packed to move away.

I have to explain that we didn't just move away. Not all of my sisters went with us. Two of them stayed in Houston.

So my freshman year of high school was itself interrupted so that I could go from one giant public school where I only knew one or two people to another giant public school where I didn't know a soul, in a town I had never seen before. With two of my sisters left behind. But I had new relatives.

At school I tried desperately to stay off the radar and make some friends. Eventually I found a group that accepted me, but not before I began smoking cigarettes and experimenting with every drug available that did not involve a needle. Within a matter of weeks of arriving in Richardson (Dallas) I was back to blackout drinking. But I also started dropping acid (LSD), smoking pot, and (within a couple of months) dealing speed to finance my drug use, oh and my "Hot Tamales" candy habit which hit six boxes a day. I was still just fourteen years old.

My daily life was fueled by "white cross" amphetamines, my six boxes of "Hot Tamales," and a joint or two; the monotony only broken by the occasional hallucinogen or a good pass-out drunk. Interestingly, my scholastic achievements didn't seem to suffer. I was still making straight A's. But it all was so easy. The coursework was no problem at all, once I remembered it from the fourth grade. Many of my fellow students were completely illiterate. Starved for intellectual challenge I joined the debate team. And the debate team was the perfect cover. My partner and I even made it to state competition.

At one point well into my drug and alcohol involvement, one of my sisters confided that the family was "worried" that I might be smoking cigarettes. I was smoking a pack and a half a day, popping acid, dealing speed, smoking pot, and getting snot-slinging drunk every chance I got. I privately laughed at their concern, which seemed to suggest that there was nothing to worry about. I was off the hook. It was all just too easy. It was all absolutely, horrifically and unfathomably easy.

One story I will never forget is the evening that my friends and I shared a number of "hits" of "purple microdot" (a hallucinogen). We were "tripping" in the front yard thoroughly enjoying the color and structure of the grass in the yard and I was just fine, but for the fact that I knew my sister was going to come pick me up in an hour. That meant that in an hour I would have to "maintain" (pretend not to be stoned). The problem was that on purple microdot, or any other hallucinogen for that matter, time is incomprehensible. You can stare at your watch and understand the intricacies of its function in a way you never dreamed possible before, and have no idea what it is telling you. But I needed to know how to know when my sister would be there so that I could hide my cigarettes and chew some breath gum.

After trying many times to explain to me how long an hour is, my friends sort of gave up, and broke it into more understandable measurement for me. They indicated that since I had three cigarettes in my hand and I smoked a cigarette about every fifteen minutes, when the three cigarettes were gone an hour would be up. My sister would be arriving.

It seemed a perfect solution. I had no idea what an hour was, but I knew I had three cigarettes and that when they were gone that meant that my sister was about to arrive. Then I had two. But a guy in the group had stolen a pack of his mother's long skinny cigarettes and then decided that he didn't want them after all. He asked if anyone else wanted them and I said that I did, so he dumped them into my hand. All of the sudden I didn't ever have to go home. My sister would never show up.

I was absolutely content. I would be able to enjoy the texture of the grass and the colors of the whole world forever. No one was ever going to come get me.

But then her car arrived. "Your sister's here," my friend said and it was like they had just thrown very cold water all over me. The universe had veered off on a sudden tangent and disobeyed the very laws of time. I couldn't wrap my mind around it. I half imagined that if I showed my sister my fistful of cigarettes, the car would immediately throw itself into reverse and she would disappear down the street backwards just the same way she had come. But then the family would know about the cigarettes and I would have some explaining to do. I would be busted. I had to get into that car much like a condemned man walking has to eventually enter the chamber. I pretended not to feel well, so I didn't have to make eye contact.

The drive home seemed to be going well until she offered me a deal. She would stop at the convenience store and even pay for my Milky Way if I would go in and get her a Snickers candy bar too. I desperately wanted to say that I didn't want a Milky Way but I knew she wouldn't believe it. I would be busted. So I had to get into that store, locate a Milky Way and a Snickers candy bar, navigate a conversation with a person behind the counter, somehow manage to figure out the proper payment although I could not in the farthest reaches of my imagination figure out how *that* was going to work, receive change and get back into the car with both candy bars AND the correct change, and all with an air of nonchalance as though I were bored with the whole thing. It was a mission of staggering complexity and I have no idea how I pulled it off. But I did.

My problems were far from over, however. Once in the car and on the road again I opened my Milky Way and took a bite. I chewed for a bit and thought everything was going to be okay and the candy was pretty good after all. That's when I learned something new: purple microdot renders a person incapable of swallowing.

I kept chewing the single bite hoping that it would just disappear somehow but it didn't. Enough time went by that I thought surely I have to take another bite or my sister will suspect something. And I'll get busted. So I just kept taking bites at what I thought to be the normal time and proper intervals, even though not one of them was dissolving, or disappearing, or going anywhere. Soon I had the entire Milky Way in my mouth and in addition to being unable to swallow, I was unable to talk. Fortunately we were almost home by then, and she didn't ask me any questions, and when she parked the car I took the candy bar out of my mouth without her seeing me do it, and threw it under the car.

But the story continues. When I got into the house everyone was sitting in the den watching TV. I knew instantly that there was no way I could handle that. It was just too much. I would surely do or say something really stupid or strange, and…yes, get busted. So I thought the answer would be to go upstairs and take a shower. That would be something normal that a person who wasn't out of his mind tripping on acid, seeing colors slur from any movement of any object, and having just come off of a really freakish Milky Way encounter, might do. And I could be alone.

It would have worked out, too. But once in the shower I noticed that the tile was "breathing." Each tile was moving in and out as though the entire shower stall was alive and the tiles were undulating. It was fascinating. I was mesmerized. But it only got better. As I watched it, I noticed that they were moving in and out to a discernable cadence. As I sat there enthralled by the intricacy of the rhythm and the perfectly coordinated phraseology of the tile movement, it was as if the volume on a stereo was being gradually turned up, ever so slowly, from absolute silence to full forte, and in what could only be described as a celestial epiphany I recognized Beethoven's Third Symphony, E Flat Major, Opus 55, the "Eroica." Who knew that a simple shower could take on the epic glory, the grandeur of a full on Beethoven symphony? But it was happening all around me.

The Eroica, like some of Beethoven's symphonies, is a longish work. And this particular performance repeated itself. And then it would modulate and slip seamlessly into the third movement – the adagio of the ninth. I was enthralled. When I had finally tired of the music and the choreographed tiles…and once my skin had become so wrinkled as to be painful, I decided to turn the shower off and get out.

The house was absolutely silent, and completely dark. I made it to my bedroom only to see the glowing red alarm clock digits "2:30" which had to be two thirty in the morning. I had been listening to Beethoven and watching the tiles for over four hours. To this day I have no explanation for the fact that no one came to investigate why I was in the shower for so long. But the realization did dawn on me that if a four-and-a-half-hour shower didn't get me busted, I could rest assured that I wasn't in Catholic school any more.

We remained in Richardson for the school year, but events took their toll on my mom's marriage and after it broke apart we returned to Houston and moved into an apartment building a short walk from the house we had left before. I was once again in the neighborhood of my friends before we moved to the Dallas area, and got enrolled at the large public high school there that I had left when we moved.

But I was already a completely different person.

I quickly reunited with my old friends, as did my sisters, and it was good to be back among the familiar. But I brought back with me a new sophistication. The drug abuse and alcoholism did not abate; they just moved into a new context albeit decorated with old faces. It didn't take long for my old neighborhood friends and I to "feel each other out" and learn that we were all smoking cigarettes now. These were not my friends from Catholic school; these were neighborhood friends. After I left Catholic school I never saw those friends again, and haven't to this day.

I think that the move away and the entrance into the world of drugs and alcohol was a departure from the innocence of grade school that made any kind of return impossible. There was a wall between that past and me. And even if I had thought to want to go back to my Catholic school friends I knew that in some way I could never do it. I would never know how. It was just as well that they were off and gone, further into growing up good and normal people. I just wasn't that way.

In the new high school there were three classes of students: jocks and popular girls, nerds, and what we called "freaks." I was a freak but with strong ties to the nerd culture which was my origin. I continued to play the piano daily and was even taking lessons from a French concert pianist who lived in the Houston area. Drugs/alcohol, and the piano were the two facets of life for me…each strong and defining. Notice that drugs and alcohol have come up alongside the piano at this point.

But they did not cross over on each other. The people in my drug life had nothing to do with the piano, couldn't understand it, and more or less considered it an eccentricity. If anything it just perpetuated the image that I had with them. I was a nerd to begin with, and no matter how well a nerd can roll a joint or hold his scotch, a piano-playing nerd was still, after all, just a piano-playing nerd.

School was still very easy and I was matched with students who could not read, just like in Richardson. This time, however, I did fit in with a small group of old friends who were now as much preoccupied with drugs and alcohol as I had become. Getting stoned and/or drunk was a daily event, and there were weekends that were nothing more than a solid binge. I can look back on numerous episodes in which things happened that I really shouldn't have survived.

A couple of friends and I once went to the top of Addicks Dam and sat watching the sun go down, and getting drunk. The steps up to the dam were concrete and had to have numbered over fifty. As we stood to leave, I passed out. Helping me down the steps was Pond John. He lost his grip on me close to the top of the stairs and I tumbled down those steps ending up with a double concussion. For some unknown reason I never rolled off the stairs onto the nice grassy slope just adjacent, and they were fairly narrow stairs.

But you know me, always getting injured. Actually I think those two were my third and fourth concussions, the first happening in fifth grade.

It is amazing I wasn't injured more, and what is really astonishing is how few of my injury accidents happened when I had been drinking. I can remember only one. It seemed like I was always in one of four states: stoned, hung over, looking to get drunk and/or high, or playing the piano. There were dark, heavy times too. One Christmas, in particular, everyone was drunk all the time and the house remained dark. My sisters who did not drink had already left home.

I'll never forget the sinking feeling I had one early evening noticing that the house was dark, bottles of liquor cluttered the countertops, Christmas was a matter of days away and there were no decorations, no lights, no candles. Even in the overlap of hangover and fresh "buzz" I realized that in all the partying the key central element was missing – joy. I remember thinking that it was really pathetic, and that I was really deeply unhappy. But I didn't pick up on the fact that I was also gradually moving toward some serious mental problems.

There was information that was beginning to settle in but only in the most inconspicuous way. There was a hint of realization that was thickening in the air but I somehow missed breathing it in…unnoticeable moments of something ominous, too subtle to be identified with any clarity. Something like the local water supplies suddenly drying up for no reason. And slight tremors too.

The more I kept myself drugged and drunk the more entrenched became my desperation, even though I didn't know it. But I persisted in a blind and reckless yet absolute certainty that everything would be fine later somehow, and for now there was nothing more important or worth doing than getting high. The future was assumed, and the present was obliterated. It was an equation that was supposed to equal happiness but it didn't. It just equaled drunk and drugged. Had anyone suggested at that time that I would be deceived by that state for another some thirty-seven more years I would have scoffed at the insanity of the idea and tucked back into it, fully embracing it, laughing. I had no way of knowing that down in the foundations of my soul was a very deep and very dangerous crack. I was seriously ill and I had no idea that anything was wrong.

High school is a period where young people naturally explore limits and reject much of what they have observed growing up to that age, making room for whatever their own constructs of life might be. I know you have told me about your own experiences at that age and how you first called into question your dad's conservative bent. In me this process took place with something sinister in the background. It was not as if I had a solid sense of the way the world was ordered and I wanted to change it through my own independent decisions. It was not as if most but not all was well with the world and but for a little tweaking here and there, a spot of my own interests in this corner, and the things I like to study in that, it would be a perfect life. It was not as if there was a perfection I could expect to life of any sort. There was nothing. No plan, nothing to look forward to but getting away someday to somewhere, and in the present moment getting away any way I could. There was a cynicism that took hold, I suppose, and rested in the background.

But time, and looking around in the moments of sobriety, deadened the laughter – shifted it back stage – and what was once laughable was just stupid. I became more and more cynical and began to harbor a real hatred. I think that hatred, left all by itself, is a really dangerous thing. If it's pointed at someone there's a chance that it can get resolved. But unattached it is more like a grenade than a rifle, and it shreds all in its vicinity. Even its owner.

I have come to believe that the central most critical difference between children and anyone else is this capacity for hatred. Perhaps that is why God speaks so clearly of His love for children…so much so as to admonish us that we cannot enter the kingdom if not as a child. Children do not hate. Oh they may say they do, but for them it is really only the superlative of anger. For a child to say they hate you is really only to say that they are furious with you.

And God forgives anger. It is an emotion He himself knows. Scripture doesn't even say "do not be angry" it says "in your anger, do not sin" (Ephesians 4:26), and children are given a healthy capacity for anger. But true hatred is an emotion reserved for those of age and consequence, those who can stand trial.

A friend of mine had become very interested in witchcraft. He lived in the same neighborhood as I did and I went to school with his younger brother. He was a budding young artist and I spent as much time with him as with his little brother. Many a stoned experience included him, and there were long hours we spent together with him describing artistic scenes to me while I would put them to music at the piano. I'll call him John, "Mushroom John," for reasons that will make sense a little later.

One of my Aunts professed to be knowledgeable about witchcraft and was very involved in strange religious beliefs. Although no one specifically told me this, I came to believe that I had a legacy of witchcraft in my family if for no other reason than that my Aunt seemed to know all about it and did not deny her involvement. She, in fact, was the first to tell me about the astral planes, astral projection, and other wisdoms she termed "esoteric." I decided I was born to it. It was a right of mine, and that if anyone could really successfully conjure the spirits to do their bidding, I could. After all, they knew my family. It even gave me a position of some regard, from Mushroom John.

My friend and I had books on the subject and books on spells. We began practicing spells and conjuring and even formed what we considered to be a coven. We would meet late at night in our robes, with our paraphernalia, light candles and dance around them chanting spells and incantations.

For us it was not just a game. It was not a charade to break the monotony or to ease our boredom; we always had plenty of psilocybin mushrooms for that. We were serious. We truly believed in the dark spirits and we believed that we could call them to us and they would empower us in ways that no one else was empowered. We believed that we could cast spells on people and they would suffer for it. We wanted to do that. We wanted to cast spells on people and we wanted them to suffer for it. But we also just wanted the power.

Practicing witchcraft as an outlet did not ease any anger I may have had; it only nurtured it in some strange way. Like the old adage about the man who comes to his minister and tells him that he feels torn up inside, like there is a huge battle going on inside him between two Titans; one that is all that is good, one all that is evil. When the minister asks him which one wins, his answer is "whichever one I feed." It was a little like that. Isn't it strange that an emotion can actually feed *itself*? All that it needs is a mind that is open and accepting to it. And for anger, my mind was very fertile ground.

On one occasion I had been practicing a technique that was supposed to develop the ability for astral projection, for about six months. I was tenacious with it and practiced it at least twice a week, each practice session taking anywhere from one to three hours. But I never had any results.

Undaunted, I kept practicing the sessions just as I had had them explained to me. I don't know if you have had astral projection ever explained to you, but it is a simple concept really. It is the idea of separating your "spirit" (or soul) from your body while you are still living. I think that if you are able to do that, you are supposed to be able to travel the world as if you are flying. And some believe that you can visit the "higher plains" of astral consciousness. Doesn't that sound like a tasty bit of esoteric-ness! I was very open with folks I knew at high school about how I was practicing astral projection and one friend named Debbie told me that once in the shower she suddenly had a sense that she was being watched and even called out my name and told me to go away! Come to think of it, if astral projection really were possible, just think of the boon to voyeurism it would be. The porn industry would collapse overnight!

One evening I was deeply into a session, lying flat on my bed next to the bedroom window. Everyone was gone and it was very unlikely that I would be interrupted. At one point I think I fell asleep; I lost awareness of the process. Suddenly I heard the crescendo sound like a hydraulic crane switch being thrown on and something hoisting up. The sound was low in pitch but climbing just as in volume, and it had a shrieking metallic tone. It was like some giant electric generator filling an auditorium coming to life. I awoke.

But I was more than awake. The room was filled with a light that had a silver shine to it and I could see in every direction. I noticed that while I was still reclined in position, I was hovering about three feet *above* my body. I could see myself sleeping, and at that height I could see out the window, which was an oblong narrow window about two feet above the bed. During that experience there was a constant hum not unlike that of the giant transformers at the tops of major electric towers. I realized that I was "projected." I was suddenly certain that I was out of my body.

The freedom to fly to Hawaii for the evening and the elation that I expected to experience should I ever achieve such a state was not at all what I felt. I felt abject terror. The kind of shock of terror that freezes every cell in your body and gives you an ache in your jaw.

I woke up a second time but it was more like having been thrown to the bed. The impact of me hitting the bed was so violent that the bed shook as if I had landed on it uncontrolled. I could not move at first but as soon as I could I ran out of the room, down the stairs, and out the front door of the house hoping to find someone…some brother or sister, or some friend, doing something completely mundane and ordinary. I needed to be back in the mundane and ordinary.

For many years after that event, I experienced episodes where the sound of that generator springing to life repeats itself in my head. It happens at times for no reason, completely unforeseen, and lasting about three seconds. It is such a profound loud and sudden internal sound that it completely sidetracks whatever I am thinking about at the moment and sometimes immediately afterward I am disoriented for a second or two. I used to wonder if it was not physiological. I still wonder if tiny flashes of random electro-chemistry in my brain cause it. I wonder if I did something to my brain that is now permanent, like maybe I totally fried some neurotransmitter set up somewhere and every once in a while my brain tries to send a perfectly sedate simple thought down that route and it suddenly pulls a "Psycho" shower scene and then sparkles out into oblivion.

Some would say that the entire projection event was explainable by other means. It could just as easily be the drug abuse and the varied mix of drugs with which I entertained myself. I almost used the word "experimented," but then realized how stupid that is. People don't "experiment" with drugs – well, people other than Timothy Leary don't. The rest of us shoot, snort, drop, chug, smoke, or make them into peanut butter sandwiches. We don't experiment with the drug, but rather how to get it into our body.

But personally, I do think the psychopharmacological explanation is the most plausible.

It doesn't matter, really. I was not on drugs when that evening occurred (it was strictly against the method's teachings) and the visual experiences I had in the moment of the episode, the crippling terror I felt, and the physical nature of the impact when I woke up were as real as the texture of these keys as I type.

Even though it was anything but a positive experience, it did not deter me from my pursuit of the occult. In fact, it seemed to shift it into a more serious endeavor. I began to withdraw from family and friends even further. My drug use and alcoholism got worse and my circle of friends got smaller. And what was more curious even than those strange experiences and how I was drawn to them was the fact that I began to become aware of my own growing hatred toward the world. At first I was just angry, then hateful toward the world in general with no particular object. But as the days passed my anger and hatred began to take on a focus. It was vague at first.

In the mix of everything that was going on and all that I was doing, I began to have a sense of God. I began to have a sense of my thoughts about Him almost as if I was beginning to know Him. But it would be wrong to say that I was beginning to know Him. I was beginning to believe that He existed.

This is very different than knowing Him. A person can believe that Pluto exists…can even know that it was demoted from planet to something less than planet because it is too small. This is knowing a fact *about* Pluto but without knowing the actual lump of mineral somewhere at the outskirts of our solar system itself. You can believe in the existence of something while still being completely ignorant as to its nature.

But I didn't seek Him. It is more that I just began to conduct my daily life with the assumption that He did, in fact, exist. It wasn't until later that I would realize that not only was I willing to concede that He existed, or at least I was behaving as though I did, but that I needed Him. In all the mess that was my life I needed God.

I needed Him to exist so that I would have Him to hate. And I did.

I loathed Him.

In those days I even dabbled in satanic studies, not because I had any interest in the theology of the writings or any belief in the possibility that it could make my life better, but my Catholic upbringing made sure that I knew it was offensive to God. Even the most brutish Catholic boy who looks down his nose at the strange teachings of some Catholic orders -- things like if you look at the host during lent you will go blind, or if you masturbate too much you will grow hair on your palms, be wearing a scapula when you die and it's an automatic get-into-heaven – even the boy who rejects some of these things as far-fetched bits of theological cartoonery knows that God doesn't like Satan and does not think well of those who do. The friend of my enemy is my enemy too.

In my general retreat there was something else getting stronger in me of which I was not aware. At about that same time, Pond John had moved in with us because his father had to work in another part of the world and his mother had had a nervous breakdown. She was put into an institution and his older brother was away at college, so he moved in with us and shared a bedroom with my younger brother and me. He and I had already been like brothers since I was nine years old, so it seemed like a foregone conclusion that he would live with us. And when he moved in during our sophomore year of high school we began to consider ourselves brothers as though it was official. We were inseparable most of the time, and got to know each other so well that we would even finish each other's sentences, just as twins often do. Our friends even noticed it and commented on it from time to time.

I did not know the extent to which I was becoming dependent on him as the years progressed, however. He and I became so intertwined that anytime either of us purchased *anything*, we always purchased the other one the same amount. Anytime anything (particularly drugs) was given to one of us, it was assumed that we would split it with the other. We shared our friends, we shared our clothes, our adventures, all of our interests, everything. Our first car was a Mustang that we purchased together and shared. He was with me when I got drunk for the first time when I was thirteen years old, and it went without saying that anytime I got high he was there as well.

I look back on some of those drug experiences, though, and they seem so silly, some of them.

One night, for instance, we had what was then called a "lid" of marijuana. I'm not sure of the exact amount in real measurement, but it was generally more than two people could smoke in any given single episode. But we had the idea (like many high school kids of my day, I'm sure) that if we drank a lot of coffee before we started we could probably make a good dent in it. So we planned the evening like you might plan an anniversary dinner. We had the house to ourselves until mom and the others came home sometime around ten o'clock. First we drank three or four cups of very strong coffee. Then we put the ever critical Sarah Lee coffee cake in the oven smeared with butter on the lowest heat setting possible (for when we were finished smoking). We put our big two-liter bottle of Coke in the fridge and headed up to the roof of the garage.

Our garage was a freestanding building with a four-sided roof that came to a point in the center. The side facing away from the back of the house was completely shrouded in a huge weeping willow. You could sit on that slope and set yourself on fire and no one would see it. The pitch of the roof would hide the view of your burning torso from the inside of the house, and the huge willow tree would catch and obscure the smoke.

And there was a main branch that reached out from the trunk perfectly parallel to the ground, that ran also perfectly parallel to the bottom edge of the roof (the tree was planted against the garage at the corner). You could take those cheap tri-fold lounge chairs that we used to call "banana lounge" chairs, unfold them, rest the bottom edge of the chair against that huge branch and recline on the chair fully opened on the roof of the garage, the large limb stopping the chair from sliding off. And we had planned to do just that while we smoked as much as we possibly could, our Sara Lee and Coke waiting for us when we came back down.

We had the chairs positioned close enough together that we could both remain reclined as we passed the joints back and forth. I have absolutely no way of knowing how long we were up there or how much we actually smoked. But memory does pick up as we decided we'd had enough and were ready to come down.

As John was attempting to get out of the banana lounge chair he must have jarred it just enough to knock the low lip of the chair off of being against the limb of the willow. The lip of the chair slipped above the limb, still against it but no longer keeping the chair from sliding down the roof. The chair began to shuttle down the slope of the roof with my friend still in it creating a rhythm as it thumped along the shingles sliding downward, and began to collapse to its tri fold shape, but with him inside. When the chair (and him) got to the edge of the roof, the weight pushed the limb away from the roof but not far enough to allow chair and my stoned friend to fall to the ground. No, instead he was stuck between the edge of the roof and the limb in a collapsed banana chair with two arms, two legs, and the fringes of his blond 'fro hair style making the chair look a little like a soft shell crab sandwich.

Two things disturbed the equilibrium that kept me in my perch. First, I "busted out" laughing. He started cussing at me to stop laughing and figure out how to get him out of there, which caused me to laugh even harder.

Second, his mass, the mass of the soft shell crab sandwich that he had become, pushing the limb away from the roof, slowly guided my chair down the slope until the lower third of my chair was in blue sky between the tree and the garage, and my butt was just above the edge.

Before I had the chance to realize that my predicament would be harder to escape than his, it didn't matter. My laughing caused the lip of my chair to do just as his had done (slip off the limb) and I was flipped out of my chair over the edge of the roof and straight to the ground bellow, laughing hysterically when I hit. I have no idea how he ever got down. But the night's events didn't stop there.

When we got back into the house it was apparent that everyone was home and already in bed. All the lights were off. At this point we knew we could not even look at each other or we would "lose it" and break into laughter, waking everyone up. So we methodically, with almost robotic precision, went about the business of preparing our feast and getting our butts upstairs before anyone caught us. Drinks first.

The glasses where in an upper cabinet to the left of the fridge, immediately in front of us. He stood next to the fridge and I stood next to him, to his left. We were as carefully positioned and as silent as the chief surgeon and his assistant in the middle of a life-or-death procedure. He got a glass out and set it in front of himself. He got a second one out and set it in front of me. I centered it so that it was equidistant between my right and left elbows. This is the kind of thing only a person high on pot would need to do. He then opened the refrigerator and withdrew the Coke, poured himself half a glass and handed me the bottle without looking at me. I poured myself half a glass and then set the bottle to my left as if some nurse assistant would then carry it away to biological disposal. Everything was precision, perfect order.

Now the freezer was above the refrigerator with the ice bucket in the door of the freezer (like many). He next quietly opened the refrigerator and while I was watching very intently, he very carefully, almost gingerly, got two eggs out of the egg rack in the door of the refrigerator. And then he just as gingerly with expert aim and care plopped them into his glass of Coke.

I remember thinking, *that can't be right. Eggs don't go in Coke, do they?* The chief surgeon must be making a mistake. When the egg shells broke releasing the egg into the drink it foamed over like a third grade volcano project, and drove home the certainty that, no, that wasn't right. Eggs don't go in Coke. We simultaneously looked at each other, broke into roars of laughter and ran upstairs afraid that we would be busted for sure this time. I can only imagine what my family thought when they woke up and discovered two glasses of coke on the counter top, abandoned, one with two eggs cracked into it, and a fossilized food specimen appearing to have its origins in Sarah Lee in the oven keeping warm.

My drug of choice, without a doubt, was psilocybin mushrooms. We had our own small field shaded by young pines in the corner of a vast pasture. It was always damp, and there were plenty of cow paddies, and we stumbled onto mushrooms growing there that we were sure were psilocybin. I've told this story many times and I am always a little nervous that someone hearing me tell it will trot off into the woods to pick mushrooms and get high. But even *we* knew that most of them will blind you if you do something as seemingly harmless as sniff them, and with others you don't get high, you get dead. The fact that we didn't blind ourselves is miracle. When it comes to not dying for the stupid stuff we did, one of many.

We cultivated them in the moist cow paddies, careful not to harvest any but the very mature. Periodically we would visit the little field to see how they were doing and try to add to the camouflage we had sort of scattered around the place. Anytime we harvested the older mushrooms we would make sure and take some spores from them and sprinkle them around to help cultivate the next generation.

One night about four of us had brewed a bunch of mushroom tea. It was very powerful stuff. We each drank our share and went to rest on the patio while we got past the stomach reaction (nausea) and then the fun would start. I always laughed on mushrooms, even more than on pot. Like I said, it was my favorite high.

During the early stages of that night one of our friends had wandered off and we didn't know where he was. My witchcraft friend, the one I call "Mushroom John." I went looking for him. In our neighborhood there were no curbs and the mailboxes sat on top of posts at the edge of the front yard so the mailman could deliver the mail without getting out of the truck. They were at just below shoulder height.

Well, I found him about half a block away, leaning over an open mailbox, one hand on the door to it with his face up against the opening. Then he shut the door and started walking to the next one.

By the time I caught up with him I realized what he was doing. He would open the mailbox door, lean over and sing into it for a few seconds or more, then close the door and go on to the next one. I asked him, "What are you doing?" He said "I'm delivering 'Me and My Arrow' (a popular song at the time) to the neighborhood. It really is a good song you know (or something to that effect) and we all need a shot in the arm once in a while."

It took quite a bit of time to convince him to go back to the house with me, and I never did convince him that the song wouldn't be there anymore by morning anyway, so his efforts really were wasted. When we got back to the house Pond John was gone. Someone told me they thought he went upstairs. So I went up there and looked room to room. I found him in a room completely darkened, lying face down on the bed. He said, "Close the door. Get out of here."

To make the story of a very long night short, I did close the door but I did not get out of there. I sat down next to the bed and asked him what was going on. He explained that he was afraid that if he turned on the light what he was seeing would be real and he would go completely insane. I sat with him the entire night, periodically reassuring him that I was still there, that no one was going to turn on the light, and that he was safe.

One other time we were not so lucky. He ingested a combination of drugs, alcohol and Nyquil and was taken to the hospital.

There were almost as many stories not too dissimilar as there were the days he lived with us for those three years, even though the stories were so much different than our younger days when we were boyhood friends living backyard to backyard.

What I hadn't noticed, even though he sometimes complained to me about it, was how I wasn't "independent" enough and I never seemed to "want to do anything." I was as withdrawn as I could possibly be and yet still be connected, because I only had to be connected to *him*. I never would have imagined that such a relationship, such a friendship was anything other than ideal for both of us. We had decided we were brothers after all, and brothers watch each other's backs. Isn't that what we were doing?

But in truth, that was not what we were doing. I was hiding behind him. I was completely unaware of what I was hiding from. After all, you would think that being drunk all the time would have been enough to keep me hidden from anything. But the truth is that I was scared and hiding behind a veil. Some day I would have to step out from behind him and face whatever it was that I would find there. I know that now but I had no idea of it then.

So completely thick and dark was that veil that I had no suspicion that it was even there. I could only see the part that I knew to be true. We were more than friends; we were brothers because we had chosen to be. We shared everything, like I said. I knew nothing about the future, but I didn't need to. I knew the past. And I had a pretty good sense of the present. Everything was pretty safe, most of it was fun, I was okay and things would be fine if they just didn't change. I wonder what had me convinced that they wouldn't change. I wonder how I could possibly have deluded myself so completely that I thought everything would stay fine.

It was in the final months of our senior year of high school. By then we had sold our Mustang and each had purchased our own cars. He had a square back VW and I had a Karmen Ghia. He worked at a gas station and I worked at a grocery store.

But we still always did everything together. We even double dated with my older sister and her best friend to the Senior Prom but we never made it in the door because he was caught with a flask of whiskey. So we all left, smoked some pot and had a fun night getting high anyway.

My birthday that March was like the others before it except that he gave me a peculiar gift for that birthday. No stash of weed, no six-pack with a camping trip planned. A poster. A print, actually. It was a broad field of corn painted in a style reminiscent of the dust bowl paintings, with two black-top roads cutting through the corn at right angles, intersecting, and then heading off into their opposite parts of the edges of the print, with each inch of the way more and more certainty that they would never again intersect. He said, "This is how I see us, John."

I remember thinking it was a nice picture, sort of an odd gift, but I couldn't make any sense of his comment. *The roads are not parallel*, I thought. *I wonder what he means?* It is sometimes shocking when I look back and realize how thick that veil can truly be. Even as I write you this I am caught with a tinge of embarrassment at having been so stupid.

Just as we had bought our first car together, and sold it, just as we had purchased scuba equipment together, and had it stolen, just as we had done everything together...I assumed that after we graduated we would get an apartment together. We never talked about it; I just assumed it. We both had our own jobs, we had our own cars, and soon we would get ourselves an apartment. I was planning to go to university and he was not but that didn't matter. It was not even significant enough to bring up for discussion because there simply was no doubt. When my mom asked what our plans were since graduation was coming up so soon, I decided I should ask him what he thought.

He told me that he had already made plans to move in with a friend of his from school. They had already gotten the apartment, put the deposit down, and were planning to move in right after graduation. It was a two-bedroom.

I was so deeply embedded in my delusion that the meaning of what he was saying was not apparent to me. I just thought that what he was saying was confusing; it didn't make sense. First I had the urge to get angry because he should have gotten a three-bedroom, if we were going to include the other guy, and why didn't he talk to me about it? I was actually a little pissed off at him for including the other guy without having consulted me on it first.

I don't know how long it took for the reality to settle in on me but I remember when it did. It was like someone pulled a plug at the bottom of my ankle and all the sand ran out of me like that giant in the movie "The Iliad and the Odyssey" when they punched a hole in his ankle and the sand ran out and he turned into stone.

Imagine again, that very complex box of gears, some very small, some not so small, and some very large. Each gear touching another, which touches another, and they all move at the same speed while appearing to move many times faster or slower, one from another. Imagine that it is all a perfect mechanism, each part inseparable from the others, and while being made up of all different parts, all working as a whole, a single unit. And the orchestrated spinning of all these gears moves the box forward. From the outside, no evidence of the complexity within.

Now imagine that one part, one of the smaller ones, has been missing a cog, running just a bit loose, but it has spun in its time never affecting any of the others. And the whole spins on harmoniously. Except for now.

Now the gear missing the cog slips. Quietly, almost imperceptibly, it causes another gear to slip, which misaligns cogs with yet another gear and shreds it, which then shreds another. For a time, the box will continue to move forward regardless of what is going on inside. The outside of the machine will still move along, from momentum or something, as if the insides were still working fine. As if the insides were still there…

Not only was it not going to happen that we would get an apartment together, but the plans for it not to happen had been going on for some time, and involved others, but not me. I was never even told. It was a realization that I could not process.

My mom caught wind of it and unleashed a torrent on him, throwing in his face all that I had done for him, and accosting him with questions about how he could be so cruel. She was irate with him and there are few that can turn irrepressible quite like my mom. But I was oblivious to it. I wouldn't have even known whether to try to stop her, because it was not about the apartment for me. It was not about how I had shared my room or my family or my life. It wasn't about anything I had done for him or he had done for me. It was not about anything that mundane. It was about the past, the part years back. The part that was now repeating.

They allowed me to move in with them, although I never really understood why. But it was so late in the game I was really stuck for a place to go. The two of them gave me my own room and they shared the larger room, which seemed to make sense. It was argued that I would need the space in order to study, since neither of them were going to college. It only took my sense of being "odd man out" and solidified it into the sleeping arrangements. Anytime they had parties I had my own place to go to, since I really wasn't part of the party. I wasn't really part of anything. Added to my isolation was indignity.

After those few months I moved out and moved on. We never contacted each other. Many years later when I sought him out to reconnect with him I learned that he had married not long thereafter. I had not been invited to the wedding.

3. Mushrooms and the Two Afternoons

IT WAS IN THOSE SIX MONTHS while I was still living in Pond John and his friend's apartment that I first became aware of how seriously alcoholic I had become. One day I discovered that I only had enough money to buy some wine to get drunk, and not even as drunk as I'd like, but couldn't also buy food. I bought the wine. There were many days like that.

I took on the new frenzy that any freshman year at college brings with it.

I made new friends, got involved with classes and took on a new interest in health, nutrition, and weight lifting. I joined the canoe club at University of Houston and went on weekend camp-out trips with a group of others where we would canoe the "upper" and "lower" Guadalupe River. It was great fun, and I was even sober. It would seem as though after John stepped aside and left me to face whatever was out there in front of me, it wasn't so bad. In fact it was nice...parts of it.

The turbulence and insanity of the previous eleven years had been lifted off of me, for a time. It was almost like it had been lifted all the way up and gone. I could move about and interact; I could deal with life. But it wasn't off and gone. It was still above me, and the straps straining to hold it there began to hum with a strain making a sound that I would later come to call "the white noise."

I was out from behind, but within a year the straps would fail, and I would be crushed and fighting for my life.

I was a music major at university. My mom didn't much approve of that because she considered all musicians as starving artists...the starving part being the most important. I was studying piano under a very sought-after concert pianist who prohibited me from playing any more Chopin. He chastised me saying that I had been spoiled to spend my time on nothing but the romantic composers and it was time I got some discipline. He even suggested, more than once, that there was still time to salvage my hopelessly poor development and might even make it to a serious competition. Eighteen years old was probably too old for that, he would argue, but he was willing to give it a last ditch effort. No concert pianist has a real career unless he/she has won a serious competition by the age of seventeen. But he thought it might still be possible for me; not because of my talent but because of his.

He insisted that I spend six hours a day practicing and started me on what he called "the Russians." I worked the Number One Prelude by Rachmaninoff – the "Bells of Moscow," and he promised me that if I was up to it I could work the First Concerto B Flat Minor, the very piece I had listened to as a four year old in my father's lap. That was enough motivation for me.

But during those days of endless practicing I was bothered by the thought that I didn't want to be a concert pianist; I wanted to be a composer.

A requirement for all music majors was an ensemble class. Instrument majors would join the orchestra to meet their ensemble requirement, and piano and voice majors would join the choir. Those pursuing composition could join either. I joined the choir.

The choir turned out to be one of the most enjoyable experiences I ever had. I loved it. I loved being part of the group (we were about 110 voices), I loved the music, the camaraderie…everything.

One memory that I still consider with great fondness happened during Christmas. We were rehearsing for the annual Christmas Concert that we performed in Jones Hall with the Houston Symphony. The music building for the university was a big four-story square built around an open-air courtyard. Each floor had classrooms that opened to an outside balcony that overlooked the courtyard. On the ground level in one corner was the auditorium.

You know, I just was in Houston a couple of months ago and I visited the University of Houston campus. I walked all over the place and apart from new buildings here and there, much of it is exactly the same as when I studied there in the late 70's. I went to the music building and stood in the courtyard, pleased that it is exactly as I remember it. But back to then…

One day after rehearsal at about 3:00 in the afternoon, we started filing out of the auditorium and a small group of us collected and were chatting. Someone started singing a Christmas carol, and the others after a moment, joined in adding the harmonies that were in our range (soprano, alto, tenor or bass). Well, as other folks came out of the auditorium, books and music in hand, they just sort of joined in. Before too long there was at least thirty of us singing every carol we knew in four-part harmony. Within a few minutes the doors to the classrooms on all four floors began to open and people were streaming out and lining up along the balconies to watch and listen to us. This just encouraged us to sing more, and more of the choir members to join in. At the height of the impromptu concert there were about fifty of us singing and well over a hundred students ringing the balconies on all three upper floors enjoying the music.

I think it was the year we had been rehearsing for a performance of Bernstein's "Chichester Psalms" to be performed with the Houston Symphony at Jones Hall.

Now I'm pretty sure I told you about this piece of music; I've told so many. It is a difficult piece to sing. Beautiful without a doubt, but no simple Christmas carol. It is broken into three separate hymns, sung in Hebrew, and consisting of some of the most beautiful and lyrical music ever written. One of the things I like about it, besides the music, is the history of its composition.

At the time Bernstein wrote it he had already showed his brilliance with "West Side Story" and he rocketed to fame as an brash new composer doing all kinds of bizarre rhythm work and off-the-map tonal clusters. He won the commission to do the psalms. No doubt they were expecting something new and edgy. But after being sequestered with it he came back not with bizarre new ground-breaking music that they may have expected. No, he came back with exquisite tonal music. It is soothing to the soul with its lyrical phrases and rolling melodies. But it is extremely complex and difficult to sing.

Well, the choir had been rehearsing it for weeks and we were not getting anywhere. It was questionable whether or not we would ever be able to sing it as a group. The concert was already scheduled and our choir director must have been getting nervous that we would not be ready. He was visibly more and more frustrated, and becoming intolerant with every little episode in which he didn't hear what he wanted. We were also getting frustrated because he seemed to stop us every two or three measures and make us start again.

One day we showed up for rehearsal and he was not his cordial self. He wasn't even smiling or saying "hello" to anyone. He was shuffling his papers at his music stand up on the stage of the auditorium with his back to the seating, where we were all filing in and sitting in our seats, chatting and getting ready for rehearsal.

That day he didn't have to tell us to be quiet to start the rehearsal. When he turned around to face us he had the expression on his face that only Jack

Nicholson ever really perfected when he smashed through the door with an axe proclaiming "Here's Johnny" ("The Shining"). Silence fell in parts of the seating and then traveled in waves like some form of death, as more and more people took note of his startling transfiguration.

We did not know what was going to happen but we were pretty sure we weren't going to like it, so we all just sat there as if our collective and absolute silence could somehow placate the wrath that we walked into. Whoever it was at the music stand up on that stage staring down at us looked a lot like our director, probably was our director, but he was obviously possessed by something that wasn't the director we had previously known. He seemed possessed by something like a surrender to the decision that if we could not sing the psalms, we would all be killed. Hacked to pieces with that music stand

He didn't speak to us. He growled. His shoulders were humped over and he looked at us out from under his brow and spoke very slowly and very softly. You could imagine that he thought speaking slowly and softly was an acceptable end of the spectrum, and he knew he was at risk for flying uncontrollably to the opposite less acceptable one if he even began to lose control of himself. An option he clearly seemed he would have preferred if he could get away with it.

He had had it. We were going to sing the psalms to perfection or suffer.

The speech he gave us included a history of his years of exposure to self-absorbed vocal narcissist "prima donnas" that made him physically ill. And he spewed forth the bitterness with which he experienced years of his career as a choir director experiencing laziness and incompetence that even he couldn't believe he had actually experienced. And none of it compared to the heights of self-centered baseless musical pomposity or the depths of abject worthlessness he had come to know with us. Something like that.

He told us that we were going to have a day and a half to learn our parts to perfection and then at our next rehearsal he was going to put all one hundred and ten of us into individual quartets to sing the entire collection, if we had to stay there into the small hours of the morning to do it. Rehearsal started at 2:00 in the afternoon. If any of us didn't like it, we could resign our position with the choir right then and there. He'd rather have a single quartet that could sing the hymns than a hundred that only thought they could.

And if any one of us failed the quartet "jury" we were out. That minute, turn in your music and don't let the door hit you in the ass on your way out. We all looked at each other stunned, like *He wouldn't really do that, would he?* In our music-major world that was a catastrophe because it could well mean not having the necessary prerequisites to get the degree. Unless we found our way into some stupid quartet or something. Imagine the voice majors' chagrin at the possibility of having only a high school bit in "Oklahoma" in their folio, oh and an eviction from the university choir.

With his speech punctuated by the "ass" comment, he turned back around to organize his music and start the rehearsal. There was dead silence in the entire auditorium. The kind of silence only a room of a hundred prima donnas envisioning a hundred doors hitting them in the ass on their way out of their nascent careers in stage and theater could produce.

Just then we heard one of the doors in the back of the seating (the auditorium sat about a thousand) click open. One of the tenors who was considerably late arrived oblivious to the tirade we had just experienced. He knew absolutely nothing about the fact that the director was experiencing a serious anger management moment and could be set off into who-knows-what with even the slightest provocation. The tenor was a rather effeminate young man, and just out of pure pleasure to be at rehearsal and to sing again, he skipped the double step side-skip down the sloping aisle just as Dorothy and the others had done, singing in a falsetto (even for a tenor) "You're out of the woods you're outa the dark you're outa the night… step into the day, step into the sun, step into the…"

The choir director froze with his back still turned to us as the tenor truly did skip right into it

Fortunately for the other one hundred and nine of us, the same door clunked shut with a loud but muffled bang as auditorium doors usually do, and there was left no doubt that it was the late comer narcissist prima donna skipping and singing. Not the one hundred and nine of us narcissist prima donnas who were on time that was gracing us with the music of Oz.

We eventually did learn the psalms, although probably not to perfection. Even if we had prepared ourselves to perform it to the complete satisfaction of our choir director, circumstances intervened during the performance.

When a choir rehearses, it usually rehearses in sections: soprano, alto, tenor, and baritone / bass. But when it performs everyone is mixed up so the harmonies are smooth to the ear of the listener.

Well there is a section of the psalms wherein the basses are singing this long phrased sort of sweeping melody lines, while the tenors are singing triplet figures (three notes in rapid succession) against the other melody line. The effect is nothing short of amazing, and beautiful. But those triplets are hard to sing with appropriate punctuality, you have to breathe through them. You demarcate, or punctuate, one note in the triplet from the other by very short interruptions of breath.

I sang in the bass section and during performance I was one row up and two people over from a very talented tenor who was dead-set that he was going to perform it to perfection. I'm pretty sure he was a voice major. In order to fully punctuate the notes of the triplet figures his rapid-fire breathing to really get those triplets to sound right was exaggerated (as it probably should have been). I was singing along with my music in front of me when I noticed in my peripheral vision what seemed to be someone having some sort of fit. It vaguely resembled what you might imagine a nervous disorder causing spasms, or perhaps someone trying to shake a mouse off of his back while still holding his music in performance in Jones Hall.

What made the whole thing particularly visually startling was his physical proportions. He was short, and pretty round. You wouldn't say "portly" because he was too short for that. But neither was he fat, really. He was very round in the middle but his limbs and other features were quite normal, so they seemed too small for the rest of him. Well, when I got a good look at him jiggling to his breath and sort of in a measured rhythmic cadence swaying from one side to another as though making sure he would spray his triplets equally distributed between the right side of the hall and the left, I cracked up laughing. He looked like a wind-up Santa Claus, or one of those things people used to put in the back of their cars, little statues on spring legs.

I couldn't sing because I couldn't have him in my peripheral vision without laughing, so I lifted my music so that the director would not see me laughing, and tucked my head to the side and tried to stop. We were performing in front of thousands of people after all. A good friend of mine, also a tenor one row up and over to my right, saw me laughing and crouching behind my music, and when we made eye contact he had a questioning expression on his face as he sang. Like, *What are you laughing at?* I motioned my head in the direction of Santa Claus and the next time I looked up he had his music up covering his face. And he was jiggling too, although not because of the triplets.

After the performance we were off-stage talking to our choir director (the actual performance was directed by the conductor of the Houston Symphony, not our choir director). There were about five of us including my good friend the tenor, and Santa. Our director seemed pleased with the performance but at one point he got this confused look on his face and asked, "What happened? During one of the psalms it seemed like the whole middle section of the choir lifted its music and stopped singing?" I didn't know that it extended beyond just my friend and I, but apparently everyone up above the little round star of the triplets' performance, and radiating out up to five or more abreast, had caught the visual and lost it like I had. But no one wanted to say anything because he was standing right there.

That tenor friend that I mention was actually one of two identical twin brothers who were both in the choir, and both tenors. We became very good friends, sang in a barbershop quartet together, took a drama class together, and even ended up rooming together. But I met them in the choir.

They were nutrition and health fanatics, and were very religious about working out and weight training. They got me interested in it and I signed up for it with them. Soon we were in choir together, and in weight training together (gym). Those early days of my university experience were actually very happy for me. The two brothers were awesome guys – funny, hard working, talented, but most of all...innocent.

I was intrigued by their innocence. Neither one of them had ever been drunk...neither had even had a single drink. They had never had sex, and seemed to be planning to wait until marriage. They had an all-American innocence and I was captivated by it. Sometimes I would catch myself thinking about how we could not have come from more opposite backgrounds.

One night we were at their parent's house were they lived and their parents had gone to bed. We were going to stay up and watch "Court Jester" with Danny Kaye in the starring role. I was spending the night. At one point the two of them went into the kitchen and retrieved about twenty bags of cookies. There had to be every marketed cookie brand known to modern man in their hands except for maybe the Mexican knock-off equivalents but had we been closer than 600 miles to the border there might have been a few of those too.

One of them would take some cookies out of the bag and then hand the bag to me (I don't like cookies) and I would pass the bag to the other. Soon they noticed I wasn't taking any cookies.

They eventually asked, "Don't you like cookies?" To which I answered, "No, I never really have." They looked at each other like I had just said, "I'm from a foreign country where we don't eat anything at all. Anything." (Not weird enough to be dismissed out of hand, but too weird to understand). Now you have to picture that these two were so identical that the number of people who could tell them apart without a second look numbered less than five, near as I knew. Identical features, even their hair fell exactly the same way, and they had identical expressions.

After a moment of staring at each other in disbelief they must have concluded that my statement might have been too universal and that's why they couldn't understand it, but that if they polled me on each cookie they would discover one that I either liked or thought was okay.

"Do you like Vanilla Wafers?"

"No I don't."

"How about Chips Ahoy?"

"Nope."

"Pecan Sandies?"

"Not at all, too dry."

They were beginning to show signs of concern that their inventory of cookies to ask about would run out. (They had asked me about a lot of cookies I had never even heard of and don't remember, so can't mention here by name.)

"You do like Fig Newtons, right?"

"Not really."

Another stare into each other's faces.

"Oreos" ...and they had the cautious tone of voice and expectant expressions such that you could tell they had pulled out the big guns. If I failed the "like test" with Oreos then all reason was impossible. All hope for me would be lost.

"Not them either."

"YA DON"T LIKE OREOS!!" It was too much. For a second they both looked at me in astonishment, and then looked at each other. I had just informed them that I don't like the little black cardboard discs with unidentifiable sweet paste in the middle; that I did not like mom, apple pie, baseball; and the jury was probably out on cute little babies as well.

I must have been a real mystery to them regarding food preferences. At that stage of my life there were only two things that I simply could not eat because they both caused a gag response in me: lamb and mayonnaise. I would eat cookies if I was very hungry and there was something to drink to make them possible to swallow. But lamb and mayonnaise were out of the question. To this day I cannot even be in a house where lamb has been cooking.

The very first night they invited me over to their house for dinner (this was a few weeks before the cookie episode) their mother, a very sweet and lovely woman, made a special meal. When I walked in I smelled the lamb and my immediate thought was, *Oh no. How am I going to get through this?* I then thought, *I'll just eat large portions of whatever else is being served and try not to throw up from the smell of the lamb.* (It smells like a wool sweater that's been left in the sewer for a few months, to me.)

First she set the plates in front of us and I think the lamb portion was a chop. Small, but I knew I couldn't even work on it. Grilled green beans (which I love). What she brought to the table next was something the likes of which I had never seen before, could never have imagined, and I actually began to question the sanity of the others in the room as a consequence. They were "the salads." A small plate with a canned pear half upside down and covered, completely covered like snow covers the North Pole, like an avalanche covers that one unfortunate squirrel in the wrong place at the wrong time... with mayonnaise. It glued the pear half to the plate and there was so much of it there was no approach left to me to take to try to get to the pear. And sprinkled on top of the ungodly white were little shards of carrot too few to ever have anything but a visual effect...such that one carrot could produce a hundred "salads." Oh, and three raisins. Raisins. I couldn't imagine the logic of it.

The situation called for a new strategy. I apologized and said I was not feeling well even though the meal was awesome and I very much appreciated all the trouble and expense. The guys both asked me if I was going to eat the chop and I said I was not. Then forks came at me in a flash; one of them would score the other would not. They jumped up from their seats to be the first one to get the chop, so much so that their mother severely scolded them right in front of me. Even I was a bit taken aback by the ferocity of their competition for the lamb chop. I probably should have cut it in half before I indicated that I wasn't going to eat it...had I known how hungry they must have been. Or how rarely they were fed lamb chops.

The three of us became very good friends and, like I said, shared some classes in addition to Choir. Before long we started talking about the possibility of getting an apartment together, since they had never lived away from home. Their parents were apprehensive at first, but we chose an apartment close to where they lived and they were able to visit home often.

At first everything went well.

At that time my family had a boat and would go out into the gulf and fish. One weekend we caught something like twenty pretty good-sized kingfish, maybe about three pounds each. I took two or three home with me and decided to barbecue them on the grill. Smoked kingfish is so wonderful that your life is really not complete until you've had it.

I figured I would smoke one and freeze the other two and we could eat that afternoon and have leftover smoked kingfish all week. We ate both of them in one sitting. I thought they might tear the aluminum foil into strips and stick it in their cheeks like chaw. I truly have never seen anyone eat that much in a single sitting, but they really liked the fish. It was a great afternoon.

And we would go up to Austin to camp and hang out above Barton Springs.

But gradually at first, my emotions became more and more intense toward them. And I seemed to have no control over the situation, my emotions, or anything. Behavior that was strange even to me began to creep into everyday life, and I began to get scared. I knew that things were not going well but it was all internal. They knew nothing about it. I sometimes thought that I should talk about it but I didn't understand it myself, and so had no idea where to begin. I sensed that I was losing my mind.

I would react jealously when they made plans that didn't include me. When either of them would purposefully seek out time with a different friend that they already had, I would smolder in resentment, sometimes for days. I would act very angry but give them no way to guess why, and they would never have any idea why. It must have been extremely confusing and frustrating to them.

There were things we did do together which spoke to the very thing I most admired about them – their innocence. We went to a high school competition from the school they attended before and they were both kind and attentive to everyone, even the freshmen that didn't know them. And the girls would flirt with them. But they themselves were not at all flirtatious, just kind. They were both handsome men, and although my emotions were very mixed up, I guessed that it was another characteristic of which I was jealous.

But in a twisted way, rather than celebrate their qualities and be glad for them, I began to be resentful. Particularly their innocence. I knew deep inside I was so far gone from it myself that there was none left in me to even nurture. Even if there was I would have to consciously cultivate it, and innocence cannot be cultivated. It only preexists. It either survives or is destroyed but it is never regenerated. I knew that fact with such a bitter certainty that I began to obsess over it.

It was the first sign of illness, but I didn't see it coming.

The second sign introduced me to a new room in hell. Even though I was aware of painful and twisted emotions that I was feeling toward them, that had been largely the totality of my problem. But now it took on an entire new desperation. I began to have sexual thoughts toward them.

I am profoundly ashamed to admit that, even now, these thirty-four years later. And I am quite sure they did not suspect it. I had had sexual experiences with my girlfriend in high school and they knew it. There was a beautiful girl in our drama class that they both commented on frequently. For some reason completely unknown to me, she pursued me and at one point it became obvious that I was in a sexual relationship with her. I think jealousy on their part may have kept them from asking about it or talking about it, until I broke up with her. She was too weird. (Imagine how weird that would have to be for *me* to think it!)

When they asked if I had stopped seeing her I told them "yes" that she was just too weird.

I told them that the sex was good, but sometimes she had to be on drugs and that spooked me. One of them almost angrily said, "Then let me have her!" before he caught the words coming out of his mouth. He had no way of suspecting that much of what would lead me away from her was more than her drug habit...it was a deeper thing.

I was tortured by the sexual curiosity I felt toward them the entire time that remained of our stay in the apartment.

There's a brief story that I have to interject at this point. It was an event that further fueled my confusion and the terrible struggle for sanity in which I was locked at that time.

My high school friend, the one that I call "Mushroom John" contacted me while I was living with the twins. We were still friends and although I had briefly lost touch with my drug and drinking friends, he contacted me to get together again. The twins were out of town with a church trip and so I invited him to come over for dinner. Maybe we would go out and shoot pool or something.

He came over and we cooked some food and decided to stay in and just drink some beer. At first it seemed a little awkward because at that point I had stopped drinking, and we never drank in the apartment when the twins were around. But we finished off plenty of beer.

Then John informed me that he was gay and asked if I'd like to experiment. I was horrified and told him that not only did I not have any interest in that, if he even mentioned it again it would be the end of our friendship. Looking back I feel sure that my indignation was authentic, but it was certainly mixed with doubt. I wondered if he knew, if he could tell. I wondered if it was obvious.

Some time later another episode occurred with him.

This is one of those memories that are hard for me to talk about. It touches on a myriad of emotions for me that are all difficult. It is coated in shame, more out of my own stupidity than anything. But there is quite a bit of anger there, too.

Mushroom John was involved with an older man who had a lot of money and lived in a high-rise condominium complex on Memorial Drive. I think he owned a dance studio. John invited me to come over because they were having a party and it should be a good time. I was free and back to drinking at that point (when I wasn't around the twins) so I told him I would. In fact, it was during the period when my old drinking and drugging life was back to claim me, even though I thought I had left it. They do that. Lives like that will come back and claim you when you're not looking.

When I got to their condo there were no other people but John, his friend and me. No one else showed up and at first I thought that was odd, but the alcohol flowed, and I dismissed it. I remember that we talked about music as it relates to dance, and his friend who was Latin explained that much of the Latin dances were misunderstood. I remember that he said that "Malaguena Solerosa" was written for its comedic value and I thought that was absurd.

By the time we were pretty drunk the conversation turned to sex and the two of them started trying to make the argument that sex was just for fun and that we should be open to trying anything. When it became obvious that they were interested in a three-way I indicated that I needed to leave. When I argued that I was not gay, they laughed as though they shared an inside joke that I didn't understand at the time, but would some day. I was aware that I was the object of their condescension just as I was the object of their sexual interest.

The next thing I knew I was waking up in a very large bed, alone, naked. Both of them were gone.

I can't tell you how bad that day was. There was no obvious evidence that I had been raped, but there was no explanation for the circumstance. Besides, I was nineteen years old.

I woke with such a bad hangover and I was so dizzy that I almost immediately realized that I had been drugged. I dressed and went down to the garage in a blur. Once I was in my car I drove mindlessly down Memorial Drive, and back up it. Memorial is a very long street winding through some of the most beautiful parts of Houston, and it always calmed me to go for a drive there, when I was upset, or scared, enraged, or in this case, all three.

I considered going to the police, but what could I say? What evidence did I have? Then my thoughts would turn to Mushroom John and I would go numb with the shock of the betrayal. I considered killing him. I considered killing myself. I was blank with the sense of filth that had happened to me, and that ultimately *was* me. And added to the torture of that condemnation was the knowledge that I could not tell anyone. After all, maybe it was obvious and maybe all that I would be doing would be admitting to others what I could not accept myself.

The weight of the internal conflict within me became more than I could bear, and the friendship with the twins was more strained than ever. And now the chasm between their innocence and my lack of it was wider than even I could have ever imagined possible. And I couldn't explain it to anyone.

But the third and I think final evidence of my illness was not just internal. It became something of which they were very much aware.

Remember, I was a nineteen year old that had been practicing witchcraft a scant two years earlier. I was no atheist; I was a God-hater. In fact, I was a young man so filled with anger and hatred that I was incapable of seeing it in myself. I looked at everything and everyone through my hatred, so I was not able to look <u>at</u> it. Like sunglasses. When you wear them you see through them, but you never are looking at them.

The twins were both religious in that they attended church. We even attended their summer church camp together, early on when things were new and fun. This was before I started taking the friendship for granted.

One of them, however, had a love for God and a gentleness of heart and demeanor that could only be explained by a close relationship with the Holy Spirit. He was what you hear called a "godly man." He was a wonderful guy by any measure. But he was no match for my ability to debate, my sense of logic, or the shear force with which I could argue when motivated.

For some unknown reason and without even being clear that it was what was happening, I took on a mission to dismantle his faith and belittle him for having it. Remember those conversations we had on our walks, about what it's like to be disrespected because we have faith? Remember when we discussed the feelings of frustrated resignation when people disrespected us for our faith? I think I told you that there are members of my family that still think I am an idiot for believing. But not only was I one of those who see faith as stupidity and who can argue, who can dish up condescension fully buttressed by reason, I was gifted at it.

On one occasion we had a routine argument about the existence of God that I started. But I started it in absolute deception, saying that I was curious about it. I lured him into the argument. I was giving him a chance to explain his faith and maybe make mine stronger. (I never presented it that way but I knew he would have assumed it.) To give you an idea how hateful that was, remember that I knew that believers tend to latch on to someone who says they are "curious about Jesus." That is one heck of a good way to get them started. Many Christians take a person who says that at face value, and believe them.

They think (rightfully) that it can be the Holy Spirit moving in the person and drawing them near, and usually it is.

But they do not often consider that it can also be the height of condescension. They do not (at least initially) consider that the person is lying and only wants to bait them into an argument. They don't give a thought to a different spirit that sometimes moves people to speak. And I think it is because they are looking through the lenses of their own goodness, and don't expect the loss of focus that those lenses can effect.

The argument became forceful and increasingly tedious, but I never gave him enough of an objection to bail out of it. I was careful to keep him in, careful to keep lying to him successfully.

These arguments about his faith occurred more than once.

But the next time it happened it was not so academic. It was one night when we were at home. He and I shared a room and the other brother had his own. We were sitting on our beds and the argument started. But it turned dark – far beyond intellectual. Eventually I was tearing into him like a lion in the Coliseum, not so much to kill him or even to make him suffer, but to feed my own hunger. He was baffled; caught off guard, I am quite sure he could not fathom why I would be doing it when I was a friend of his. I began to sense desperation…not mine, his. And I fed on it. It was like I had attacked his intelligence as perfectly parallel to the absurdity of faith in such a way that he had no choice but to doubt, even if only briefly. Then I would dig in stronger and deeper. It wasn't just unfriendly; it wasn't just unfair; it was demonic.

The argument ended when he was reduced to tears and had to leave the room. And he was not a man commonly given to tears.

I was left to enjoy it and while I simmered in the experience only wishing I could have had more, his brother entered the room. He looked at me with calm stunned disbelief. And he said only one thing. He asked, "How could you do something like that?" and let the question linger as if he wanted to know if there *was* an answer, more than so much what the answer might be. His question revealed that he understood the entire set-up. He understood the purposefulness of the entire thing. Then he turned and left.

Most people would have been hit with remorse by the question, or at least snapped back to lucidity after such a feeding frenzy, but not me. I look back on that night as one of the early of many great regrets. There would come to be more. Regret that you might know for things that were done to you is child's play compared to regrets for things that you yourself have done.

If I could beg his forgiveness today, I would.

When our six-month lease came up, they told me they were moving back home. I wasn't surprised. I was dead inside. I bounced around living with friends and relatives in brief stays, and slipped ever more seriously and with accelerating descent, into deep depression.

Some weeks after moving out of the apartment with them I woke up and realized that I had started considering suicide pretty much every day. Even though I was still functioning in school (to some extent) I knew I had to get help. But I couldn't let my family know. I went to see a family friend who was a psychiatrist and who knew me since I was nine years old. It took every ounce of courage I had, and all the money I had, to see him. I told him about the abuse and was even able to tell him about the fantasy feelings I had discovered. He explained to me that the events of my earlier life had left my sexuality, to use his word, "diffused." He knew I needed help but I could not afford him so he referred me to an associate in his office…an ex-priest who had become a therapist. There was so much our psychiatrist friend just didn't know.

The other therapist was a nice enough man but in the months that I saw him my depression deepened and spread to other more confusing characteristics of insanity. I could not hide it from my family anymore and I was connected with the Texas Research Institute of Mental Sciences (TRIMS). They used graduate students and their fees where considerably lower. During the year that I would remain in therapy at TRIMS, the question of whether or not I would end up institutionalized was always on the table. Actually, the question of whether that would happen before I killed myself seemed to be the first and last question for every session. I believe I had two sessions a week, but my memory is very cloudy of that time.

Much of the time I spent at TRIMS was spent trying to unravel the abuse, as though understanding it would neutralize the effects. I underwent hypnosis multiple times to try to reconstruct "the missing hour" that I told you about. The situation got worse.

I got to the point where I could no longer function at anything. I couldn't study, and could not engage in *any* relationship of any kind. The only constructive thoughts I had were when I spent time considering the best way to "do the deed."

The only comfortable waking hour I could spend was in a completely darkened room, alone, quiet, uninterrupted, and incapable of doing anything other than just being in pain.

There is no good explanation for what being suicidal is like, and I suppose it differs with every person. In many though, it is an experience where the pain you feel is so great, mixed with the thought that it will never end, that suicide seems like the only rational idea. If you've ever had something fall against you that burns, you will do *anything* to get that burn away from you. It's not unlike that. If you are in so much pain and so deeply hopeless, suicide seems like a perfectly rational option. It seems almost as though it can be the *only* rational option. You know like in those war movies where someone gets injured so badly and they are in so much pain and there is no chance that they will ever be rescued so they ask the other soldier to shoot them? And they DO? It's because they both agree that it's the only rational option.

For me it was all those things. It was the intense pain, the inescapable truth that I was seriously broken, and that nothing would ever change it.

Looking back now across all these years since TRIMS I realize that my emotional state did not improve as a result of that process, because it was pointed at the molestation(s). The focus was in the wrong place.

It was not those events that left me unable to live; it was the consequence of them in my father's life, in my friends' lives, and in mine. Much more corrosive to my soul was my father's living abandonment of me, his emotional and mental abuse, and his death. My sisters lost a loving and wonderful man. I was finally abandoned complete.

At the age of seven I knew something was wrong with me because things had happened that hadn't happened to others. By the age of twelve I had been convinced that my father hated me, by the age of eighteen I had been taught that the scorn and disdain did or would extend beyond my father to the entire community of men, and by the age of twenty I learned that the damage was permanent. I was not equipped to live in a world with other people, and I needed them much more desperately than they seemed to need each other. I was trapped in an isolation that was so vast as to be beyond even my own comprehension, let alone anyone else's.

That agony of constant suicidal ideation lasted a full year. I will never forget it. I didn't know it was possible to suffer that much and I remember wishing that it had been me that died rather than my father.

My family grew weary of the problem I was living and it took a huge toll on my mother. She feared every day wondering if that would be the day I would be gone. At one point, in desperation, she called out to me through her tears "If you're going to do it then just do it and get it over with! I can't stand this anymore!" And ran to her room crying.

That was the first moment that I realized I was hurting others.

But it made the dilemma worse. I couldn't stand *my* pain but neither could I bring myself to hurt my family. It was a predicament worse than being suicidal alone.

One day when I was in the living room, because the curtains were so thick they could block out all the light, my sister came over to the house. I suspect that my mom called her. She was the middle one, the genius of the family. I had been sitting in the room staring into space for who knows how many hours.

My sister came into the room and told me she was going for a drive and wanted me to go with her. Next thing I knew we were in her car driving down Memorial Drive. We were at the end toward Addicks Dam, where it courses through tall pines with beautiful homes on either side. The street was uncharacteristic of a big city, and even one time in the winter it snowed enough so that the snow clung to the trees and you could have been in Maine to look at it.

At that time they were beginning to build out Memorial towards the dam, the scene where I was dropped down the concrete steps. My sister decided we would go look at the houses under construction. I didn't care what we did.

I walked around with her pretty much silent because I could not see the point of anything to say about anything. She never once said a word about anything that had to do with my illness; she only talked about the neighborhood. "I wonder…" this. "Do you suppose…" that.

We approached a large "McMansion" as I think they call them now. We were both peering into the same window as she was commenting on the room layout and how big she thought it might be. You know how you have to cup your hands around your eyes so the sun doesn't obstruct your view? As we were standing side by side peering into the window, without any warning, without any lead-in, simple meteor out of the blue…she quietly said,

"Don't kill yourself, John. We can't fix that."

I turned my head and faced her, stunned.

A year of intense therapy, countless hours of hypnotism, psychiatrists, priests, therapists, lab people, hundreds upon hundreds of hours of abject confusion, and at least three minor attempts…ever getting worse and no one able to even touch it. And she made it through.

I suppose it was the simplicity. Or maybe it was just talking to me like I wasn't some impossibly fragile monster from the mental illness kind of life. I really don't know.

Everything leads up to a point in time where it sort of turns a tight turn, the way a switchback does on the side of a mountain. After that point you can look down on the length you just traveled along. But until you turn that point you really can't see things with the same perspective. Staring into the window was the point of that turn for me.

Within a week of that day I went back to University of Houston and sat at the fountain that I believe is in front of the library and spoke to the illness within me as if it were an animate being. I said: *I've had it. I have had it with this and with you. Bring it, do your worst because I don't think you have anything you haven't already thrown at me and I am still here.* It was shreds of strength.

Some night very shortly thereafter while I was in my bed I found myself lying there with my arms around my chest as if I was holding my body together. I surprised myself. Why would I care? Why would I even care? But I knew that I did. I know it sounds maybe a little awkward, or stupid, but I actually cradled myself like I was holding a wild animal that had been hit by a car. Cautiously.

I was on the ascent from hell.

Now many years later I sometimes think about the twelve years after grad school for clinical counseling, the private practice, the work at the VA and the time I spent as a therapist at the residential treatment center in Hawaii. I try to count the number of times I have had a person sitting in front of me telling me how there just wasn't any reason to go on... that they just couldn't take it anymore. These were some intense conversations, a lot like some of the ones you and I have had, except much darker, about things much too difficult to bear. And it amazes me that there has never been anything better I can say. It strikes me as odd that although I know the pain well, and I know that the person brave enough to want to talk to me about it wants – no – *needs* to have some deeper wisdom to match the depth of their pain...all you can do is love them with everything you've got and hope it is enough.

But I also tell them that they may never know when the day will come that they find themselves at a window and out of the blue someone says something so simple and pure that it makes it through. So I tell them to wait for it, even if they don't have the strength to. Wait anyway. I tell them what I was told. I say to them, "Don't kill yourself; we can't fix that."

For the rest of my undergrad, and actually for grad school too, I battled the odd depressive phase but they were aftershocks, like the rumble of thunder as the hurricane moves on.

I've always been good at school and never had to study much so it was pretty easy. I majored in Philosophy and focused on logic and the Philosophy of Mathematics. When you say "Philosophy of Mathematics" to someone they usually go silent in hopes that you won't start talking about it.

But I enjoyed the complexity of it and the fact that it took my mind in all kinds of abstract directions. And by my senior year it was pretty complex.

One exam was one sentence on the top of about twenty blank pages stapled together, which would be necessary for the symbols alone; words were not used: "Prove Goedel's First Incompleteness Result."

Logic bled off a lot of the mental energy I hadn't been able to direct for so many years. Logic and the drinking. After the return to university I stopped wanting to kill myself and I stopped doing drugs, but my drinking was making up for lost time fast.

It is evident, looking back, that none of whatever lead to the year of suicide had been healed, really. Only the actual desire to kill myself had been neutralized. I didn't know it, but everything underneath it was all still there.

My two hobbies were playing the piano, and inviting Jehovah's Witnesses in so I could attack them with logic. The incident with my roommate didn't turn out well, so now I took on strangers.

Anyone who professed faith to me was prey. I loved it; I looked forward to it. I was like some vampire lusting for the blood of religiosity, but true faith now, someone with true faith was special prey. They protested with more passion, fought with more purpose, and sometimes recognized the evil and fled. Back then I just assumed it was superiority from which they fled. But now I think it was a special kind of fear known only by someone who truly loves God in the presence of someone who truly hates Him.

Many times I would attend class so hung over that I couldn't see the teacher and would think to myself *Why bother?* I can't count the number of times I slept through class only to be startled awake by the sound of the other classmates closing their books and getting up to leave.

But there isn't a whole lot more to say about college class work than that I was either drunk or hung over almost every waking hour, fascinated with complex logic proofs and pretty much staying to myself. Oh, and playing the piano (a different and maybe better isolation, but isolation nonetheless).

It should be noted that during this time I was not attaching to anyone. I had no real friends except one, who was another Philosophy major. Whatever drew me to people before, which only led to catastrophe for me, was quickly replaced with a deepening bitterness. My anger and hatred swamped any desire I had for friendship. I had yet to know one that hadn't ended in abandonment. My Philosophy major friend was an intellectual relationship; no emotionality or even real camaraderie other than intellectual banter. But I liked him. He drank milk and drove an MG Midget and *that* was cool. I also suspected even at that time that his own brilliance caused him to have to cling to sanity, maybe a little like I did. Even though my struggle to hold on had nothing to do with brilliance. It is impossible to describe, but one who doesn't take sanity for granted can always sense it in another.

All throughout college I had to work. We as a family had no money to pay for college, but I didn't really mind. It was true for all of my sisters and my brother too, not just me. I had friends who were from families with plenty of money and they were given a full boat ride to college, and I don't think any of them actually graduated. Most went to University of Texas, but I couldn't afford anything but University of Houston. When I lived in the apartment with the twins I worked at Pizza Hut which not only gave me a paycheck but I got to eat free pizza whenever someone didn't come pick one up. And I never got sick of pizza.

My best job, though, was as a waiter at the Houston Country Club (HCC). Man, was that fun. It was hard work, to be sure. But it seemed like there was always something funny going on, or something we could laugh about. And we got to eat free Grand Marnier Soufflé every once in awhile, because they always made twice as many as they needed in case any of them "fell." I had moved up from pizza.

I have to move into a couple of stories about HCC because it was there that my illness showed itself again. And so shortly after I survived the first bout. If I were a bi-plane bouncing down the runway trying to take off, it would be the second time I hit the tarmac.

But I love telling the stories, anyway. Some of them are really good; they are HCC history and I bet they are *still* telling these stories some thirty or so years later.

First, you have to remember that HCC is the oldest country club in Houston, and one of the oldest (perhaps the oldest) in Texas. Very noteworthy Texans were members: Lady Bird Johnson and the Bushes (once out of the White House), for example. You could not show up there with your checkbook and join. You had to be invited, or have a relative die and leave you their membership. In any event, a membership had to open up to become available to anyone, regardless of how noteworthy you were. I sometimes wondered, given that the median age of the membership seemed to hover somewhere around a hundred, if whole groups of memberships didn't open up in waves. Like some generational thing.

Anyway, the place was pretty amazing. When I was there, newly hired folks were given an orientation to the place (it was huge, with many dining rooms, a ballroom, etc...) that included a special lecture on the fact that the chairs throughout the building were original Chippendales and were then worth about $25,000 each; in other words, "don't stack them," kind of thing. That was to set the tone for how we treated all the property within the walls of the HCC…and pretty much the membership too. Most of the employees, but not all, were properly intimidated. Anything you did that left management convinced that you were not in your place meant that you probably only had a few days before you were relieved of your employment. The membership expected you to know where you stood in the order of things, and management always obliged the membership.

There was an elderly lady of about ninety that used to arrive every afternoon about three o'clock. She would sit by herself in the main lounge and drink three or four rum punches until she had a proper buzz; then her driver would collect her and take her home. One afternoon she called me over to herself, I think about two rum punches in, and waved me closer to her as if she was going to tell me a secret. She said, "Waiter…" and I answered "yes, ma'am?" to which she continued, "I notice that you're, well, white."

She asked her question with a sort of kindness as though she had noticed that my clothes were all torn and tattered and was going to suggest that she give me a dollar to go buy some new ones. I just stared at her not having a clue how to respond. I almost flashed on the idea of saying something apologetic like "Well, not really. I'm half Mexican or Spanish, Cuban actually, depending on whom you ask, and I just *look* white." But I was too surprised even for that bit of honesty. I had no idea where she was going with this.

"Does it bother you to have to work here in this sort of employment?"

I have to say that she said this in all innocence, and again, with a tone of sincere empathy. I couldn't have responded with condemnation for her racist attitude because she was utterly unaware of it. I realized that I was staring at something few ever really see. Someone comfortable not only with the huge thirty-foot ceilings overlooking acres of manicured gardens, huge white pillars, and Chippendale furniture…but also with what they suggest. Someone who really doesn't have a clue when or where they actually are. "No, ma'am." I answered. "Can I bring you another rum punch?"

"Yes, please. That would be fine, and thank you so much."

There were other members, however, that were truly difficult to bear; old rich lawyers, and the drunk guys who hit on the waiters. I'm sure there were those that hit on the waitresses too, but for whatever reason we never heard about them.

Probably my favorite story involved a special luncheon for "The Daughters of the British Empire" (DBE).

I was working the main dining room, which accommodated about a hundred and overlooked the lawn and swimming pool area down by the grill.

Technically the main dining room was on the second floor, but you entered it from the main floor. Once inside the country club on the main floor you noticed that you were actually on the second floor, even though you entered at ground level, because it was built on the side of a hill. The tall windows of the main dining room looked down on the lawn from a height of about twenty feet, which gave you a full sweeping view.

I was setting up for a big lunch and an elderly lady dressed in tweed approached me and asked where the luncheon for the "DBE" was to be held. I didn't know so I asked the floor manager and he indicated where it was. She was followed by a stream of others who all had to be directed downstairs to the lawn. It wasn't long before I noticed that each of these ladies seemed to be quite elderly, several of them walking with the assistance of those clinical-looking canes that sprouted four legs just above the floor. But then I noticed that the luncheon was set up as a buffet.

I remember thinking to myself that it seemed odd to me to set the thing up on the lawn as a buffet, when most of these ladies were elderly and couldn't get around too well. I wondered why they hadn't set it up as a three-course "sit down" instead of a buffet. There were to be about a hundred guests and I tried to imagine a hundred geriatric British ladies filing through a buffet line, on the grass, plate in one hand cane in the other. *This ought to be good*, I thought to myself. So I made a point to glance down and check it out from time to time, when I was near the windows.

Well, the buffet opened at 11:30 a.m. and the line was definitely moving slow. You could see the waiters scurrying around trying to help carry the plates for the most elderly, or fetching them entirely for those who could not easily get out of their seats. The captains (captains were waiters who were in charge of directing three or four other waiters) were running around anxiously calling commands to the waiters and trying to make up for the short staff, in light of their increased and unexpected new burdens. By about 12:30 p.m. the line was completely full, and pretty much everyone who could stand was standing, with well over half of them holding plates or in the process of loading them up.

And the automatic sprinkler system came on. The managers had neglected to turn it off in preparation for the event.

Now, these were not the gentle mist sprinklers that you see in residential lawns sometimes. These were big powerful golf course sprinkler heads powering honkin' thirty-foot streams on fifteen-foot centers. Looking down on the scene you could barely even see the people under the canopy of the huge white spiders formed by the over-lapping jets of water. Immediately every waiter was gone. There was not a single antebellum green-and-black waistcoat to be seen. I caught a glimpse of the manager standing dumbstruck. And then a very elderly lady inching along away from the mayhem in an aluminum walker, one little two-inch step at a time. I couldn't take my eyes off her thinking that she would be absolutely soaked by the time she got out of the spray. Just then a jet hit her beanie and carried it off about ten feet. She stopped and sort of looked at the beanie in what seemed to be a moment of decision. Did she inch along after it, which would certainly mean a good five minutes more in the line of fire, or abandon it till later?

For the moment I lost my sense of self-awareness and collapsed against the wall laughing, next to the window. The folks seated at the tables could neither see nor hear what was happening down on the lawn, so one by one, the waiters first, then the guests started coming over to the window to see what was happening. The waiters all broke up laughing, but many of the guests seem to respond considering it like a tragedy or something. And we caught not a few looks and comments of reprimand. There was nothing we could do. By the time we got down there they would all be wet and the water would already be turned off anyway.

Another time in that same room I was serving a lunch held for a very exclusive private school from arguably the wealthiest neighborhood in Houston. It was a fund-raising luncheon and many of Houston's finest were there. It was a three-course as I recall.

The wall opposite the windows in the main dining room is shared by the ballroom, with these huge twenty-foot tall pocket doors, two of them, separating the two rooms. Because the ballroom was being broken down and re-set for a dinner and dance that evening, the pocket doors were closed.

We had served and cleared the main course and were setting down deserts and coffee. The Bursar of the school was walking to the podium to speak, for the first time during the lunch and would no doubt be talking about the wonderful year the school had had, and the worthy plans for the future. He would be making his bid for them to name their pledges of support, of course. The waiters were pouring coffee for the approximately one hundred or so guests. All the sudden, when the bursar was just a foot or two from the podium a voice came booming through the speakers at full volume "YOUR MOTHER ---- ---- IN HELL!!!" A line from the then newly released movie "The Exorcist." (This was in the late 70's.)

The Bursar was actually physically and literally taken aback. He staggered away from the podium backwards, as if Satan himself were already standing there, invisible but in full manifestation of unspeakable evil.

The next sounds were those of about thirty coffee cups dropped onto thirty coffee cup saucers and a room full of people suddenly gasping in shock. Then there was a laugh coming through the speakers… "Ha! Ha ha haaaa" upon which most of the remaining, who were still unconvinced it really was Satan, were disabused of their doubt. Others, recognizing that it was coming through the speakers, suspected the source to be human and you could almost sense the beginnings of a lynch mob mentality forming in the room.

I knew it was human, I recognized the voice. It was a waiter I knew, and I suddenly realized that he must be working set up in the ballroom and horsing around with the microphones, not realizing they were turned on and blaring in the main dining room. I ran to one of the pocket doors and shouldered it open, entered and closed it behind me hoping maybe to shield his identity (and his life) from discovery by the manager. There were two of them and I knew them both. The other one was responding into his microphone that the first one should go perform lewd acts on a particular diseased beast of burden, but his mic was not on. I called out to them "The mics are live, you idiots! We're hearing every word you say in there!!" pointing over my shoulder to the main dining room. They fled. They ran like the wind. But I thought to myself, *Schedule sheet, boys. You can run but ya can't hide. Nope. You, gentlemen, are screwed.*

I went back into the room and reported the situation to the manager who was scrambling to figure out what was going on. I didn't rat out my buddies but he let loose a stream of expletives with which even they would have been impressed. His face turned the color red it gets by saying something in a whisper and a full scream, at the same time. The pressure caused by the words trying to escape his mouth at top volume and with greatest emphasis possible, stopped by the desire to keep his country club job in the presence of his country club membership, caused the blood to back up in his cheeks and forehead, I guess.

Okay. One more country club story and then I'll tell you why I brought them up.

You know how I said there were some pretty wealthy Houstonian members, right? Well, one of them was a doctor of international reputation. His daughter was getting married and they decided to have the reception at the HCC. All the waiters that were to work the party had to attend a special meeting the Saturday morning before we set the place up.

We were told that he was having his own ballroom furniture brought to the club, his own crystal champagne glasses, and his own dinnerware for the happy couple and three hundred or so of their close family friends. It was explained to us that no matter how careful we ever were with the HCC things, we had to be doubly careful with the good doctor's stuff. For emphasis we were told that the champagne glasses alone were two hundred dollars a stem. Each! We weren't sure if this meant that if we broke one it was coming out of our paycheck, or not. Two of those suckers and we were working the party for free. Who know how much the chairs were worth.

It was an interesting party. At one point I happened to be standing next to a wall in a walkway with another one of the waiters. He was one of them that never really understood how to act around these wealthy folks. He fancied himself a "rebel without a cause" type, and he really didn't like them. As we were standing there with our arms folded behind our backs stiff in some form of attention pose, two of the ladies invited to the ball passed right in front of us. Without even turning his head he said, "Oh, look. K-Mart must be having a sale on its formals." I have a whole group of stories just about him, but I'll save them for some other time.

Toward the end of the evening I went into the side bar to kill time with my friend the bartender while we all waited for the last of them to get drunk enough to finally want to leave. I decided I'd take some champagne glasses down to get washed. Some of the doctor's glasses.

The trays each had about sixty glasses on them, and they were stacked about four trays high on the shelf in the side bar. This was a working bar where the guests usually did not come in – only the waitresses and waiters getting drinks.

I grabbed the top tray and began to slide it toward me so I could stack it on the roller to take down to the washers, only I didn't grab the sides of it in the right place. When it came off the shelf, it became obvious that I was holding it at points on the sides not quite in the middle but just a hair too much toward me. Off balance. As soon as the far lip of the tray came off the shelf it fell downward catching on the close edge of the tray beneath it, and sending the sixty champagne glasses on the top tray sliding down into the sixty on the one just beneath it. I was startled and had a sort of knee jerk reaction to the shock of breaking one of them, let alone a whole tray full of them, and in my reflex pulled both the top tray and the one beneath it whose lip the upper tray had caught on, right off the shelf. The trays crashing to the floor managed to take yet another two trays stacked beneath them and in one single event I ended up standing in a pile of trays and two hundred-dollar-a-stem champagne glass pieces. Who could guess how many I broke, but probably well over a hundred.

I'm not sure exactly what I said in my exclamation but I can tell you it would have gotten me into a world of hurt back at St. Cecilia's. My friend the bartender said, "Go. Get out of here. Now! I'll tell 'em I came in and found them and don't know who did it. Get out of here."

I was dazed and almost dizzy as I ran out of the bar and tried to think what to do, where to go. But I knew I needed to get far away from that side bar, so I decided to go down to the kitchen and get things that had been washed and dried and were ready to come back up to be loaded and taken back to the owners. There was a stack of the green plastic wash trays that held coffee cups already cleaned, dried and ready to go. There were about ten trays each holding about forty coffee cups.

The kitchen to the HCC was at the bottom of two ramps that met in the middle and each went up in opposite directions ending in side bars; one outside the ballroom, the other outside one of the small dining rooms. The ramps were about fifty feet long each and ascended to about ten feet above the bottom, and they were floored in red industrial tile.

The green wash trays for the coffee cups stacked on top of each other all fit into a frame with a wheel on each corner. I was pushing the stack on its rollers up the ramp that goes to the ballroom side bar when one of the wheels hit a small stone or something. It was just enough to stop the whole stack dead in its tracks. Well, I was almost at the top of the ramp, and at the incline that I was at, pushing the stack when it came to a sudden stop...well, I didn't. I fell on top of the stack, un-stacking the trays into a pile very much like the one in the side bar I had just left except made of bigger pieces. And I rode the pile all the way back down the ramp. One of the managers turned the corner to go up the ramp just as I was sliding on top of all the fine coffee cups mashed and ground into a pile. I was sliding along right down toward him. He yelled "*Got* DAMN IT !!! Some dumb sonavabitch just broke $20,000 in champagne glasses and NOW THIS!!! What's wrong with you people?!?"

I said, "Someone just broke a bunch of champagne glasses!?!?" looking up from my reclining position on the floor of the ramp with as shocked an expression as I could muster on top of what was left of about a hundred or so coffee cups. And they didn't fire me. They never found out that it was me that broke the glasses too. There were lots of things they probably *should* have fired me for, but never did. I sometimes wondered if they just didn't get it, that I was an uncoordinated klutz who not only broke thousands of dollars of fancy champagne glasses, coffee cups and saucers, but also once held a tray of after-dinner drinks behind a man's back serving his brandy and spilled ten after-dinner drinks of various colors all down his beige silk blazer. Or the time

I was pouring the coffee from a silver pitcher in my right hand and heard the dribble coffee makes when you spill it on the table. Only it wasn't spilling on the table. Confused, I looked around and noticed it was the coffee from the silver pitcher in my *left* hand that, while I was intentionally pouring the coffee in my right hand, was also pouring. Onto the lady's white mink coat.

My days at the country club were good days, and I had a lot of fun not getting fired. But they are particularly fond because of a good friend I made there, who was also a waiter. It was the next time and setting in which I made a good friend like my friend from Catholic school, Mike. His name is Bob, but he liked the name Chris so we called him Chris-Bob. I was in school, Bob was considering going to school, and we were working the country club. We were young and I think those were the days of the proverbial "wild oats" you hear about. I was pretty wild back then and I guess many of us were.

We played pranks on each other much like Mike and I used to. One time, for instance, we were both working the same party at the HCC. One of the cardinal rules at the HCC was that all waiters had to have our little black bow ties on at all times while on the floor. These were little black ties that clipped on.

I was serving a drink to someone and Bob swept by and just almost with a flick of the wrist as he was passing by, plucked my tie off and popped it in his pocket, walking off with it. I can't remember where I found it. But I managed to get his off in a similar fashion and took it back to the same side bar where I broke all the champagne glasses and filled it with fruit wedges and cherries on a stick – drink decorations – and set it on a display. It looked like Carmen Miranda got hold of it, but I doubt that even she could have crammed more fruit into a black clip-on bow tie.

He managed to get mine again and I could not find it *anywhere*. Finally he gave me some hints that led me to another side bar. I looked around and still couldn't find it. He motioned in a general direction until I noticed something that looked kind of like a silvery gray beach ball. When I looked closer I realized that it was a huge wad of sheet cellophane wrap, the kind we used to cover chafing dishes and had on rolls three feet wide and two feet in diameter. Just barely you could make out something black in the center of it. Took me an hour to get it out of there.

I always liked going to bars with Bob. He did card tricks and other magic tricks and the girls always liked him. So I often got to meet them just because I was around him. I could never have been that outgoing myself, and the girls never seemed to realize this. I could have been with the risen Elvis.

It was during this time that I was the busiest chasing an opinion of myself that was based pretty much on how many women I could get into bed. I guess a lot of guys go through this, but most guys who do just want to sleep with a lot of women. They never stop to count, and probably never even consider it an accomplishment. I know Bob didn't, and he was someone any guy would consider successful with girls. For me it was another facet of an illness I didn't know I had. If I stopped and considered it for a minute, even then I would have thought it was pathetic. It was a compulsion, but I didn't recognize it. Looking back I think it is ironic that at that time that behavior spoke to me of how masculine I was, how virile and manly. When in truth, it was driven by the fact that I was anything but…and in my quiet moments alone, I knew it.

For Bob it was all innocence and fun, and I acted as though it was for me too. But it wasn't innocence and fun, for me. It was a battle, and every time I came home from the girl I had fooled…every time I came home having dodged the bullet again and comforted myself thinking myself a "real man" I did so against the testimony – yet again – that it was a lie. And I ached at the pain of knowing it was not a lie for the other guys. It was not a lie for Bob.

He once told me that he always had a dream to become a circus clown, and we actually had a couple of long conversations about why he should. I told him that he should do it if for no other reason so that he would not look back one day and regret not having done it. He mentioned Ringling Brothers and Barnum and Bailey Clown College and I urged him to go. He was raised in a wealthy Chicago neighborhood and laughed at the idea of his high-powered corporate executive father explaining to his friends in the locker room at the club when they were talking about junior doing well at Yale, or struggling at U Penn, commenting, "Yeah, son Bob is down at Ringling, in Clown College these days…."

But I reasoned that if he didn't do it, he might never get it out of his system, and after all, what would he lose if he did? I'm sure there were other more lengthy pontifications but I think that was the gist of it. He decided to go.

I remember that when he made the decision to go to Florida, and I had made the decision to go to grad school in Arizona, that the life I had been living was coming to an end and I could place the date on a calendar. What had been the almost capricious speculations of a couple of buddies between work, pranks, and parties had turned into decisions. And decisions have a tendency to leave you behind sometimes, when they move to take you where you said you wanted to go.

The point is that even at that time, when all was fun and freedom, and he was the best friend I had, something was wrong. Even then, I knew it. I could sense it. My feelings of attachment to him were far too strong. I couldn't understand at the time, but in every moment that I celebrated what a terrific person he was and how much I admired him, laughed at his sense of humor, and truly deeply appreciated every word or act of kindness he showed me...all of it hurt. It hurt for no reason. It was a pain without explanation, without justification, without any provocation whatsoever. He loved me. But his love for me was healthy; it was innocent. Because *he* was healthy, *he* was innocent. He was everything that I was not but wanted to be and I was constantly choking down my hatred for myself, at my love for him. He either never figured it out, or he was showing me a kinder kindness. And that would have been just like him.

That last day I would ever see him, the day we both left for school, I almost couldn't stand it. After I boarded the plane he managed to have the attendant bring me a note he had scrawled on a boarding pass jacket which had the words to the old Irish blessing on it. "May the sun be always at your back, the roads always rise to meet you, and until we meet again, may God hold you in the palm of his hand."

My throat seized up and I put my face in my hands to hide my tears. When I looked up the lady one aisle up from me had turned looking at me with the kind of compassion you would see if it were a note from my sweetheart who I could not bear to be leave, rather than my drinking buddy from work. I accepted the lady's anonymous compassion because I needed it, even if deceived by appearances.

As I sit and write this to you; I still have that note in a little box along with other mementoes, worthless to anyone but me. I have held onto it for more than thirty years in the same box with a trinket my mother gave me more than forty years ago; a piece of bark from the log where my girlfriend and I sat on the beach when I asked her to marry me, and unnoticed, I lowered my hand and broke it off secretly putting it in my pocket. Other odds and ends no one could ever reason out, or whose justification could ever be guessed. Little bits of things stored in a box, garbage to anyone who would open it but me. I don't know what they do for me now.

I digress.

During the weeks and months just before I went to Arizona for graduate school when I wasn't at work at the country club, or partying with friends in the discos of Houston, I was spending a considerable number of hours doing pretty much one other thing: composing piano music. I mention this because it provides the context for another event that, like my friendship with Bob, could have been a sign.

It happened on April 1, 1979.

At that time I lived in the downstairs bedroom of a two-story townhouse with my little brother and sister, and my mom. The downstairs consisted of a kitchen, my room, the entryway, the living room, and dining room. There was a bathroom off the hall between my room and the entry but other than that the downstairs floor plan formed sort of a donut of a traffic pattern, with the stairwell off to the right of the entry. If the door between my bedroom and kitchen and the door out to the entryway were open, you could walk an uninterrupted circle through each of the consecutive rooms.

The piano was the spinet that I grew up playing and it was inside my bedroom.

The day my father died was April 1, 1968, "April Fool's" Day. This was another aspect of the whole thing that helped convince me that he really did want to die because he was an almost fanatical practical joker. Think back to what he did to his daughter with the duck call. If he did actually choose to die, that would be the day he would have chosen for it. I mean, the principal of the Catholic school scolded me when I called the office on that afternoon to tell them that my father had died. She made sure that I understood the truly poor taste and disrespect of such an awful April Fool's joke. Imagine the absurdity of that call from my end of the phone line.

On that particular April 1 afternoon in 1979 I was at home with a day off, I was alone, and I decided to spend the day at the piano. By that time in my life I had probably written maybe twenty compositions for piano and many, if not most, had been dedicated to someone I knew. I didn't really write *about* people I knew; I composed music that was sort of an attempt at tonal poetry, if I had to describe it. But many of the pieces seemed to be right for dedication to someone I knew and cared about, in the same way that a gift you see in a gift shop might be perfect for someone you know like it was made for them, even though it wasn't made about them.

Here's the story: I was sitting at my piano, alone in the house, thinking about it being the anniversary of his death some eleven years later and realizing that never once had it ever occurred to me to write something for *him*. I think I had forgotten or had stopped caring about the times he drug me out of bed at 2:00 in the morning drunk to play for his friends.

I thought, *Yes, I should write something for him. After all, he was my father.*

So I thought about it. I knew he would want it to be simple and very respectful. He was not a man given to displays of emotion (at least not any that would have seemed weak) and I am quite sure I never once saw the man cry. He was an "old fashioned" Latin man. Dignity. He would have wanted something with dignity.

I started on an E Flat octave. I began with a simple melody line in E Flat Major that may have been a little reminiscent but nothing else. As I varied the melody line and tried out a few modulations I began to feel pleased with the work. I thought he might like it, maybe even be proud of it. I wasn't pushing it; there was no reason to. Wherever it led, I went, and when it hit a dead end I'd just play through it until I found a more fertile improvisation.

I sometimes find myself in conversations about what it is like to actually compose music. I'm sure it is different one composer to the next, but I also feel pretty sure that in some ways it is always the same. For me it is often like riding a horse when you do not know the field. You know how to jump a stream and duck a low hanging branch…and you're always up for the full run when the terrain is nice and flat. That seamless transition to a rolling smooth rhythm, that has to be the closest thing there is to flight without wings. But you don't really know where the horse is going, or really much care. In your mind you may be taking mental note so you know how to come back to it, but generally as it happens, you are just along for the ride.

As I was coursing down cord progressions following the melody lines as they came up, lingered and then ran out of steam, my approach to the piece began a very gradual shift. It began to edge away from dignity. Or maybe the purpose of having a direction for it began to lose its grip, and a distant creeping emotion started to show up fleet and passing from the periphery, unannounced, and yet too benign to fully notice.

The melody had been a solid but simple structure and working within it was difficult without being obvious or crude, or overly repetitious. It had an innocence, if a melody can be innocent. But I started noticing passing and very brief dissonances enter the flow. Here a ninth, there a suspension. I didn't plan nor intend them, and they definitely were discordant, and might have ruined things if they didn't pass by so quickly. But they weren't mistakes.

As I continued on and almost started to get lost in the session more and more of them began to show up in the passing riffs – an augmented octave (the most dissonant combination of notes in acoustic music), now and again.

The other thing that I noticed was that the piece was becoming louder. It was not a phrase crescendo like you would put in for interpretive effect. It was building. More and more dissonance. Louder and louder.

Before long I was in triple forte (very loud) and I was slamming scales sending them flying up and down the piano. All mental or intellectual control over the process had been ceded and raw emotion was at the levers. The scales were furious, climbing up into the treble register of the piano and stomping back down into the bass. My feelings were edging toward an un-tethered violence, in the absent anchor of words. And they were becoming *physical.* As the music was getting louder and the scales more physically demanding my emotions were beginning to overwhelm me.

At one point without any warning as the piece was speeding up, getting louder, more and more reckless, I suddenly had the view from a different perspective. My perspective shifted out from under me. I was looking down out from the doing of it, above it, and watched. I could see that what was happening at the keyboard was beyond my technical ability. I did not have the technique needed to be playing what I was watching happen. I thought to myself: *I am not doing this. This is doing me.* But it did not stop. It escalated and escalated, getting louder and louder, more, more. At the top of it none of it had been enough to satisfy what had emerged and finally thrown off all dignity, all control, all respect for sentiment.

Rage.

The thing carried me off and, having nothing else to use, I just opened my hands and slapped the keys, then clenched my fists and then pounded them either to get. what. I. wanted. Or break the damn strings. Jumping back into the scales only to try to wrest control again, only to find them too ordered, too civil, and fly back into the slamming dissonance for another go.

Finally, in a split second, it was over. My energy was spent. I just fell into the keys, my forehead resting on the wood, the harmonics and dissonances still clashing, filling the room in chaotic stampede like the innocent after an explosion. I could not but collapse against the beast that had just beaten me up.

My left hand had landed on an E Flat octave, the same octave I had started with, what seemed like hours earlier. My hand was holding the octave because my chest was resting on my arms. I was crying, clinging to the piano.

I'm not sure how long I remained that way but it was long enough for the octave to fade silent. I sat up, and more out of pity for myself than anything else I can think of, repeated the opening melodic measures with which I had started because I couldn't think of anything else to do next.

The effect was disassembling.

It perfectly portrayed that after all the thrashing about, all the fighting, you only stop because you have nothing left to fight with. You never accept.

There is really no such thing as sorrow, only anger bled of strength. And in the end, you are right back where you started. Nothing has changed.

I got up from the piano and started pacing. My hands were clenched in fists up against each ear and my eyes were closed tight as I paced the circle, into the entry, the living room, the kitchen, the bedroom, back into the entry, the living room…saying over and over again, "shit, shit, shit, shit, shit, shit…"

I didn't want the piece. I did not want the composition. But neither could I discard it. I had heard it; I knew the power it had. I also knew that I could never write it. I cold never go back there and do that again.

It took six years to compose what I came to title "Two Afternoons, April 1." At one point I worked six months on the crescendo and realized that I had made the top of it too easy to predict. The crescendo had become structured which ruined the chaotic feel of it. By trying to create it I had given it too much melody and it undermined the effect at the top. I couldn't just back up a bit and change course; I had to toss out the whole six months and start over.

Six years later I started performing it.

At one performance I was invited to sit at the table of an elderly couple that was there. It was a very large piano bar that sat about 200 at small tables with this massive twelve-foot grand. When I got to the table the gentleman wasn't there. I asked where he was and she said, "He went to wash his face. His father died ten years ago. This is the first time he has wept over it."

Four months later I added another fifty measures almost as an apology.

Back in 1979 I missed the message in that afternoon, just as I miss so many. There was a warning in all those scales but I never heard it.

So on to grad school I went. I decided on a Business School, applied and was accepted. The school I selected turned out to be the perfect one if for no other reason than that through them I was able to attend Oxford University for a semester. And that was a highlight of my life. I'll get to that later. It was perfect for other reasons too, in that the folks that I met there so fully enriched my life that I began to venture out of my isolation and to trust enough to make friends. Or maybe it was just that we all lived on campus and there was no way to *avoid* making friends. But the whole time I spent there started with an experience that is still one of my favorite stories.

I already told you about the plane trip after having said goodbye to Bob. Well, I landed in Phoenix in what you might call a "resigned" state. This was at the end of May and I knew that Phoenix was a desert (I had never been there before), but I didn't really appreciate that deserts are truly hot. Things don't typically live in deserts unless they are things you would have no interest in approaching. Plants designed to hurt you if you even touch them. Snakes that are poisonous. And ever this oppressive wall of heat that you actually walk into when you get off the plane. At that time only Terminal One was in use and you walked outside under a covered walkway from the gate to the baggage area. There was a sort of benefit in that…at least you weren't deluded into thinking you had landed somewhere that is actually habitable. Not deluded for long, that is.

It was my first big adventure since going to France when I was seventeen. I did not know a soul in Phoenix, had never been there, but I was to be there for at least a year and had brought with me everything I could pack. It was only when I went to retrieve it all and get it to the hotel where the school shuttle would pick me up that I realized I couldn't manage it all. When I had left there were airport things, like carts and stuff. But there were none of those things in Phoenix that I could just load up and with which I could tool on out of the airport never to be seen again.

I knew the hotel (no longer there) was adjacent to the airport and when I got to the curb outside the baggage claim I could see it. It was too close for a cab, too far to walk. I figured that I could carry most of my things to a median, then come back for the others, and sort of schlep it all to the hotel in segments like some British army making it through the Sahara with no real continuous supply line possible.

While I was at a pause standing there trying to figure it all out, this young woman who appeared to be about my age asked me if I needed help. It didn't occur to me to wonder what she was doing in the middle of a vast mix of parking lot and traffic corridors adjacent to an airport, with no luggage of her own, in the middle of the day, in the middle of the desert. But such was my level of preoccupation with my dilemma. I told her that I did and would be very grateful if she would help me get it all over to the hotel we could both see just beyond the tarmac.

It took some effort and maybe ten minutes but as we were dragging the stuff up the curb I offered to buy her lunch to thank her. There was a little café in the lobby and people were already crowding in for lunch. We got a table for two.

Everything I am about to write happened exactly as I write it. This is not a memory about which I have any doubts. At first I started the conversation by asking her where she was from. She answered "Oregon."

I said, "I hear Oregon is very beautiful but I've never been there." To which she replied, "Neither have I."

"Oh, so you moved away when you were still really young?"

"...away from where?"

"Oregon."

"No. I don't know what you're talking about. I'm from Montana."

Now I know I've told you that my short-term memory is really bad, but I can still generally remember things I am told at least for the first thirty seconds after I am told them.

I tried not to show any confusion to her and just keep it light and not be offensive. I decided not to confront her on the apparent discrepancy in the first thirty seconds of our lunch, and press on. But something didn't seem right.

After our food was delivered she grabbed her purse and began removing from it what could only be called idols. She arranged them in a neat semi-circle in front of her plate, evenly spaced apart (about two inches as I recall). I know there were Jesus and a Buddha, and I am pretty sure there was a frog and a Mayan or maybe Aztec thing. There were a couple that looked like buildings of some sort, one of which I think was the Empire State Building. As she was very carefully lining them up making sure they were perfectly equidistant from each other, I stole sideways glances at the others in the restaurant hoping to reassure myself that they were not watching this. And then she pulled out a votive candle and I realized that they probably soon would be.

She asked, "Do you have a light?" and I answered that I did not smoke.

She smiled at me like I was a sick urchin on the streets of Calcutta and she was Mother Teresa herself, then stood up and walked to the next table with her hands clasped together in a modified universal position of prayer, cradling the candle, bowed to the table as if the Pope were seated there, and asked if anyone could provide her with fire. Yep. She did.

I watched in a pained state, as the people at the table looked at ME rather than her, with the confused and somewhat annoyed expression that spoke very clearly... *Is this wack job yours?*

It dawned on me that lunch had been a bad idea.

As soon as I could I looked over God and the burning candles and everything and mentioned to her that I was going to go to the restroom and I would be right back. Now, as I think I made clear earlier, in those days I absolutely detested people who were religious fanatics. They were beyond deluded in my opinion; they were a waste of perfectly good oxygen. So you can imagine my disdain at not only having to sit with the grand "poopah" of them ALL while everyone in this god-forsaken desert looked on, but I had to pay for lunch for the pleasure. I was furious at being trapped into it as I dried my hands and exited the men's room.

"Excuse me, sir, my name is (whatever it was – that part I don't remember) and I'm the assistant manager here." He reached out to shake my hand. "We have a situation and you might be able to help us…"

Oh great. A "situation." Like I didn't have one of my own. He very slowly and in whispers described to me that the state mental hospital (Arizona State Hospital – still there) which is a locked facility for the criminally insane was located just a block north of the airport and that the young lady with whom I was having lunch was an escaped inmate. He asked if I knew her. He was actually asking me if I was an accomplice in her escape. I emphatically responded that I did not, that she just helped me with my luggage, that I had never even been in Arizona before (and was wondering why the hell I ever thought to change that), and what was she in the hospital *for*, if he didn't mind me asking. Looking back I am surprised that he answered that, but I think he must have thought that I needed to appreciate the severity of the situation.

"She is dangerous, John." And his expression made it very clear that she was *murder* kind of dangerous. "The orderlies from the hospital are on their way now and we need to keep her calm until they get here. We can't let her escape."

At that point I think the thought flashed across my mind that I might be a little murder kind of dangerous, I was so fed up with the situation. Very reluctantly I agreed to return to the table as he assured me that the hotel would "comp" the lunch. The absurdity of the matter was so enormous that I attributed it to the whole of the state of Arizona. The airport alone could not contain it.

The orderlies did come, about four of them. By the time she saw them it was too late and she didn't even run. She never looked back at me; she just went with them as if they were the carpool come to take her to elementary school. The van from *my* school arrived and loaded me in with the others who were there and I wondered if having had lunch with an insane murderer escaped from the state hospital was apparent on my face. The story doesn't end here, though.

The school that I was there to attend is considered by many to be one of the top business schools in the country, and as far as international commerce is concerned, one of the best in the world. But I had never actually seen the campus. I went through the entire application and acceptance process without ever visiting the place. I had always hoped, no almost longed, to go to an ivy-league school. One steeped in tradition with ancient hollowed halls covered with ivy, or fig, or whatever. As the van made its way through Phoenix and then Glendale the realization slowly settled on me that there was not likely to be any such institution in a place like Glendale, Arizona. My hopes were fading fast.

I think it was the last stretch of road before we turned into what was to be the BACK entrance of the campus that finally shut me down. Cactus, a few orange trees, and cows.

The campus was an old military airport during World War II and some of the classrooms were actually in hangars. As we turned into the place this heavy sick feeling began to sink into me that I had made a huge mistake. At one point I had been considering Stanford University, and now I was driving into a dilapidated desert version of "McHale's Navy." (I know you're too young to remember that movie) I had not left home to go grad school; I had accidentally enlisted.

After checking in I was directed to the dorm room to which I had been assigned. I walked into a building that was one of the barracks. It was a fifty-year-old dilapidated barrack built well before air conditioning had been invented, and designed to be inhabited by young men who had absolutely no say whatsoever in their living conditions. The room into which I entered was a small dorm room with no less than four bunks. It couldn't have held more. But the real treat awaited me.

The bathroom was communal. At the doorway into it from my bunkroom I could see across the room another door into an adjoining bunkroom. And along the wall between the two doors was a line of toilettes that did not even have the little modesty walls mounted between them. Not only had I messed up and missed my opportunity to study in residence at some grand old bastion of gentility and learned pursuit, I had stumbled into a broken-down barrack in the middle of the god forsaken desert where I would get to attend the necessities sitting next to guys I didn't know, like we were waiting for a bus.

As soon as I settled in I decided to walk across the street to the convenience store, get enough beer to knock me out, and figure out how I was going to explain why I was back in Houston after only a day or two. And how I was going to get my stuff back into the airport without buying lunch for some lunatic.

Normally the amount of beer I drank would sedate an elephant, but I could not sleep through the night. Not because I was disturbed by dreams although if I had had them I am sure they would have been disturbing. I couldn't sleep because of the frostbite developing on my toes, nose, and fingers. The building was indeed designed before air conditioning but it was equipped with what are called "swamp coolers" that cool the air by introducing moisture into it. Since this was June in the desert, the air was so dry that you didn't need to put your laundry in the dryer. You just took it out of the washer and carried it back to your dorm room; it was dry by the time you got there. You didn't sweat in Phoenix at that time, you salted. The sweat never appeared as moisture; it just evaporated leaving a coating of salt on your skin.

So the swamp cooler was in the environment where it was designed to work most efficiently. The problem was that there was no thermostat on the thing. Those hadn't been invented either. So the only way to actually control the temperature was to turn the thing off when the room got to the temperature that you wanted, which is difficult to do when you are asleep. So as you sleep the unit just cranks more moisture into the air until the temperature drops to the point where you either wake up because you didn't think to go to sleep in a sub-zero sleeping bag and the cold pain in your extremities exceeds your desire to stay asleep, or slip into the endless sleep that usually characterizes being frozen to death.

You would think that the first full day on campus would have gotten better.

After taking my first shower in the communal crapper I dressed and tried to cover up the raging hangover I had, accented by lack of rest. There was a knock on the door. I thought *Who the hell could that be? No one knows me here!* and I answered the door.

Standing there were two very serious looking men in dark suits, who flashed badges at me as they introduced themselves. In my fog I thought they said they were with the FBI but it could have been the CIA. Hell, it could have been the AARP or the YMCA for all I knew.

"We'd like to ask you a few questions, if you don't mind…"

"I didn't *know* the girl," I protested.

"What girl?"

"The homicidal maniac I had lunch with…"

Surprised, they looked at each other then at me and answered "…You had lunch with a homicidal maniac?"

I said, "Yeah…isn't that what you're here to talk to me about?" And they explained that it was not. It turns out that the school is a recruiting ground for the CIA and they were from the CIA. One of the guys that had lived in the dorm room to which I had been assigned had recently graduated and they were in the process of performing a security check on him.

After they left I decided that I had definitely stepped off the bus at the wrong stop and resolved to pack my things and go back to Houston. There was a wine tasting for the new arrivals to get together and meet each other that evening and I decided I would go, make an appearance, and get out the next day.

While I was sitting at the table with all the other strangers, they each told the stories of where they were from and what their first impressions of campus had been. I learned that I was not the only one who was less than impressed with the World War II ambiance, but I remained quiet. Finally one of them asked me, "What did you think?" and I answered that I thought my first impression might have been adversely influenced by the lunch I had with the homicidal maniac.

To which Bob, Karen and Anne all sort of looked up shocked and someone said, "You had lunch with a homicidal maniac?" and I answered,

"Yeah, that's the reaction I got from the CIA agents, too."

"CIA agents!!"

I stayed, and we've been friends ever since.

In grad school we all worked very hard. For the first time in my life I really had to study; it did not come easy. And my drinking continued unabated. It seemed that everyone drank on campus. Again, almost every waking hour I was either drunk or hung over but I still made it through. And somewhere through the stupor I began to form really close bonds with some of the folks there.

We had great fun playing practical jokes on each other.

One of our friends, Bob, had an old Peugeot sedan with a sunroof. It was the type that you had to turn the key, wait about three minutes and then push a button to start it. I think it was because it needed to heat the oil or something. We called it the "getaway car."

Well, Bob was so meticulous about the car that when you went anywhere with him you were not allowed to have food or drink with you. Like the presidential limo or something.

He made the grave mistake of leaving the sunroof cracked, once, and we had the great good fortune to discover it. We purchased several of those huge bags of popcorn that cheap bars purchase, you know, the ones that are the size of a big pillow except maybe four feet long. I think we had four of them.

We were able to slowly work the sunroof open but we left it partially open so that we could pull it closed again, and then filled the limo with popcorn. There was so much of it that it came up almost halfway in the windows. I have no memory of what was done to clean the car, or what was done with the popcorn. But Bob remained, to his credit, a friend to us all.

One of my favorite pranks was when we broke into a friend's room and took every picture on the wall, every piece of furniture, and even the thirty fancy bottles of who knows what that she had on top of her chest of drawers, and turned them upside down. Exactly where they were.

And another in our group of friends constantly complained about the barricades with the yellow blinking lights on them because the campus roads were always under construction. It was a small campus (maybe 100 acres) but there were a lot of them. Now this guy was a very heavy sleeper. You could have a rowdy game of poker going on replete with cigars and drunken scoffs right next to his bed and it wouldn't wake him. We didn't know this at first, but we found out when we collected about forty of the barricades (that he called "winky blinkies") and very carefully, very quietly began setting them up in concentric L-shaped lines radiating from his bed, and he never woke up in spite of our giggling. The yellow lights were still blinking – forty of them. There was no possible way he could get out of bed because they were right up against it.

I secretly hoped that when he woke he would freak out thinking he was in an episode of "Twilight Zone" and that we hadn't done it; no one had done it. They had all marched there cognizant of his disdain for them. We would know if he showed up for lunch at the cafeteria with a really confused expression on his face and said nothing about it to any of us.

I borrowed that very same friend's car and as I was out with it noticed a tiny little nick in the windshield. I stopped at the store and bought heavy-duty masking tape, the blonde colored kind with fibers in it. When I got back to the parking lot I put strips of it from top to bottom, half an inch apart, and from side to side, half an inch apart. I left a note saying that I had found a nick but not to worry I went ahead and taped it so it wouldn't spread. And left the tape to melt in the Arizona summer sun.

At one point I had to leave campus and return to Houston for a family wedding. I would be gone all weekend. Of course I knew they were going to try to do something while I was gone since I had been in on every joke. So I spent about a week figuring out ways to secure my dorm room. By that time I had left the barracks and secured a real dorm room in one of the newer dorm buildings, along with my Brazilian roommate who just never could get the English language ("I'm burning down..." "No, you're burning UP..."). I had it so secure that I was certain they would have to come through the cooling duct to get in. But just in case they did, I left a little plate of candy on the study carrel with a note next to it reading "Be nice. Paybacks are a bitch."

When I returned I unlocked my door and opened it. I was facing a sheer wall of crumpled newspaper from floor to ceiling. Immediately against the door and hanging from string right at eye level were the crumpled candy wrappers all bundled together. My entire dorm room was filled with crumpled newspapers, fifteen large garbage bags full of it. It took me an entire day to get the newspaper out of there and another to clean the ink off the walls. It turns out they had been collecting newspaper for months preparing for such an opportunity.

One time I was out and about somewhere in Glendale driving in my Volkswagen beetle. I paid a hundred dollars for it, and it only had one front seat, so we called it "The Mexican Taxi," because back in the late seventies all the taxicabs in Mexico were VW bugs with only one front seat. It seems like no one's car has a nickname anymore...have you noticed that?

Anyways, this was when Glendale was still pretty rural and a lot of the intersections looked like they could have BEEN in Mexico. At one intersection in particular there was a spot where someone had an old van loaded up with junk they had purchased in the markets in Nogales probably and brought back to sell on the street corner. Little clay things: statues, birdbaths, garden pottery of every variety looked like it had all spilled out of the van and miraculously everything landed top side up. You knew these things had not been fired, like actual porcelain pieces, for the bright colored spray painted highlights. It was fun to stop and take a look at it all just to try and find a piece that someone would actually pay *for*, rather than to have hauled off with other clutter. I mean, most of the junk wasn't worth the label necessary to get twenty-five cents for it at a yard sale. And even if it did, you'd feel compelled to comment to anyone actually looking at it, "Oh this was some junk in the back yard when we bought the place...funny, huh?" And then pick something else up to look at and dust before they figured out that you were lying.

But that day that I was passing by and seated right at the point of the corner of the intersection among all the lesser pieces was a poodle. She was seated upright on her back haunches and I knew it was a she because her fur puffs were all spray painted light bright blue. And she had a bow. Had the man at the van collecting the money and presiding over the whole collection actually been the artist that created this little gem I am quite sure she would have been the pride of his portfolio. She was regal, and I had to stop and get a closer look.

Yes. She was a standard poodle perfectly coiffed into a series of expertly balanced fur puffs adorning her legs, paws, ears, crown of her head, and ass – if I'm not mistaken – all spray painted blue. She had an absolutely stoic expression on her face. Queen Elizabeth herself, as she would later remark on the year she dubbed *Annus Horribilis*... "Upon which we shall not look back with undiluted pleasure." The year Chuck and Di split up and Windsor burned. This dog had it all, and only five bucks.

I bought her because I thought she would make a perfect gift for my friend Anne. And when I got her back to campus I did give her to Anne and told her that her name was "Fifi." Anne needed a companion that could also serve as a guard dog too.

Well, Anne appeared, at first, to share in what had come to be all our affections for Fifi. Anne had a dorm room right around the corner from mine. We were in what were called the East Dorms that were a collection of one-story buildings that radiated out from a central point like fingers of a hand. Each long building consisted of a row of two-room dorm complexes with two bedrooms that shared a kitchen and bath. Anne and I often had lunch together and I would walk around the end of the building to her room and from there we would head off to the cafeteria together. Soon after giving Fifi to Anne I noticed as I walked to her room that the dog was seated *outside* her dorm room, next to the door. All the rooms opened to an outside walkway that ran the length of the building. I thought it must have been a mistake. Or maybe Anne was mopping the floor and Fifi was outside while this was going on so as not to become overwhelmed by the soap fumes or something.

When Anne came to the door I very politely and patiently made eye contact with her, glanced down at the dog, and gently pressed, "Anne, Fifi is an <u>inside</u> dog."

No amount of explanation was ever enough to convince Anne that Fifi did not belong outside next to the door, that she belonged inside. And every time I thought I had talked sense into Anne about this, I would still invariably find the dog outside next to the door and not inside where she belonged. Anne secretly treated her not like the blue fur puff poodle I gave her, but more like just another Heinz 57 mutt with no breeding whatsoever.

The others and I hatched a plot to kidnap Fifi and we even made a ransom note by cutting out newspaper letters and gluing them to a piece of construction paper:

W E H a V E f I Fi

The note went on to say other things but I can't remember the exact wording. The point was along the lines of how we would not bring her back until and unless Anne could demonstrate some willingness to take proper care of the dog. After all, there was no protective agency to which we could make an appeal or to whom we could complain about Anne's mistreatment.

All throughout the hostage ordeal I had Fifi hidden in the closet of my dorm room on the shelf above my hanging clothes. But what really surprised all of us, I think, was that the news of her kidnapping even got a mention in the school paper, and in fact it became the subject of coffee house small talk. *Who kidnapped Fifi, how could anyone be so emboldened to do something like that, what would be the punishment for such a thing if they were ever caught, who actually IS Fifi* (for the uninitiated), and such. And the whole thing just sort of died down and everyone forgot about it. I forgot about it.

One day in April we learned that "The Wizard of OZ" was going to be on TV and so we planned a party. We put the TV and the blender on an extension cord outside my dorm room (in the little lawn that was there) and moved all our chairs outside. Anne, Bob, Karen, and our other friends all gathered to make Margueritas and watch the movie. Since it was April, once the sun had gone down it got pretty cool and Anne asked if I had a sweater she could borrow. I told her I did and just to go in and help herself to whatever she wanted – completely forgetting about Fifi in the closet. The next thing, Anne came out of the dorm room clutching Fifi to herself with her arms wrapped around her, and stormed off miffed and unapproachable back to her room, refusing to speak a word.

And Fifi was returned to her vigil outside Anne's dorm room door.

There were lots of stories like these about the time on campus; I've just included a few of them. I was really happy there, then. I had close friends, I was intellectually challenged, and life was a lot of fun. But I have to confess that I was drinking very heavily through it all and I really don't know why. I didn't need to drink, the others didn't drink as much as I did, and they all seemed to be loving life. A few of them were regulars for Irish Coffee Night in my dorm room when we had a lot of studying to do, and we would take a break. But every night was Irish Coffee for me. And then there was cocaine. But I'll move on – you don't need me to ramble on like some AA speaker's night thing.

I do need to fill in some background before I explain the events of one April day in particular. The April before we all graduated and I went off to England.

At about that time in grad school I was torn over what I was going to do when I graduated. I knew business school was a good practical education, but I really wanted to be a composer. I began tossing things over in my mind, *business or music, business or music?* This was really troubling to me because the two career paths are so different. One of them (music) would throw out all the money and work I had invested in grad school, which would seem like a crazy thing to do in anyone's book. And I was considering it. Even my grad school friends knew that I was thinking about dropping out and moving to

Austin. They were concerned. Before too long it became almost an obsession. I was no longer just considering the difference and weighing the options in a practical way; it was angst.

For my birthday that year my sister (the one at the window) and her husband gave me a bible. In it they had written a note just below the words that they loved me, "Proverbs 3:5-6." They had recently converted to Christianity.

They knew that I was struggling with what we considered a major life decision and one whose parameters were not exactly *practical*. I mean, it's not like I was weighing the difference between being an import-export analyst in New York and a partially refined crude oil trader in Houston. I was weighing the difference between being a respectable professional in the field of international commerce utilizing a very expensive and noteworthy education, and a boheme. While they very graciously and patiently gave me a bible with a verse cited in the cover that seemed to bring God into the equation...anyone else would have just held it to a heart-felt "What are you, NUTS!!" and left it at that.

They had a clear understanding of my dilemma, they had a pretty good picture of my past struggles, and my sister had even been the one with me at the window the day I began to reconsider suicide. But they had no idea what was in me toward God. I had never even opened a bible, let alone owned one.

I took the bait and read the scripture ("Trust in the Lord with all your heart and lean not on your own understanding. In all your ways acknowledge Him and He will make straight your paths.") This sounded to me like a promise. Now I had some ammunition I could <u>use</u>. I decided that after all the years I had been toying with Jehovah's Witnesses and Jesus freaks, now I had a shot at the main man; I could sink my teeth into the real thing.

I decided to cut class for a full day and call Him on this promise, that He "would make straight my paths." I would lock myself in my room, take the phone off the hook, and wait. He would tell me whether I should be in business or music, or I would have proof He was a liar, or if silent, that He didn't exist. I. Had. Him. Check and mate.

Remember, my hatred for God had been a prop for most of my life by that point. I hated Him – hated Him with a passion – because even if He had only allowed what happened to me and hadn't caused it directly, He was equally at fault in my mind. As the day approached, my hatred swelled and came to the surface. I did not go into the day honestly seeking guidance. I went into it seeking revenge in the form of "outing" Him and His reckless promises that were not real.

So I locked my door and unplugged the phone. I did not want to be interrupted.

After preparing myself a little bit, I spoke to Him. I admitted to Him as politely as I could that I had no use for Him and that I thought that any God like Him was not worth a second glance. But that in His recklessness above and beyond the crap I lived through as a child, above and beyond the filth that had been perpetrated on me during HIS watch, He had neglected to keep me from discovering this promise He had stupidly made. And now I was going to cash in on it, or call Him on His bullshit and walk away forever.

I told Him that I needed to know whether to stay in business school or leave and go pursue a life as a composer. I thought that I was calling Him on His bluff, challenging Him at His word, and it felt good. It felt like power against Him. My sister thought the verse would be inspiration to me, but I saw it as weaponry.

"If you exist and mean what you say, you will answer me, and I am not leaving this room until you do. If at the end of the day I have received no answer, then I know for sure that you do not exist."

I never considered how utterly lost I would be if I didn't hear from Him. Like I said earlier, my hatred for Him served a purpose.

I waited, sitting on my bed, turning over in my mind what might be the form of His answer. Would the unplugged phone magically ring with a call from a business recruiter? Would it be a knock on the door with someone saying there is a telegram from an agent who heard me perform in a recent concert? I imagined a voice in the room saying "Go to Austin" or "Stay in school." I mulled all sorts of possibilities over and over in my head, but each and every one of them centered on an answer to the question, a choice between business and music. Nothing more, nothing less, nothing else. I waited.

I think there were times when I took a break and then went back to it. In the last round I was beginning to get tired of the whole thing. I started to feel my heart sink and my anger begin to sort of melt into a gut-sick sadness. I think about an hour went by but it felt like many. And then it happened.

"I love you."

Those words happened in my head, very distinct, very clear, as if someone had said them to me in a voice I had never heard and did not recognize. Not my own voice. Now you have to know that there is no way that I would or could ever have thought those words. Love in any conceptual sense was as far away from my speculation as it could possibly be. It would have been more likely that "Who's the leader of the band..." sung in Chinese to the music of a Zydeco band would suddenly pop into my head.

And I cannot begin to tell you how completely taken aback I was. I can't find the words to describe it. Not just that words would occur in my head that I didn't put there in a voice I didn't recognize, but THOSE words. As soon as I got over the initial shock of them I completely disintegrated when I had to consider what the words meant. Whatever had occurred in my life up until that very moment seated on that bed in that room was undone. I was undone. I couldn't do or think anything; I just began sobbing. I couldn't stand it but I couldn't let go of it either...and I was destroyed. Then I heard it again.

"I love you and I will be with you."

I spent the rest of the day crying like a newborn slapped by the doctor into breath. I went to bed that night exhausted of years, exhausted of everything.

The next morning when I woke and considered it I realized that He had answered me as only He can. Whether I stayed in school or went off to be a composer didn't matter. What I did could not have mattered less. I hadn't given Him a tough enough question.

What mattered is that I was loved in that moment, and I knew it. I felt it. It was real. It is said that while we were yet in sin Christ died for us. For me it was even worse. I was beyond simple mindless sin. I hated Him with every fiber of my being, and yet He came and got me in my dorm room that afternoon to tell me that He loved me anyway.

So that is when I became a Christian. That is the moment when I had something else to know.

Now when the Jehovah's Witnesses ask me if I have found the Lord, I like to answer, "No. I never found anybody. But do I know Him? Yes. He came a pretty good distance to find <u>me</u>."

And I don't argue anymore.

4. The Bohemian Years

For about fifteen years now I have had a friend named Geoff, who is a radio talk show personality but also a writer and director for plays.

Years ago he directed a play about the dust bowl days in the United States and he asked me if I would consider writing music for it and I said I would, and I did. It was a great experience for me, and we got pretty good reviews. Geoff liked the music so much that he told me that he would be interested in having me write music for any of the plays he does in the future.

One time about ten years ago or so, he had the idea to do a production of <u>A Christmas Carol</u> and he had already adapted the script. He asked me if I would like to score it, I said I would, and he sent me the script. Geoff explained to me that it was theater of redemption (but I really didn't know what that meant) and he explained how he saw the whole process that Scrooge went through in the context of redemption.

I started to conceptualize the score using some sampling ideas that involved the music reaching its apex at the scene of the grave when Scrooge begged the ghost to "expunge" his name from the gravestone. When I talked them over with Geoff, he disagreed. He insisted that the point of Scrooge's redemption was the next morning when he woke up. For some weeks we went back and forth on it, with me thinking the moment of redemption was his surrender at the grave, and Geoff insisting that it was when he woke up alive. We never produced it. And I don't think Geoff ever produced the play without me.

But I think of it because I had my own morning like that.

When I woke up the next day I was a different person. I know Christians always say that, and I also know that it is at least true in my case. I woke up laughing. All of the sudden I had an urging to read the bible, and not even a hint of memory about how ridiculous I would have considered the idea a scant ten hours earlier. I was excited to tell someone. But then I thought, *my friends aren't going to believe this. They aren't going to have anything more to do with me now.*

But it didn't matter.

At first they were a bit taken aback. The girl I was spending time with wasn't openly displeased but I could tell in her expression that she thought something had gone wrong with me – or maybe that I had given myself over to some lesser form of eccentricity, one not so much fun to be around. Those first days were a wait-and-see proposition for her, with no obligation to stay in if she decided it was time to pitch the freak and move on. But I pressed ahead, and started reading my bible during a lot of my spare time. This was in April, so graduation was just about a month away anyway. You know, *everything* significant in my life always happens in April.

We worked hard preparing for our finals, and everyone seemed to be completely preoccupied with studying and finishing up, graduation looming ahead. The last day when everyone was going to be on campus as we were all packing our things to leave was a day of tremendous sadness for all of us. We had grown very close over the time we spent together, all the funny times we had had, the jokes we played, the work and hardship in studying we had endured together, and now we were scattering – literally – to the world.

That last day most of my small group of friends spent drinking, laughing, and crying with each other. I remember one scene out of all of it.

I had a little Volkswagen bug that I had jammed with everything I owned. I was going to quietly drive away so that I wouldn't have to face the absolute moment of "goodbye." I lived my entire life up until that day with plenty of separations (and some pretty profound ones) but never once having the opportunity to say "goodbye." I didn't know how to do it. Somewhere deep inside of me I knew I couldn't do it as an equal with the person from whom I was being separated. I found the situation of someone caring enough about me to say the words, knowing that we both have to, too intense. To this day saying "goodbye" is difficult for me. I'd rather not do it. I'd rather leave as if I would be back in an hour.

The time I spent in graduate school with my friends was the first protracted period of time since before my father died that I had been a part of a group of friends, accepted as one of them. Even though I spent much of it in a drunken stupor, it was without rejection, without pain. And now it was to end without abandonment, which was something I was not equipped to handle. Abandonment I knew; "goodbyes" I did not.

As I was getting into my bug to go away, a car pulled up and Karen jumped out and ran to me crying. She threw her arms around my neck and said through her sobs, "You were going to leave without saying goodbye?"

I just sobbed into the hug, tore myself away from it, got in my bug and left for Houston. Even if I could have found the words to explain, it was not the right moment.

The next few weeks were spent in Houston preparing to go to England. I was not going to hit the streets and look for a job right away because I had been accepted to do a semester at Templeton College, Oxford University, England. Finally, against any expectation, I was going to get to go study at an old hallowed hall somewhere. And as hallowed halls go, Oxford is tough to beat. I could not have been more excited. My friends and family all seemed to be pretty impressed, and I might have allowed them to be more than I should have. I mean, it's not like I was a Rhodes Scholar (which most Americans associate with Oxford). I wasn't a scholar at all, just a guy going to England for a semester.

When I landed at London's Heathrow the plans were all set for the duration of my stay in England, which was set to be about four to six months. I had an apartment lined up in Abingdon Borough and a couple of friends and I had planned to share an apartment at the end of our duration there in London.

To attend school in that location was the dream of a lifetime, but there was much to figure out, a lot to familiarize myself with, and a lot of things to get prepared -- with little time to do it because lectures started very soon after we arrived.

The school was about three kilometers from my place so I would walk to the bus stop and take the bus to campus. I noticed that at that time in Abingdon Borough, there was only one small grocery store (sort of) near my place. I would pass it on the way to the bus stop, but it was never open. I thought to myself, *When do these folks buy groceries?*

But one day coming back from class I noticed that it *was* open, so I ran back to my flat, threw my books down, grabbed some cash and ran back. While I was there I figured I should buy as much as I could afford because there was no way of knowing when/if the store would be open again. Besides, I was hungry. You know the adage; don't ever buy groceries when you're hungry.

Baby food in a jar looks good if you're hungry enough; you just figure you'll use it for dip with apples or something.

I think I had about two weeks' worth of groceries, but as the lady was ringing it up, no one came to bag it. I thought it was pretty odd, because the groceries were really piling up at the end of the register.

The lady looked at me kind of funny as I was beginning to look confused, and when she saw me looking at all the groceries and then around to see where the bag-boy was, she stopped ringing in mid order and asked if she could help me. I asked her if there were any "baggers" working that day. It was the first of several times the fact that I was *from* South Texas would collide with the fact that I was *in* Central England. She did not have the beginnings of a clue what "baggers" were. I explained that baggers are people who bag the groceries. She looked at me like it must be another one of those hopelessly pedestrian American ideas. Don't you have a "tote"? I did not have the beginnings of a clue what a "tote" was. But the nature of the circumstance was suddenly clear. They didn't have baggers and I didn't have a tote.

I had this nervous feeling in my stomach that you get when you completely overreact to a situation. I mean, it's not like my sail boat just sank out from under me in the middle of the Atlantic. But it kind of felt like it.

How was I going to get two weeks of groceries back to my apartment? One relay with arms full of junk at a time? It hadn't occurred to me that even if they had all the baggers in Houston flapping open the newest, crispest paper grocery bags at the ready, bread on top…I could not have carried all the bags home anyway. I guess I was just so elated that I finally caught the store open that all otherwise careful planning necessary to get the groceries home from the grocery store was overlooked in the frantic excitement of the rare twenty-minute window of opportunity to actually buy some groceries.

They had pity on my poor, stupid South Texan soul and gave me some boxes that I could fill, close, stack and carry home. Now, had I been in Ireland, the whole town would have pitched in to help me and carried two or three items back to my place singing "Sally Garden" the whole way and saying their "farewells" when we were done, like it broke their heart to leave me there all alone.

You might think of this grocery experience as the first of what would be a string of incidences in which the culture of Houston in which I grew up did not exactly match the one in which I found myself for that semester.

The second cultural disconnect occurred in and at the bar (or "pub" actually) next door to my apartment in Abingdon. Abingdon Borough is one of a number of old villages in an area of England referred to as "The

Cotswolds" named for the stone from which the cottages are all built. When I was there it was a time when the little country pubs were truly little country pubs. I've been told that since then (this was thirty years ago) they have all either closed or become "theme" bars. I'm not sure what a "theme" bar is exactly. Maybe it is a bar decorated to suggest that you are not where you actually are but are someplace else, like New Orleans. Back then I was in rural England and the pub didn't need to be decorated, because being in rural England was just fine. I don't know why that would need to change.

I was seated at the bar drinking my "bitter and mild" (room temperature beer) and soaking it all in, talking to the bartender and keeper of the Pub. A girl about my age sitting next to me spoke up. Now, you may find it hard to believe that I remember almost every word of this conversation exactly as it occurred, but you'll just have to trust me. So much of it was a surprise to me that it seared into my memory even as it was happening. I just wasn't used to things of this sort. I was used to girls in disco places shooting you down with wise cracks and laughing while they were doing it. This was very different. First, I didn't say a word to her; she spoke to me.

"You're American, aren't you?" I guess she had heard me talking to the bartender.

"Yeah, I am." I answered.

"So where are you from?"

"I'm from South Texas," I said.

You could see her shoulders slump like she had just been voted off the island. This was 1980 and I was used to having people ask me "Who Shot J.R.?" almost as a knee jerk reaction when I let anyone know I was from Texas. I did not watch that series and couldn't have cared less about it. So I had developed a series of answers to dismiss the question. My favorite was "I'm from Houston; we don't give an airborne fornication what happens in Dallas." But that was usually a little over their heads. It alluded to a rivalry between Houston and Dallas that they had absolutely no way of knowing about, and the phrase "airborne fornication" alluded to a little bit of alliteration that most certainly was not common in the Cotswolds, although we all knew it well in South Texas.

But I had others answers to that stupid question ("Who shot JR?"). "I did. Why do you think I'm over here?" or 'The cameraman. Turns out he and that actor guy were having a spot of a falling out." I digress...

"I could tell by the accent." She said almost to herself as she looked back down into her glass of wine.

I didn't know that I had one so I replied, "I didn't know that I had one."

"Yeah, yeah. Do you ride horseback?" And she asked the question with the kind of air and tone of voice that you might use to ask someone if they chew their fingernails. Now first, I had not started up the conversation with her; I had been polite and assumed that she did not want to be bothered by some guy in the pub she didn't even know. So why she would open a conversation with me and then switch it into condescension gear just because I was from Texas was initially annoying to me, and I doubted whether I even wanted to answer any more of her questions.

"Yes, I ride but I don't own a horse. I helped take care of a neighbor's horse when I was a kid, though. We rode him all the time. I even learned to ride bareback."

The expression on her face told me in an instant that she either didn't believe me or was just exasperated at stumbling across yet another stupid clod in a lifetime of talking to stupid clods she didn't know, in bars. She looked down into her drink again and said to herself only barely loud enough for me to hear, "the way you treat those poor animals…"

I answered, "Excuse me?"

"I said, 'the way you treat those poor animals.'" She squared off with me, resolute.

"How do we treat them?" I said this without thinking that it might open the gate to the full extent of her opinions on the matter. Which it did.

"Well, you don't know how to care for them, that's for starters."

Knowing as I do that horses in Texas rarely fall over dead leaving people standing around scratching their heads saying, "Welp, I guess we just don't know how to take care of these things" I had to protest. She explained.

"For instance, you feed your horses, stable them, ride and water them all in the same pasture."

*Yes, that we do…*I thought. All I could manage was an educated, "So?" (Which won me no points on the equestrian intellectual charts in this apparently equestrian intellectual conversation I was having. I might just as well have added "nonny nonny doo doo, poo on you."

"How would YOU like to spend your entire life in the kitchen!?"

This is weird, I thought. *This girl probably has pictures of horses in her bedroom, and little plastic ones in the bookshelves, and horse bedspreads, and maybe a horse outfit. Besides, what do you say to that kind of question?*

"I don't think the horses mind…"

Wrong answer.

"How would you know? That's the problem, isn't it?" (Why do so many English people always finish their statements with the question "Isn't it?" or "Doesn't it?" And do they ever get the come-back "Yes, it is" or "Yes it does" followed by "Doesn't it?" and you could go on forever until you accidentally say it at the same time and someone says "Coke!")

The conversation became tedious within the first thirty seconds or so, and it was dragging on. The more we couldn't agree, the more she seemed fueled to press on. I didn't want to be rude but I was really a lot more interested in my bitter and mild than in talking with her. Actually I would have been more interested in a conversation regarding the complexities of foreign currency fluctuation risk management in the emerging European Economic Community (which reminds me of another story) than in talking to her.

"And what, exactly, do you call that monstrosity that you strap to the poor animal, what with all the loops and hoops and hooks and things?"

"That would be a saddle," I replied flatly.

"Why, whatever compelled you to leave off the kitchen sink?"

"Look," I said, "in Texas, as in many other parts of the United States, a horse is a working animal. We don't prance them around because they're pretty, or at least most of us don't. That horn thing on the top of the saddle is for one end of the rope, which if you're having a good day, has a cow on the other end of it. All those hoops and straps and things are for putting your feet in. And besides, I was a kid. I just rode the horse for fun!"

"But you don't even know HOW to ride a horse!"

I came to conclude that this girl had probably spent the previous three years (ever since the first season of the show "Dallas") waiting for a guy from Texas to come in and sit down next to her and order a bitter and mild so she could unleash her personal frustrations regarding horses against someone from any part of Texas who had ever so much as smelled a horse. It was her lucky day.

"You yank the head of the horse around by the teeth and jaw to get him to go where you want, whipping him the whole while mercilessly! Everyone *knows* you use the reigns to position the front and head steering the front of the horse, and you steer the back of the horse using your ankles!"

"Well, excuse me, but in Texas we figure that wherever the front of the horse goes, the back of the horse is likely to go too."

In abject frustration she exclaimed, "You prove my point!" spun and stormed out of the pub.

Finally having the opportunity to go back to my beer in peace I said to the bartender who had witnessed the whole conversation standing there behind the bar, as I lifted my mug, "what a bitch."

"Yes," he said, "she's my daughter."

His name was Pete and he and I became pretty good friends (I was in there quite a bit). In fact (I have to tell another story about him and that pub...) he explained that in England it was the custom that at the pub you normally attended, you brought in your own mug. When you came in, the bartender would grab your mug and pull your pint in it. I told him that I didn't have a mug but maybe I could get one.

I had a "BritRail" pass that allowed me to travel anywhere in the country by simply getting on the train. I had to go to several different locations throughout England to do research and I was very poor there. So without having arrived with it I would have had considerable trouble getting my research done.

I was in Nottingham and passed a market where they were selling all kinds of tourists' things and odds and ends from what seemed to have been a lot of garage sales. At the tables I saw these glass pint mugs just like the ones you see in all the pubs in England. Except these had a little white picture of Robin Hood painted on a cameo smooth spot on the glass.

When I was a child my two main heroes were Roy Rogers, and Robin Hood. I loved all the Robin Hood movies and probably saw every one of them. In fact, I started shooting a bow when I was about eight years old, and by nine my friend and I would hunt squirrel with our bows in the woods near our house. I bought a group of the mugs (they were cheap), one for me and one or two for some friends.

At that time (this was when it was legal to advertise liquor on TV) there was a beer commercial that had Robin Hood come into a pub, and when the maiden offered him and his men tankards with the lids up, he smugly replied as he slapped all the lids closed, "I'm Robin Hood, a famous swash-buckling hero, I don't drink ordinary beer!"

Well, I brought my mug in to Pete at the Pub. He looked at it closely to try to see what the white spot on it was. It was thin and white and you had to look closely to tell that it was Robin Hood. "Wot's that?" he asked, looking at the little picture.

I said "I'm Robin Hood, a famous swash-buckling hero! I don't drink out of an ordinary mug!" imitating the TV commercial.

Pete cracked up laughing and repeated over and over in his very thick English accent, "'eee's Robin Hood. A fa-amous swash-buckling 'ero..." and would crack up laughing again.

Well, weeks had gone by and we stopped laughing about it long back. Every day I'd come in, he'd grab my mug and pull my pint and I'd sit and we'd shoot the breeze.

One day a friend I was spending time with decided to come visit me in Abingdon. She lived in Oxford. We both went into the pub so I could introduce her to Pete and the others. He saw me come in and pulled my pint off the wall and poured my bitter. When we got up to the bar she looked at the mug and the white thing on it and said, "What's that on the glass?"

Pete jumped in with, "'eee's Robin Hood, a fa-amous swash-bucklng 'ero. 'Eee don't drink out of ordinary mug!" and started laughing all over again. I still have that mug, but now it holds pocket change.

I love to tell the stories from that period of time but I jumped ahead of myself and skipped the most important one.

When I first arrived at Oxford, the first order of business, of course, was to secure a piano on which to practice. Groceries were important, yes. Even the odd bizarre horse conversation with a local "bird" (English slang for girl) was fine, even if it was a complete waste of time. But the piano was a necessity.

I figured I had about two weeks before the stress of not being able to play, on top of the stress of being in grad school in a foreign country, would begin to, well...affect me.

I asked around. Did anyone know where a piano might be that I could play, and if so where might it be? I heard that there was one at a pizza parlor called "Sweeny Todd's." So as soon as I could get some time off I got the address and spent an afternoon finding the restaurant. Once I had found it I was able to get in to see the manager and told him what I was looking for. He said that indeed there was a piano upstairs in a storage area not being used, and I was free to practice on it. When I got upstairs I was a little disappointed at the look of it. It was on old dusty upright, the keys were stained, and the case was cracked. So I didn't expect it to sound all that good. But hey, it was a piano.

I sat down and started playing. The action was not bad, the bench seemed sturdy, nice private room above the noise of the pizza parlor. Only one problem: it didn't make any sound. There was no sound at all! I opened it up and there were no strings.

So I went down and mentioned to the manager that his piano upstairs had no strings, and he seemed a bit amused, actually. My first search effort was a bust. And I was about a week into withdrawal at that point. I couldn't help wonder on my way home, *what are the odds that the only piano in town has no strings?*

After a few more days of lectures that prevented me from looking again, I decided to check out a piano repair place that someone suggested after they searched the local listings. They had come up with the idea that if there was a piano sales place, I could go *there*. No piano sales, but we did score the location of a piano repair shop. Off I went.

I had to take the bus to the edge of the line and then walk about ten blocks to the very edge of town. In the cold English rain.

I got to the location only to discover a sign on the gate saying that the shop had moved, as if only to keep the apparent absurdity of this search going, to the opposite edge of town.

Clearly there was not enough time to get there on that same day so I would have to schedule another day's afternoon to make the next trip. As I was on the bus home, ten days into withdrawals, I was beginning to feel the need to tape my fingers together to keep me from looking like an amphetamine addict what with the fidgeting. I began to consider how much I would deserve the piano whenever or wherever I found it. After all I had been through to get to it.

I think it was another three days before I could get away for the afternoon to trek out to the new location of the repair shop. This afternoon was very similar to the previous. Bus ride to the edge of the line, ten blocks in the rain to arrive at the location. I could see the sign perpendicular to the sidewalk indicating the piano repair place was just up ahead.

By this time I was fully two weeks into withdrawal and although I was constantly on edge, I was beginning to think that not being able to play the piano was survivable, after all. But only just survivable. I really did need to find one. As I got close to the sign and the gate I noticed what looked like a chain and lock on the gate immediately beneath the sign. Not a good indicator, at three o'clock in the afternoon.

"OUT OF BUSINESS."

My heart sank in my chest. Maybe withdrawal from piano IS fatal. It sure felt fatal.

First I wanted to tear the chains and break in just in case a straggler piano had been left behind. Even if not, it would have been a good way to bleed off the surging rage within me. I turned around and leaned against the gate, getting soaking wet in the rain and not even trying to stop it. It was as if I wanted someone to cuss out. I was a baby Christian at that time, only five or six weeks from the moment I was saved and converted to Christianity. In those early days everything was of God, nothing random. Sort of like some of us forget but then return to years later when we wake up to our faith again.

My rage turned to silliness and I started laughing when I considered what God might be doing. It seemed like He was teasing me and I wondered if He was having fun with this. So I spoke out loud to Him along the lines of...

"I am sure you must be enjoying this right now...but guess what? You have had your laugh. I am not trekking back and forth on the edges of this place in the cold pouring rain anymore. Your little game of "keep away" is over. You can stop tossing the piano now. If You want me to have a piano you are going to have to ROLL that sucker right up to my front door, because I GIVE UP."

Now I know this seems irreverent but I guess I have to chalk it up to immaturity, looking back. Anyways, soaking wet, I hiked back to the bus stop resolved not to lift a finger to find a piano, even if it was fatal.

I don't know how many days later, the new status of being without piano was rerouting the nerve pathways in my brain, so a lot that happened during that time was not recorded in memory. I used to go for walks along the Thames River and in other locations throughout Oxford. I loved the area near Deer Park and the cherry tree pathway there.

One afternoon I was walking along a pathway that ran alongside a tall wall. I thought I heard piano music. It was like some switch in my head flipped back on...or while walking along a dry river bed I saw the beginnings of a little stream of water trickling toward me and suspecting it to be a torrent further along up the slope of the riverbed.

Yes, it was piano music, and it was live. I could tell that it was coming from the other side of the tall wall I was walking along but there was no way to get over it and no gate. When I got to the end of the wall I turned right and walked further along it until I got to a gateway, or rather, entrance archway through a building. The building looked to be maybe three hundred years old. At the end of the archway (maybe thirty feet in length) I entered into a courtyard surrounded by old buildings four stories tall. I was facing an ornate entrance at the opposite end of the courtyard such as might be the entrance to a City Hall, or church, perhaps. The piano music was coming from inside there. So I walked straight toward it and got to the outer doors. As I was entering them the piano music stopped. I was in the entrance facing another wall. But I heard what seemed to have been heavy doors closing with a "clunk kunk" sort of sound around to the right.

I walked around to the right and found doors on my left that had to have been the ones that had just closed, but no one was in sight. I walked up and tested the doors and they were unlocked.

The room I entered was a recital hall. If I remember correctly (this was thirty years ago) the ceilings were about thirty feet high and along one wall were giant glass windows overlooking English gardens. It was stunningly beautiful. And there at the far end of the room was a stage. And on that stage was a twelve-foot grand piano. My knees almost buckled.

Cautiously, as if some heavily armed police force would suddenly start streaming out of hidden doorways, I approached the piano, sat down, and began to play. If memory serves, it was about three o'clock in the afternoon.

I don't know if I can describe the sensation. Being given a glass of cool water after a three-day thirst might get close to it, although I don't really know; I have never gone three days without water.

I do know this. As I began playing I fell into the keyboard with my forehead resting on the piano itself and my chest close to the keys, out of sheer love for the instrument. Almost the way a child washed down a raging stream might collapse into the arms of a parent upon rescue. I had been gone much too long. Later in life I would know much longer absences from my place there, but never a return as sweet.

The joy of it was indescribable. As soon as I got over the sensations of the piano as I was playing it, I began to test the piano. There seemed to be nothing it couldn't do. No trill was too fast, no contrast from triple forte to triple piano too abrupt. No number of fortes the piano couldn't reach. It was as if, had there been enough strength in my arms, I could break those thirty-foot windows with the power of the piano, but it was more powerful than I was strong.

The finesse of which it was capable was like nothing I had ever experienced in the twenty years of my twenty-four year life sitting in that spot, on that bench. I was spirited away in the music and the reunion with the object of my life-long passion, and I didn't notice the hours passing; not a single rest, never once stopping, one piece seamlessly flowing into another until I looked up and it was pitch dark. I could no longer see out the windows. Night had fallen and I had no idea what time it was.

I made it home that night to discover that I had probably been playing without interruption for somewhere between three and four hours. I was spent. Every bone and muscle in my body was more completely relaxed than I ever would have thought possible. I entered my flat, made it the ten steps to my bed, and collapsed into a deep sleep until the next morning.

The next day my abilities to focus and concentrate were even more impaired than before. All I could think about was getting back to that hall and spending another afternoon like the one before, except that this time I knew exactly where to go, exactly which gates to approach and doors to enter. I felt certain that there would be no "moved" or "out of business" signs this time.

When I got to the hall my heart was pounding and as I went to open the interior doors to the hall they were locked! This couldn't be. I couldn't find anyone in the deserted hallways. Panic began to set in and I began to have the dread feeling that I would have to get permission this time. Something in me told me that yesterday was a stolen afternoon, but this time it would have to be given, proper.

I hunted everywhere and finally found a student who suggested that I speak with the bursar and that she would be the final say. She told me where her office was and I went to speak with her to ask for permission to play. I had to wait what seemed to be about half an hour to get in and when I did, I wasn't quite sure how to tell her what I had done, or why I was there. That part of the conversation I don't remember. But I do remember her looking at me like I had just planted my face full on deep in the middle of her five thousand dollar wedding cake the very moment the guests were arriving.

"Do you know where you ARE?"

She asked, incredulously, when I asked her if I could play that piano again. I answered that I did not. She informed me that I was at Lady Margaret Hall, which I would later learn was an all girls' school and for some reason I remember to be the music school for Oxford University (but I may be mistaken about that). I told her that I was a student at another college in the university and that the bursar of that school also was my landlord and could give me a letter of recommendation if that would help.

She looked even more incredulous, as if she could not quite get her mind around the unbridled presumptuousness of this, this, this American. She almost reeled back to physically engage in her retort giving it the full weight of her body and not just the energy of her objection.

" WE DON'T EVEN ALLOW OUR OWN STUDENTS TO PLAY THAT PIANO."

She went on to explain to me that that particular piano was a twelve-foot Bechstein grand piano. I thought the better of it and elected not to remind her that I knew that already. She trailed on one sentence leading into another without any punctuation as if it were all one big message hoping to get it all out before I responded with anything so I was to be sure to realize the abject stupidity of such a request.

"...That piano is not only arguably of the finest construction, far surpassing Steinway, even Boesendoerfer, the piano is seventy-five years old! It has never been disturbed; it is one of the most EXquisite (sometimes the English put the accent on the first syllable of that word) pianos in all of Oxford, perhaps all of England, possibly among the best instruments in Europe!!! That is our RECITAL hall...no one practices on that piano, the very idea is, is...do you know where you ARE???"

I began to suspect that permission would not be forthcoming.

Just at that moment the cleaning lady who had been emptying the waste bins behind her desk as we were having this conversation spoke up.

"You really ought to hear him..."

As it turns out, she had been in the hall, which turned out to be named "Talbot Hall" for quite a while as I was playing the afternoon before. When she heard me she hid out in the back row and sat and listened. I did not notice, probably because I wouldn't have noticed half of Ringling Brothers and Barnum and Bailey Circus filing in and taking their seats, elephants, cotton candy and all.

To make a long story maybe a little shorter, she managed to convince the bursar to allow me to play the piano again. And what is more, not only was I given permission, but a key, and a range of hours when I would be allowed use of the hall each day for as long as I remained in England.

I believe in angels now. I saw one emptying wastebaskets. But when I was on my way home that afternoon sitting in the bus still in shock and not really believing the events of the afternoon...I think God took the opportunity to make the final comment. You know how I said about sometimes getting a thought come into your head and you know it isn't yours? That's what it was. I wasn't sure whether to laugh or cry...but I am pretty sure I did both.

"Okay, I'll give you a piano."

I stayed in Abingdon for about four months and there are other stories about stuff I will remember for as long as I live, but I think I'll save them, maybe put them in a different letter or something. It was a wonderful time in my life. While in England I worked hard at my lectures and preparing my papers, and I lived with a sense of adventure that being in a foreign environment can bring you. It was my first time to ever experience culture shock. I always thought that was weird because when I was younger I had spent considerable time in Mexico and in France and never had any problems. I speculated that it was because in those countries I was forced to be around people speaking a different language, but in England there was no language problem. So I theorized that it was because things were so close to life in the US (no language barrier), but still just enough different, that I was not braced for the cultural differences and so went into "shock." It was a little like depression only crazier.

But the drinking did not abate. Right after arriving, I quickly associated with two different groups. One consisted of other students from a variety of countries other than mine that were together with me at Templeton, and the other consisted of local friends I had made at Abingdon Borough. I think, as is so often the case, I fell into these groups because they were all heavy drinkers; otherwise, why would one of them have consisted of scholars several of whom had credentials far outstripping mine, and the other consisted of milkmen, carpenters, and mail delivery folks? Not that one is more desirable than the other, but they are very diverse.

No, the only criterion I needed was that you spend your free time slamming back as much bitter and mild as you could hold before 10:30 p.m. when the whole of the countryside of England fell quiet. I loved my local friends, and I loved my student friends. We did different things when we were sober, but sang the same songs in the local pubs otherwise.

I missed them all dearly when I left, and we promised to see each other again, each promising to make it a priority to visit the other. And I promised to return some day. You know, lately I have had this weird desire to go back to England and I'm not sure why. Maybe writing this to you is affecting me, but why there, of all places?

Back in the United States, I picked up where I left off with a girlfriend I had in Texas, went to work for a large oil company, and settled in at what I thought to be the threshold of a happy adult life. I became engaged within a few months of my return.

In Houston the patterns that had permeated high school, college, and England re-established themselves but with new and different faces…different things we did when we were sober, and different songs sung in different bars when we were not.

I still referred to myself as a Christian; I supported a child somewhere in South America. I even had a bible lying around somewhere. But my fiancé and I never once attended church together, and never once did we ever give a moment's thought to whether the life we were living would be pleasing to a God who loved us. She was sympathetic to my faith (such as it was) but did not really profess to have one herself.

She was an innocent and beautiful woman, and in no way influenced by debauchery. On the contrary, it was I who was a bad influence on her.

In those days I had a beautiful apartment in an older part of town where the oak trees formed a canopy over the winding streets. My apartment was filled with antiques. I had a new sports car that cost a fortune by any standard, a beautiful fiancé, an impressive (sounding) job on the twenty-seventh floor of a major oil company's operations tower and all was looking good.

Whether there was any joy in my life I couldn't tell.

I used to walk to work, since my apartment was just on the other side of a bridge from the tower. I recently went back to Houston and the apartment building has since been torn down. I think there is a strip center there and a new street that runs behind it, along the garish line of shop back doors at the ass end of the little businesses. But when I lived there, it was a fifty-year-old apartment complex with vacant lots here and there.

One day as I was walking across the empty field adjacent to the bridge back up to my building I noticed on the ground a porn magazine partially open enough to reveal that it was indeed a porn magazine. When I picked it up I noticed that it was filled with pictures of nude *men.*

While my sex life with my fiancé had been very active and satisfying to both of us, the thought of the magazine there on the ground sent a current through me that left me horrified. It was the first sight of the fact that there were things about myself I did not get to decide. Up until that time I had always believed that whatever I did or wanted to do was a decision under my control. But this…this was different.

The magazine began to intrude into my thought life when I was alone. And I began to drink even more heavily.

At this stage I was at a fork in the road but I didn't know it. I could have confessed the situation to my fiancé, returned to my faith, sought a way to live through this in balance between my disgust and my fascination with my desires all in check no matter how conflicting. I could have sought Christ and thrown myself on the banks of the river and began what would be my own all-out wrestle. I could have run as far and as fast as ever I had run before. I could have run like Joseph leaving even my cloak behind.

I ran, but not with purpose like Joseph. I ran like a man in flames, blinded and directionless, overwhelmed and scared.

There began in me a deeply profound confusion that came from a destroyed sense of certainty about anything. The situation that had been life for me had taken a new turn for the worse, and as worse things go…this was a big one.

I began to question whether I was in love with my fiancé or with the idea of having one. We began to argue on decisions we had already made and it was clear to me that she was having doubts too. Nothing was secure to me anymore. I was more and more miserable in my job and feeling sentenced to it. The prospect of working in the corporate giant for the next forty years, trying to climb the corporate ladder pressed on me like a wet blanket suffocating me. Every hung-over colleague of mine that showed up at work red-eyed and blurry (and there were a goodly few) was proof that it was a killing damnation. I even began to refer to the tower, which was visible outside my dining room windows, as the "great white beast." Not having been given a usable answer in that dorm room on that day back in some April ago, I had chosen wrong. All my choices were wrong. My furniture was stupid and laughable, the thrill of my sports car had worn off but the payments and the insurance costs would go on for years. And my fiancé didn't know me so how could she love me. And worse, how could I love her.

The volume of the white noise became intolerable, and even though I was drinking quite a bit I could not shut it down. Somewhere in all of the thoughts constantly bombarding me I latched onto the idea that I had indeed made the wrong choice back in grad school. I should have gone to Austin and become a composer. My state of mind and emotions had returned to the point *prior* to when God reached me. This is important. The situation I found myself in put me right back into the ways of thinking that were so natural to me before that day alone in my dorm room when I first heard Him.

My fiancé and I broke off our engagement, I resigned from the oil company, and loaded everything I could fit into a Volkswagen bug, gave away everything else, and drove away heading west. I was throwing it all away to go be a composer.

That drive from Houston to Albuquerque was among the happiest fourteen hours I had ever lived, up to that point. I felt free. It was the freedom of an escapee in those first hours away from the bondage, an intoxicating freedom.

You know, for many years after that I looked back on that drive as the first time I truly experienced joy. And for almost all of the years looking back I never questioned the joy I felt in that single day. I have never so much as doubted it, to the point where I have many times wondered how to get it back. I've asked myself *how do you live life with that kind of freedom of spirit,* to break away from the weight of other people's expectations and be content with your own. You know as well as I do that it was a ruse. I hadn't left anything in

Houston but a car, some furniture, a boring job and a truly wonderful woman who deserved better than me.

I went to live with the same sister that spoke to me at the window, and her husband. Both were relatively new Christians and it was a tremendous opportunity for me to find peace and to collect myself. I had reasoned that it was a chance for me to get back to my faith and to follow the true path I was meant to travel. Although I hadn't specifically articulated it to myself, I somewhere harbored the belief that all would be right if I did, and the monster that reared up at me would stay back in Houston, away from me.

For the next three or four months I was safe and stable and everything seemed as if it would be fine. I was lonely for some friends, but my sanity seemed to be restored and I even found it easy to remain sober. I reconnected with Christ, read the bible again, attended church regularly, worked a simple job that I loved, and rode my bicycle everywhere I went. I was in great physical, spiritual, and even emotional shape.

In the months that followed I did make new friends. But within six months of arriving at my new home I was drinking again, gradually at first. Then I moved out on my own, surrounded myself with a new group who did yet a new set of things while sober, and sang a new set of songs every night.

For seven years I went in and out of relationships with women, but this time never being able to be sexual with them unless I was completely drunk. When you and I have had the conversations about how you feel as uncomfortable around women as you feel compelled to get beyond it, I sometimes wonder to myself, *At what point does that stop being the normal angst all guys feel and become some kind of real problem?" At what point does it reveal that it is a problem you cannot get beyond, and what do you do then? What do you do if you can never get beyond it?*

I was quickly returning to the bitterness, anger and even hatred that I knew so well before that day in grad school. Only this time God was left out of it. I was not angry at Him anymore; I just ignored Him. It is said that if we insist on our sin, God will eventually give us over to it. I wish I had known that.

Those seven years were a blur of partying, chasing sex for its own sake, and drunken binges lasting for days on end. Nothing would shake me of it. We all had jobs and we all worked, but none of it was serious. Those were working days like you had in high school when there were other things you did out of a more long-term view of things. But I was in the phase of life where the long-term view of things was supposed to be working itself out, or I was supposed to be working it out. I was just chasing a good time. My friends and

I would party till three in the morning and then decide to get in the car and drive for three hours into the mountains to party at a cabin there for another day or two. Then I would go back to my place and nurse a hangover until I was feeling good enough to do it all again…about two days.

But there was a story I was telling myself that made it all okay. There was a script running in my head that kept me from noticing how stupid the life I was leading actually was. I think that in order for any of us to do things we will later look back on as really stupid things, things we will someday regret or times we spend that we will look back on as having nothing good in them… we first have to be telling ourselves something.

In my case it was this fantasy that I had that I was the suffering, eccentric composer. I had actually romanticized the drunkenness and even the poverty that I was experiencing all as part of the life of a tortured artist that would one day be discovered. I imagined these interviews that would be conducted with me. One day I would be sitting across the table from Charlie Rose, in my rightful place behind the likes of James Baldwin, Joseph Campbell, and Benjamin Netanyahu. I would be expounding the depths of my philosophical understanding of music and what it is to be a composer. And more importantly, all the drunkenness, all the "acting out" would become part of it and so would be excused. No one ever condemns Jacques Brel for all the whiskey he drank in those dimly lit nightclubs or the unnumbered packs of cigarettes he smoked that ended up killing him with lung cancer. His songs justified all of it. No one has anything but compassion when they consider all the needles that found their way into Janis Joplin's veins. Her performance at Woodstock was the bloom on that stalk of thorns and so all was okay. And it was like that for me too.

I have to mention that I was encouraged. There were a growing number of people who liked my performances and usually both attended them and showed me a little guarded worship at the receptions that often followed. I was always the gracious artist who feigned humility covered in gratitude. Like the very first performance in New Mexico…

My sister and I had been planning it for weeks. It was difficult to find a place to have the performance that didn't cost too much, wasn't too big or too small, and had a nice enough piano. But we did. We arranged to have the recital (concert?) at one of the larger churches in the older part of town, in a hall that could accommodate about five hundred.

We also made arrangements for a reception at my sister and brother-in-law's house after the recital and prepared invitations. We sent or delivered invitations to everyone we knew and as many of the people the people we knew knew as we could. It was one of those things that being in a friendship makes you think you have to do whether you want to or not. But I think there were some who actually thought it might make a nice evening as long as it didn't go too long or cost anything. And there were quite a few people there who were willing to show me support not because they had ever heard the music or even believed they would want to, but because they were good and generous people.

Even members of my family came from out of town to attend, including the woman who had been my fiancé.

The performance consisted of all my own compositions and I had prepared about a dozen to perform with the entire recital to last about an hour and a half. In those days I always included the piece of music that came to be called "Two Afternoons April First" that I have already told you about, but I never played it in any position other than last. I couldn't play anything after it, usually. I think in all the years I performed that piece publicly it wasn't until the fifth or sixth time that I did it in concert that I could get past the crescendo without losing composure. I have told people that the piece of music is not sad, or even angry. Over all it is just pathetic. It makes a spectacle of the performer and (if it is performed with the kind of abandon with which it was composed) solicits not sadness from the audience, but pity.

One of the last times I performed it was in a concert in Santa Fe. We had the opportunity to hold a recital at a very large piano bar there. It was filled with small tables and probably sat two hundred. My friends and I were up there one night drinking and listening to the resident pianist, who was actually quite good. The place was clearly designed for piano performances with a beautiful twelve-foot grand piano set in front of a massive mirror hung from the wall behind the bench. The mirror was situated such that the audience seated at the tables could see the hands of the person playing.

During a break, one of my friends went up to him and asked if I could play while he was on break. He reluctantly agreed. As it turns out, the bar had a policy that no one other than him could perform there, and I learned later that many had requested the opportunity to perform in that venue because it was quite popular among the artsy set of Santa Fe. But the policy was strictly enforced and it had never happened.

I played a couple of compositions and afterward went over to the pianist to thank him. His name was Doug, as I recall. He was very kind and generous with his words and I instantly liked him. He seemed to be not only truly gifted as a musician, but also had a humility and generosity that you don't often find in that mix. And he asked me if I would like to come back some evening for a full performance. On the drive home I was drunk with more than the beer.

The night of that performance there were about two hundred people in attendance and I played for about two hours. The last piece I played was the "Two Afternoons." After I finished I went back to join my friends at their table and slam back a few beers. One of my buddies came up to me and told me that there was an elderly couple who had asked him if they could have a word with me. He pointed to their table, so I got up and walked over.

This is the story I think I told you when I described writing the piece, earlier on. Only a lady was sitting there; her husband had left the table. After introducing myself to her and she inviting me to have a seat, trying to be polite, I asked where her husband was. She informed me that he was in the bathroom washing his face. You remember, his father had died some ten years earlier and his wife calmly told me that it was the first time he had shed any tears over it. I didn't see any anger in her face although my first reaction to the thought of what had happened was one of guilt. I felt guilty, like I had jumped up from the piano and ripped open his shirt to reveal to the whole room how wimpy was his chest, and now he was back in the bathroom buttoning it up again. I had an instant flash of fear come over me sort of along the lines of *what the hell am I going to say to him when he comes back?* Nothing I know better describes the piece of music than the events at that table that night.

And back at that first performance in the church recital hall, my very first time to ever play it publicly, the audience gave me a standing ovation and seven, no less than seven curtain calls.

My family and I went back to the reception in separate cars. I was in a fog like the haze of hope when things first begin to happen. Or that you think are beginning to happen. The kind of fog that makes fools of anyone, even the most resolute and austere.

A couple of days later I learned a little about the conversation that occurred in the other car, the one in which some of my other family members and my ex-girlfriend were riding. I wrote it in a journal I kept back then. One of them said, "He doesn't stand an ice cube's chance in hell." And another, "I was bored to tears." They never found out that I knew this or the many times my thoughts went back to knowing it and silently, absently pleading with them... *but they gave me a standing ovation and seven curtain calls.*

Those years were full of recitals, and composing, and the small clutch of fans encouraging me on, regardless of what some members of my family really thought. And I actually fell in love. I'll call her Mary, although I know that if she knew I was writing this she would wonder why I didn't just use her real name. Like so much of what would become what I thought of as deference, she would consider just silly.

My friends and I were at a bar and I spotted her across the way, sitting with two other women. I mentioned to my friends that I was <u>sure</u> I knew her from somewhere. I couldn't place her but I knew that I knew that face. I started going through the possibilities with my friends at the table. "I wonder if I met her in England, or maybe she sang in the University of Houston choir or something." They finally told me to get off my ass and go ask her. I screwed up the courage and made my way over.

I'm sure you can imagine the expression on all their faces when I said, "I know this will sound like a line, but I am pretty sure I know you from somewhere." What turned out to be her sister just threw me a glance of instantaneous and abject dismissal as she rolled her eyes and swiveled around in her chair turning her shoulder to me to wait until I would just go away. Her mother just started laughing. But she decided to play along, and I think that was what sealed the deal for me.

She decided to pretend that it was actually possible that we did know each other from somewhere and that it was not just a line. But her part of the conversation never lost the patina of it being just a line. Were you to be her mother who was witnessing the conversation rather than trying to ignore it and suffering the moments it was dragging out, you would not be able to tell who was toying with whom. I suggested England. She said no, she had been to England but never to Oxford. I tried the University of Houston Choir and she told me that she did indeed sing, but never with that choir.

After a while she figured it was time to bring the exchange to an end and she wrapped up with the pronouncement that we were "twins, separated at birth." And gave me her phone number.

The very next morning, which was a Saturday, I called her. I think it was about seven in the morning and I didn't even stop to consider that we had both been in a bar just the night before and maybe seven was a little early. And I never went through the old angst routine of whether calling so soon would seem "needy." It never occurred to me. All I knew was that I wanted to talk to her again.

And it never even dawned on me that after the fourth or fifth ring, she was probably sleeping. But it sure dawned on me when she finally answered.

"Hi, Mary, this is your twin brother, separated at birth…"

"Do you know what time it is?"

"I, uh, I…"

"I'm hanging up on you." And she did.

Like any somewhat rational person, I figured that I had blown it and would never get the chance to speak to her again, would never know where I knew her from, or what she was actually like now. Until about seven in the morning on a Sunday a couple of weeks later.

I heard the phone ring in my deep sleep and was instantly hit with anger. It was Sunday, for crying out loud. Who the hell calls you on a Sunday morning at seven o'clock?!?

"John, this is your twin sister. You know, the one separated at birth..."

We started hanging out together and I found out a lot about her. She did indeed sing and she had an absolutely beautiful voice. One of the prettiest voices I had ever heard. I even began writing music just for her to sing. She had one of the best senses of humor I had ever come across, and she was an aspiring actress. I always knew that she would (or should) be an actress because she had a fantastic and delightful theatricality about her.

Often when we went out we would play a game. The rules of the game were simple. Each of us would choose an accent that was not natural to us. We were to carry on the entire evening's events in the accent paying particular attention to speaking to the waiters or waitresses we would encounter or to any other folks we would run into that we did not know. Our task was to convince them that we actually were from the country from which the accent originated. It didn't matter what accent we chose, but we could not change it once we had started it. Failing to maintain a British accent, for instance, did not justify me switching to Italian. It seems like she always chose Russian.

She was so good at a Russian accent that I even started believing she was from Russia. Had I ever been to Russia I might have begun to suspect that Russia is where I had met her before, and she was playing a very long joke on me.

And she was beautiful. Her face was flawless and her emotions flashed across it with ease and grace. When she smiled it was as if nothing in the world could cloud the moment.

During the weeks and months that we dated her mother was diagnosed with breast cancer. It devastated both Mary and her sister, and I felt helpless to do anything about it. I couldn't be part of it. They had a mock funeral for her while she was alive and I was somewhat repulsed by that. I kept quiet about it because, thankfully, I had the presence of mind to realize that I had no say in how another person grieves. My opinion could not have mattered less and I knew that before I ever gave away a hint of it. But it did seem like surrender to me. Some sort of surrender that we're supposed to object to.

I saw Mary suffer sadness while her mother was sick and when she finally died. It introduced a dynamic in our relationship. Or I should say, another dynamic in a relationship already so full of dynamics it could have been a software engineering convention.

The friends I hung out with all got to know her and she quickly became part of the group. She even went to work for the same new-home builder that most of us worked for, and so we all saw each other pretty much every day. My best buddy Ted was paired up with another sales person who I will call Charlotte in one model home, I was paired up with a Norwegian woman who another salesperson once referred to as "Doris Day on Steroids" but I referred to as the Volga Boat Woman. She was actually a very sweet and kind woman, but you did not want to cross her, man. You did not want to cross her. And Mary floated, at first, between model homes. She eventually became part of the team with Ted and Charlotte.

Life in those days was like a cross between the TV series "Friends" and the movie "Debbie Does Dallas." Charlotte was secretly sleeping with the president of the company, who was married to the person assigned to write all our mortgages, and with whom we also partied regularly. We all knew it, because Charlotte couldn't keep her mouth shut…and I think she enjoyed the sense of power that she imagined, having the boss under her control and all.

But his wife didn't know it. One time Charlotte even suggested that I have an affair with her so that she would be distracted and Charlotte and our boss could go about their merrymaking unimpeded. The idea was out of the question, but in my innermost thoughts I was flattered that she might think I would consider it. Interesting that I could have considered the idea that I would throw myself sexually at a married woman who was otherwise my friend with complete disregard for her probably already broken heart in a deceptive plot to make it easier for another friend to wreck her marriage by screwing her husband, as a personal favor. And then to think that being asked to do it was a compliment. Charlotte had already fully concluded that the marriage was over so it couldn't really matter, could it? And besides, it would probably make her (the wife) feel pretty. Don't have the right shade of lipstick today? Hop into bed with a friend and cheat on your husband. You'll feel pretty.

When we would get together for drinks we would laugh and joke about things and pretend that we didn't know anything about all that we knew.

One time Mary showed up unexpectedly at Charlotte's house to help her sew a dress. Charlotte nervously let her in keeping from her the fact that her lover who was the president of the company we all worked for was hiding in the closet, naked. Mary spent more than an hour sewing on stuff before Charlotte was able to coax her out the door. Within twenty-four hours everyone in our group of friends knew about it. As did half of the sales force of the company and a few of the folks we hung out with at the title company.

It sure put a twist into our weekly staff meetings. I mean, it was weeks before any of us could make eye contact during any of them, while our illustrious corporate captain of the industry stood before us lecturing us on current issues with home sales. More than once I was painfully tempted to ask about closet space in the newer home designs. You know, opening with a question like, "In your experience, do you think our customers are going to find the closets, um, generous enough?" While everyone else would be thinking, *enough to comfortably while away a few hours trapped inside naked?* I could be certain that I would lose my job, which I needed. But I otherwise just didn't have the guts.

I think Charlotte truly believed that he was going to divorce his wife and marry her. And we all thought she was an idiot. We were sad for her, I believe. After all, she was a friend, even if she did steal a good number of Ted's clients with absolute impunity. But more than once during our frequent nights in the bars when no member of that little love triangle were around, we quoted the old adage "Never fall in love with a married man: they make lousy husbands." That assumes, of course, that someone cheating on his or her spouse *wants* another spouse. But we all knew that Charlotte did desperately want to be married to her lover, and so felt justified in all of it. I'm sure that while we were getting drunk quoting our adage *du jour*, she was getting sexed up trusting hers: "All's fair in love and war."

My friend Ted was a very outgoing and fun guy. Everyone liked being around him and he always had more women throwing themselves at him than we could keep track of. He was the heartiest partier I had ever met or to this day have ever known. Together he and I drank more beer in more pool halls and dive joints than you would ever believe, even if I could estimate it. He was tall and good-looking and always, always had multiple girls chasing him. He had steel blue eyes that were the instant ticket to conversation with women, so he never even had to do anything to initiate it.

One of the many times we were in a bar drinking beer by the pitcher, the waitress showed up at the table without her tray, which was always a sign that she wasn't there to take our order. She leaned against the booth, put her hand on her hip and said to him, "Has anyone ever told you that you have the most *gorgeous* blue eyes?" I wasn't really that drunk actually. But something in me just sort of snapped, a little. I had heard that question posed to him by one too many waitresses in one too many dive bars, and I couldn't restrain myself. The comment rolled forth free. "Oh please. The man is thirty-five years old. Do you really think you are the first?"

I shocked both of them. He looked at me stupefied like little sparklers had just emerged from my ears and nose in full flaming smoking sparkle, lighting up the table. She just turned and walked away. The next night in a different bar he had a grin on his face and said "I have something for you." He reached in his pocket and pulled out a plastic pair of glasses that had these huge bulging plastic blue eyes, with little holes in the pupils so that you could see out of them while you were wearing them.

He and Mary became pretty good friends. It was inevitable. But as their friendship grew, so did my jealousy. My best friend, who every woman seemed to desire, and my girlfriend with whom I was quickly losing all control of my emotions.

You see, I really did love her. Truly I did.

But I can't say that I *lusted* for her, even though I secretly wanted to – lust for her. I did want to sleep with her (I mean fall asleep in the same bed), and I did want to have sex with her even though I was terrified by the prospect. When we first started dating, Mary made it clear that she was not going to rush into sex. But it wasn't something we talked about at first. Each of our dates would end with an awkward period of affection in her living room at her front door, then she would turn me toward the door to leave and I would look appropriately dejected. I think it was a role I was playing, because I don't really remember being frustrated all that much.

And at some point, I am not sure how long into our relationship but I think it was a few months, I told her that my feelings for her were strong and that I wondered if marriage would be possible for us. What a stupid clod. How ridiculous to think that a woman would actually favorably respond to an intellectual curiosity about whether the most significantly passionate thing a man can do (ask to marry his girlfriend) would be consistent with the circumstances. Were the tables turned I might have responded, "Do you <u>want</u> to marry me, or are you writing a thesis…"

I think that when a guy asks his girl to marry him, he should do it with every ounce of passion he can muster. I should have abandoned myself to the passion and had no doubt for a second that the entire universe had already conspired to put us together, and were we both not to lock that reality into place I would know I would suffer a life too painful to consider.

Appropriately, Mary was noncommittal and it threw me off balance, making my descent into jealousy and confusion even more rapid.

But one night, after our time together when we were standing in the living room and I turned to the door to leave, in her best John Wayne, she took my hand and turned me back toward her saying, "C'mon, pilgrim."

Her mother's illness worsened and even though I loved every minute with her, there was a seriousness that never evaporated. Nothing could burn it off. Our lovemaking was never good, and I often thought it was just that she was going through such a difficult time that there was no way it would be good, given the situation. Maybe after things got better, maybe if her mother recovered. She was usually willing to accept my advances but never once did she ever make any of her own. And there didn't seem to be any joy in it for her. This was tortuous for me, because I was already saddled with my own doubts about myself. Doubts that she could not know.

After a period of time I started to get angry. All of the little things that fueled my jealousy together with what I felt to be her lack of desire for me started congealing and I became angry. Trust me, anger is not going to soften a woman's heart and turn her affections toward you. That along with my growing certainty that she probably didn't want to have sex with me, and didn't want to marry me, took its place in the chain of instances proving my talent for figuring out the obvious.

Mary's mother died. Her friendship with Ted became closer and closer; I became more and more jealous and angry, and one day I got a call from Charlotte. She asked me to join her for a drink after work; there was something she wanted to talk to me about.

My first thought was that she had another idea about how I could help her by distracting the attention of the wife. But I couldn't fully expect this because I had been so resolute that there is no way I would ever do that. By this time everyone pretty much knew about things between Mary and me, so I thought maybe it had something to do with that. I really didn't know, so I was actually kind of anxious to find out.

We started out just having some drinks, killing time in small talk, and making jokes about things. Charlotte had a way of making you feel like you were special to her, and maybe I was, who could know? I think she was the kind of person who could find a reason to consider almost everyone special in one way or another. I asked her what she wanted to talk about.

She got this sort of sheepish expression on her face like it was really bad news and she didn't want to be the one to deliver it. She looked at me with compassion I did not yet know I would need.

"It's about Mary."

I knew that the two of them were good friends and probably talked a lot among themselves about their deepest things, or everyone else's deepest things. In my mind I put the apparent concern and gentleness she was exhibiting together with the probability that Mary had spilled her secrets to her and braced myself to hear that Mary was probably going to break up with me completely, or ask that we just go back to friends – which is worse. I instantly felt a slight pang of fear that Mary and Charlotte had discussed the lack of passion between Mary and me, and wondered if I should be embarrassed.

"She's not exactly being faithful to you."

This was worse than all. *On second thought, maybe finding out she just wanted to be friends (and no other bit of news) would have been okay...* A rush of several different thoughts all flooded into my head at the same time. *Why wouldn't Mary tell me this herself, privately? Why would she send Charlotte to meet me in a damn bar and add embarrassment to this pleasant little surprise? Why would Charlotte know? It's Ted, it's got to be Ted, sonovabitch. That f--- in sonovaBITCH.*

After the moment or so that I must have looked shocked and dejected, trying to get my thoughts all sorted out, it occurred to me not to ask Charlotte who, I already knew who, but for some reason my gut reaction was to ask her just "How do you know?" I think maybe it was because I expected her to give me some answer like "Oh, I just know, a woman knows these things." In which case I would order a shot, slam back my beer, and content myself that I had dodged *that* bullet. I would dismiss Charlotte with some comment like "Get outta here, you don't know what you're talking about."

It must have been the crack in the inflection of my voice, or some other subtle indication that I was wading into this fully knowing I was going to get my guts ripped out. She had Mother Teresa on her face as she gently leaned into me and put her hand lovingly on my knee and said, "I am the other person."

Sometimes abject astonishment can be so intense that it blows every other emotion you might otherwise feel clean out the door, out of the neighborhood, the city, state, and right off the face of the planet.

What I remember is her telling me that they didn't plan to have it happen. They were in the hot tub having a glass of wine…I told her to stop. I didn't need to hear any more. Even asking her something like "Does Mr. President know?" would have seemed petty and retaliatory. Too small. He probably would have seen it as a positive development, anyway. Always the mover and shaker, he would have considered it a growth market situation, the slime. I hated them all.

Having told you about this period of time now I have to tell you the hard part. Having explained about life as a boheme when it was full of just drunken binges, laughter at bar tables in the two layers of smell, and this woman I fell in love with who chose an adulterous lesbian over me, now I have to tell you the other stuff. I can't express how hard it is to keep writing right now, but I have to do it. The rest of this will not make any sense if I don't. I know you care for me and we have been like brothers in our faith. I can imagine you on one of our walks saying to me that you won't think less of me, maybe even saying it to yourself; I also know that you will. You will think less of me. But I am convinced that everything that happens affects what happens next, even if it takes years, decades, to play out. And I can bear my own disgust better when I consider that.

Up to this point I have included a number of stories because I thought they portrayed the other side of life for me, the humorous side. I reasoned as I decided to include them that they demonstrated how things were never really in balance...it was always one extreme competing with another. Then Christianity came into the picture and became just another extreme, sometimes leading events, other times not. Sometimes driving my behavior, other times not.

But while the stories that occurred during the seven years of my descent were laughable, they were not funny. It was not the joy of life that brought out the laughter in my drunken binges; it was the delusion of escape. In a sense, there was no happiness in the center of things, only the rush of chaos. The laughter was peripheral, uninformed.

I had been what you hear called a "black-out" drinker for at least ten years by the time I lived in New Mexico. And my years in New Mexico just dug the trenches deeper. Another label that could have easily been applied to me was the term "dipsomaniac" (someone who could not control their urge to get drunk). That was what they used to call a particular type of alcoholic back in the infancy days of psychology when they were all hunting for clinical-sounding names for things. But interestingly there was no term (of which I am aware) for someone who simply couldn't control *anything*. I wonder what you might call a person like that. What with so much of the events in life that are outside of our control, and so many ways we can respond to each of the things that can happen that we can't control, would that describe all of us?

I don't think so. Most folks can control some things. It seems like most folks can control most of the things in their life and keep the things they cannot control away, at bay. But I had come unhinged. I couldn't control any of it.

In that time where I lived, there was an area of town where prostitutes and people in the fringe, runaways, drug addicts and dealers hung out. All towns of any size have them, I guess. But it's something I wish I never learned. I am not sure how I learned of the place, or exactly how I came to know the precise location. But I surely did.

At first I fought the temptation to drive to it and just drive around checking it out. On days when I was alone with no responsibility, and usually drunk or drinking, I would get this weird desire to go there. It was strange and would cause this physical pain in my jaw. Sometimes my heart would start racing too. I would pace around in my apartment not really sure what was going on, and even my thoughts would get jumbled up. I would end up slamming back my drinks even faster, and wake up sometime the next day on the bathroom floor or in a completely inexplicable position on the bed… and take inventory looking for cuts or bruises. The classic. It was true for me too.

What was cooking a brick in my throat was not that I would drive around there and see pretty girls dressed obviously enough to advertise that they were there for sex, any kind of sex, and no one would know if I did go there to drive around and find them. What caused me to fill with a weird kind of tension – a buzzing energy – was that I had heard that there were men.

In these days as I sit here writing you this, the confession a guy might make that he had a sexual fascination with men is considered no big deal. So what? Guys "out" themselves every day. I have known more men than I ever thought I would meet who fought against these things and then gave up, coming out of the closet trumpets blaring, balloons, and their rainbow flags waving. Some with shattered wives and devastated children left behind too young not to know it's not their fault, all because dad has to be "himself." And no one even notices anymore.

But that is not what I am telling you.

It doesn't matter that the focus was about sexual activity with men. It could have been about women with red hair, Japanese women who never talk. It could have been about feet, or some famous chick singer who cashes in distracting us away from her utter lack of talent with her innovations on Victoria's Secret.

No sexual desire is healthy if it causes you torment, regardless of the object of your desire.

And whether or not you were born with it, or ended up with it because you failed out of "Webelos" when you didn't happen to bond well with other boys, or some mean-spirited reckless jerk fathered you and then treated you like a turd he would rather leave behind, or a couple of sick wack jobs down the street forced sex on you when the objects of your fantasy were still "Count Chocula" and seeing Wile E. Coyote finally nab that bird...couldn't matter less. Irrelevant.

Because of all the things about which I had no choice, I COULD choose who I wanted to become. I HAD chosen the man who I wanted to be, even if I never consciously knew it. And the guy fascinated with the seedy side of town because he might run into other guys looking for sex was not that man.

I don't remember the first time I gave in and made the trip. But I do remember the drive toward the area and the weird physical sensations I was having. My arms felt shaky and weak as I held the steering wheel, and that strange dense feeling in my throat was back and strong. I remember the exact image of the street that you had to turn off from the interstate onto, and I remember thinking how mundane everything looked. How could something as intriguing and potentially scandalous be happening right here, right around here, when everything looked so...normal? The donut shop had people in it just buying donuts, not having sex or even looking like they were there for it. And exactly where would these people be, anyway? Would they be propped up against buildings smoking cigarettes like in the cop shows? Would the *guys* be propped up against buildings?

I knew the boundaries of the area. Again, I don't know how I knew or from whom I had learned them. But I knew the streets that formed the outer edges within which all this stuff was supposed to be happening. So I made my way for the area. Once there I drove circles up and down the streets doing what I would later learn is called "cruising." As I write this I almost have to laugh at myself. The Catholic kid who in eighth grade thought that people who smoked cigarettes also robbed banks on Saturday nights...cruising.

I'm not certain, but pretty sure that the first time I went to the area I didn't see anything. Nothing stood out to me; no scene seemed unusual, no prostitutes, no guys doing what – I wasn't sure. I gave up and drove back to my apartment half convinced it was all a hoax, or maybe I had the area wrong.

But I didn't stay given up. It wasn't long before I was right back there again. It quickly became exciting to be back there driving around staring down alleys and stuff, even though I never saw anyone. It was like a game, an exciting game I was not supposed to be playing. If I were found out, I am sure the shame would have been so great I would have to kill myself, and as they say, maybe that is what hooked me into it. Every time I made it back to my apartment without being stopped, arrested, and paraded in front of the media that very same day to be splashed all over the five o'clock news, I returned home with a trophy. Even if I never stopped or spoke to anyone.

All these years later one of my remaining fascinations is to watch murder shows on TV. I don't like the fake ones, you know, the series shows based on the idea of murder. I prefer the real thing. I am fascinated with how peoples' lives can descend to the point where someone ends up murdered and so many lives are shattered. It fascinates me how someone can drive their life to the very pit of hell, which I think prison really is, and never even be planning to end up there. Never even seem to suspect that they will end up exactly there.

Or maybe they do. I have to admit that while I have never once in my life entertained the desire to actually kill anyone, or have sex with a minor, or abuse anyone in any way – stuff that is really messed up – I can fully understand the drive to be doing something forbidden just because you are getting away with it. I can fully understand how it draws you in and holds you. How it causes you to come back time and again, even if you never end up stopped, arrested, and splashed across the five o'clock news. And I confess that today as I watch these murder shows, part of me experiences a sense of relief seeing that things can end up very bad, but they didn't for me. They didn't end up *that* bad. Now, looking back, not in the slightest way tempted to get caught up in that kind of thing anymore, I observe from the safety of time passed. I watch stories of others who didn't make it through, and it brings to my awareness the safety I am now in. I can only imagine the true depths to which I might have descended but for the grace of God.

But now I know that you never get away with it. You never get over seeing yourself on the five o'clock news even if no one else does, even if it never happens. You live with that fear the rest of your life because it is so unique and goes so deep. You cannot ignore the fear you have of the monster next to you, just because he doesn't know you are there. Nothing can ever wash it away other than the worst actually coming to pass, doing its ultimate damage. Maybe it is because you know you *deserve* it.

As I write this to you I am approaching the toughest part. It's getting harder to even think how I have to word this, to be honest, to tell you what I need you to know but not too much. Not so much that it just becomes like slowing down on the road next to an accident with injuries. You're fascinated with the accident; who knows why. You're fascinated with the fact that people are hurt, maybe even killed. But you don't want to actually see the blood and pained faces, hear the cries. That's too much.

I kept going back there often. I wanted to be in the stream of people living at the bottom of the garbage can. I wore the filth inside me and I sought the comfort of proximity to others who did too. I wanted to be with the others that didn't matter. They didn't matter so completely that even if they knew about me, even that wouldn't matter.

By then my drinking had progressed to the point where there were days when I would wake up still drunk, not just hung-over. Usually there would be a brief period of time when I would argue with myself about whether I should just live through the hangover and try to get back on track, or plunge back into a deeper drunk. The question was almost always answered by figuring out what I had to do that day, who I had to talk to, call, who might come over, did I have to work? Did I have any responsibilities? More to the point, did I have any responsibilities I couldn't postpone or get out of altogether?

I had gotten pretty good at doing a sort of preemptive thing, where I would call people I thought *might* call me or drop by to make sure that they wouldn't do that while I was drinking. I would clear the day to make sure my drinking wouldn't get discovered, and after doing that I would feel this strange sort of delight that I had gotten away with something I hadn't even done yet. I'd celebrate my cleverness and pour myself a shot for congratulations. It wasn't long before these days started to be strung together one after the other, and even got to the point where there were stretches when the sober days were the bookends, not the other way around. And that wasn't even yet halfway through the forty years I spent drinking.

It was a day like that. I think it was a Saturday. I remember that the skies were blue and the air was cool, but the sun was warm on my skin. Funny that I can remember extremely minute details of that day even though it was almost twenty-five years ago, and I was pretty drunk the whole time. My apartment at the time had a parking space right in front of the sliding glass door to my living room. Close enough so that I never had time to talk myself out of getting into my car, or enough of a walk to stumble or fall along the way and thereby come to my senses at least enough to go back and forget it, whatever it was.

As I said, I was still drunk from the drinking I had done the night before and I decided to keep drinking. At some point I had the idea to drive to the cruise spot, not really certain that I would talk to anyone or meet anybody, but just to head out and see. I drove around aimlessly until I happened on two young men walking along a side street. They seemed to be a little younger than me and I would guess their ages somewhere in their early twenties.

There was a spot where I could stop the car and be positioned so that they would eventually pass by walking along the driver-side window, which was opened. I knew they would be walking right toward me with my car positioned there and would see me watching them out of my window, so they were bound to know that I had an interest in talking to them. When they came up to the car I struck up a conversation.

They indicated that they were on their way to an apartment where they could make $50 for being in a porn film being produced by some guy that lived there. We talked about the whole thing and they seemed a bit surprised at the good luck of getting paid to go have sex, but that didn't really surprise me, because of the neighborhood. The whole area was like that.

It is amazing to me looking back how there was, like, a righteous indignation that rose up in me at the idea that they were heading to a place where they were going to be used by the guy, taken advantage of, even if they didn't see it. Even if they were perfectly aware of what they were doing and lucid enough to decide to do it. In my confused state I judged that he was going to be using them in the foulest and most despicable way – for sex. That guy was nothing but a "perv," a predator, and he was planning to take them for his own sick business. But even while I was thinking that in the back of my mind, I had the idea to offer them an option to come home with me instead. As long as they were going somewhere for sex, why not go home with me? Not that I was making a film, of course. So in my mind, my offer was somehow clean. The two talked about it a little right in front of me, then one said that he wanted to go to the apartment and be in the porn film, and the other came home with me.

It was clear that the idea was a stupid one when we got back to my place. He wasn't really interested, and strangely, neither was I at first. But he was in my apartment; I had brought him there after all, and wondered to myself when I would ever have a chance like this again. I think a part of me also figured that the deed was already done, whatever would happen I was already guilty of it so I might as well have the payoff. We went back into the room and started things. But after a time, he stopped them and told me that he didn't want to do it after all. He said that he liked women and wanted to leave.

I instantly felt a crushing weight of shame. My offer had not been clean after all. It wasn't something he wanted to do.

I apologized to him and assured him that I would take him back right away. I stumbled through a lame explanation that I really liked women too but was just curious, as if there was any possibility that he would believe a shred of it. I instantly wanted him as far away from me as would be cosmologically possible. I wanted to be as far away from *him* as possible. I couldn't get him back to the street where I found him fast enough. And as clearly as I remember every nuance of that day, the weather, the visuals of every single transient event no matter how miniscule even to the tone of both their voices...I cannot remember anything about the drive back. Not a single moment of it. Nor can I imagine a memory of driving home from dropping him off. It is all completely blank.

But my memory picks up again at the moment I walked back into my apartment.

I was so deep in disgust that I couldn't even drink it away. When you win in the hunt driven by your darker appetites it isn't just the prey that is left laid out and torn to shreds.

I lay on my bed in a fetal position literally sick to my stomach, and wept. I knew that my life was changed forever. From that moment forward the hatred that I had grown up with coming at me from all over the place external, against which I had thrown up walls of dependence on drugs and alcohol, was no longer outside those walls. In the early hours of my new and lesser life I came to face a closer hatred, not the one I had known from others but of a deeper, searing and sickening drape. And I recognized it as my own.

Once hatred makes it inside, the enemy can relax; his work is done – handed off to an executioner even more savage, of even more implacable cruelty and new unfettered access.

All I could do was sleep for I don't remember how long. It was a drunken sleep but there was an insanity in it too. It was the kind of sleep you have the same day that you smash yourself up bad and the drugs knock you out, but only mostly. Not enough, not completely.

Then I woke like that guy in the horror movie, in the middle of a field he doesn't recognize, after a night he doesn't remember, naked and bloodied, in the pale light of the morning and the waning moon.

5. There. And Back

I THINK IT WOULD BE ACCURATE to say that the episode I just described to you was the low point of my life. I almost wince at the thought that there have been so many, and they have each been so different, that it's kind of hard to tell. But this is the point where what I had planned to tell you about reaches a sort of bottom. The rest of the stories I have for you cover the time frame from this last episode up to the year 2004 (around seventeen years) when I made a turn. But there aren't *that* many stories left.

The point is that sometimes when you hit bottom, or maybe in my case when you hit *a* bottom, it isn't itself a turning point. Sometimes you don't hit it and turn around. Sometimes you hit it and stay there.

I'm not going to dwell on the stories from these next years, or draw them out too much, because we are getting to the end of the point where the stories contribute much to what I have to tell you. But don't let the fact that there aren't as many stories in this part as before cause you to miss the fact that we *are* talking about seventeen years and that is a long time in anyone's life.

I have debated in my thoughts whether to refer to these as wasted years and decided that I wouldn't do that, and so I'd like to prep you not to think that that is how I consider them. I think I understand what they mean when they say that you can really only waste the present. I can see now that the future isn't ever guaranteed to us to do anything with: waste, conserve, give away, store in the bank, or make tacos out of. It just isn't ours. And the past... well, nothing's wasted.

But sometimes when I find myself picking over the rubble of my past looking for pieces that I can recognize, pieces I can polish a little and make them look better to myself (and others if I have to) they seem to bear resemblances. This one looks like that, but nothing like the other. This one draws a smile out of me, that one tightens my chest, and a few here and there I just don't know where the hell they came from or how they got there.

There's a true story that happened about ten years ago in the central mid-west, as I recall. As the story goes, an elderly couple had just retired and purchased a large mobile home to head off and see America. Maybe they figured they would travel for a time and see all the national parks, all the coastlines, and everything they always dreamed of visiting. And then go home to settle down to a peaceful relaxing time together.

They put a banner on the back of their RV that had some cute saying on it about how they were retired. You know, like "Newly Retired: No Kids, No Cares, No Money" or something like that. And they attached a small car, like a Celica or something, to the back that they were towing behind the RV. Well, if I have the story correct, they were on a two lane highway in Kansas or Utah or some state like that, and noticed that people would occasionally change lanes to pass them and come up alongside them waving their hands and calling something out. They thought it was quaint that well-wishers would still do that kind of thing, read their banner and go to the trouble to let them know how happy they were for them. Perfect strangers on the road.

Their windows were closed and I imagine that the driver side window was probably quite a bit higher than the level of ordinary cars too, so at first they didn't really know *what* the well-wishers were actually saying or calling to them. The area was heavily forested, the road winding, and they couldn't really see the cars approaching them from behind, or really *anything* behind them all that well.

What they didn't realize was the fact that a tire on the back of the little car they were towing had gone flat at some distance back, and for miles they had been dragging the thing on nothing but its steel rim, throwing a steady cascade of sparks off into the brush like some sort of freakish water truck, and quietly setting mile after mile of Kansas on fire. The cars passing them were frantically trying to get their attention to the unfolding disaster as they were comfortably inside their new RV, open road and adventures ahead, noticing the kind drivers congratulating them and thinking, "how nice." In the end the poor couple was assessed something like three million dollars for damages caused to the state parks.

If you changed the story a little bit and had them slamming back shots of Cuervo the whole time, it would be a good little metaphor for those seventeen years for me, and I think I'll pick it up here with that.

After the incident with the porn movie guy I slipped back into a sort of low-intensity insanity like I had experienced when I was a freshman in college. Except this time it wasn't marked so much by depression and thoughts of suicide as it was with paranoia. I could not get the events out of my head and I entered a phase where I only slept a few hours at a time, at most. Since there was absolutely no one I could talk to about it, no one I could tell, my thoughts began to morph into very strange things. I was living in a constant state of abject fear. And I tried everything to reason my way out of it. Many times I seriously considered just walking into the police station and turning myself in to be arrested. But for what? I knew, I just knew that at any moment a bevy of cop cruisers were going to come screeching to a halt all around me as I walked down the street, with agents leaping out of them landing perfectly into half-kneeling poses, weapons drawn. The media would arrive seconds later. It would be funny, if it wasn't so crazy. I was losing my grip on sanity, and I knew it. But I also knew that there was nothing I could do about it...I could not afford a therapist, and there was absolutely no one I could tell about it.

To make matters worse, I had started to do more concerts at that time and had even been invited to perform an outdoor concert for the city. After the performance I received a call from a young woman who I assumed had been in the audience. She wanted to go out on a date with me. She was asking me out for a date.

She had no way of knowing it, but in my frame of mind that would have been like asking a soldier who was crouching behind a pile of rubble shattered by shell fire, grenades blasting all around him, gunfire searing off nicks and pieces of walls everywhere, if he would like to play a game of ping pong. All I could manage in response to her request was a lie that I was in a committed relationship and not looking to start seeing anyone else.

But she kept calling. When I continued to rebuff her, she eventually got rude with me, and then started threatening me. It made no sense. I thought she must be a crazy person, like a stalker. It got so bad that I actually called the FBI who informed me that they could put a tracer on my home phone. I explained that she had anticipated that and already informed me that she was calling from pay phones, knew where I lived, and recommended that I keep a good watch over my shoulder. She was threatening my life.

To my complete horror she told me that she knew porn movie man (the guy I had brought home) and had gotten my phone number from him. In my shame and remorse I had given him my phone number before I took him back to the street and offered to help him any way I could. I was desperate to vindicate myself with him and even though I didn't know how I would or could help him, I had to do *something*. She was not a fan. She was never at the performance. She was probably a homeless porn movie candidate herself who smelled an opportunity for extortion, or maybe she was just out for a pound of flesh of her own.

In the ensuing phone calls from her she unleashed the full measure of her loathing toward me. Probably the full measure of her loathing for all men, for the guys behind the porn movie cameras I supposed, and every single person who had ever hurt her, cheated her, or asked her to come home with them because they were filthy and selfish and knew she probably had nothing better to do. And I deserved all of it. I was flat out terrified.

When I told the FBI that she had said she wanted me dead they became very interested. Apparently threatening someone's life over a pay phone is a Federal offense. We filled out a report and they put a tracer on my line. When she called again I told her that the FBI was involved, that my line was tapped, that threatening someone's life from a payphone turns out to be a Federal offense, and that as for my home address, well, the FBI had it too. She never called again.

But it was all just too much. Looking back on those months I don't really know how I survived it. I can't remember how I managed to go to work each day…I walked around in a constant state of fear far beyond anxiety. I was afraid for my well-being, I was afraid I would be discovered for who I was and what I had done, and it progressed to a point where I was afraid for my life.

Ted, my friend with the blue eyes and the waitresses, moved away from the town and it ended up being the catalyst that convinced me that I could leave too. I had to move away and start over. I had so thoroughly trashed the environment I was living in that I could no longer stand my own stench and I desperately needed a fresh start. I moved to the San Fernando Valley, hoping to pursue a career writing music for the movies, but really I was just running away. Even if I never wrote a single note for anyone, getting lost among the millions was enough.

I quit my job, packed my car with all my belongings for a second time, and continued on heading west.

LA has everything: beautiful beaches, weird foggy mornings, weirder people, and very cool places where they all hang out. Life was as good as it could be for someone like me, and the bohemian fantasy thing I had going on in my head was in full bloom. I was dirt poor, but I was a composer living in LA. Someday I would be talking about this in my interview on a late night talk show. And everything, all of it, would end up justified by the hauntingly poignant music the world would come to know and love. All creativity is born in pain, and all that.

While I was there I spent most of my time with Ted. But this isn't another story about me being secretly overly dependent like others I have already told you about. Although we were both a little dependent on each other there briefly. Nope, this is more along the lines of living life unhooked, so to speak. I guess that as I sit here thinking about it, I might say that the time frame falls into the category of running away. I didn't just run away *to* Los Angeles; while I was there I just kept running. He and I had a lot of adventures together...

One time we were skating at Manhattan Beach. I've been a pretty good skater since I was a little boy and used to get into races at the rink while I was growing up. So I was in my element on those roller skates. But I was very new to the beach scene in South Bay, and no one had yet explained to me about how some folks dress down there. As we were skating along, I was going pretty fast, and just happened to look up in time to see two young women who had very nice bodies skating toward me and just about to pass me. They were completely naked. Out of pure reflex I craned my head around to see them just as they passed and slammed dead into a telephone pole, separating my shoulder. It turns out they were not naked, they were wearing what I later heard referred to as "California Butt Floss" that was beige – the same color as their skin.

Laying there in a heap at the bottom of the pole everyone around me was laughing and rushing to help me, aware that the accident had been caused by the two beauties who just continued on down the sidewalk gracefully swaying their arms as they skated, long hair streaming behind them seemingly oblivious to the admiring glances that they were all too used to, but permitted just the same. I was some kind of innocent hero whose hapless boyish curiosity got me slammed into a telephone pole. But it wasn't like that, even if no one knew it.

I am also a strong swimmer, not fast, but with a lot of endurance. So is Ted, as it happens. And he is also one of the very few people I know who is not afraid to be in the open ocean. So we used to go over to Catalina Island at every opportunity to snorkel the cold waters off the island and party in Avalon.

One time we decided to stay at Two Harbors because we had heard there was a rock just off shore, sticking out of the ocean about a quarter mile out. We heard that it was full of fish – big ones. It was a ways out there, but you could swim out to the rock and rest a while on it, snorkel around a bit, and then swim back. So we went to check it out.

The first afternoon there we were killing time at the bar there and joking around with the bartender who invited us to become members of the "Two Harbors Yacht Club." We explained that we didn't have a boat but he told us that it didn't matter, all we had to do was finish three "Buffalo Milks" in five minutes and pay a dollar. Buffalo Milk is a drink that they made up there and named after the island's feral buffalo that are still everywhere, brought there for the filming of "Vanishing American" (1925) and just left there because it was cheaper than shipping them back to LA.

The drink is a combination of every kind of alcohol they have, (the buffalo) and the addition of some Half and Half (the milk). One will turn you into either a weepy sentimental who misses the days when TV shows were pure and simple, like when Ricky and Lucy didn't even sleep in the same bed. Or a prophet of modern political theory whose mission in life is to finally bring to awareness the fact that the entire democratic party is nothing but a bunch of "gotdamned" ex-Nazi's who have infiltrated it in order to turn America socialist. Never mind that the "gotdamned" Nazis were not socialists but rather fascists but that doesn't matter, you see, all part of the cover, all part of the cover.

Three of them will make you see two bartenders when there has ever only been one, long lost friends you haven't seen in twenty years back at the table over by the restaurant door to whom who you have to go say hello now…and a member of the yacht club.

The next day we were so hung over we didn't even know what city we were in when we woke up. But that very day we hiked from the Bed and Breakfast we stayed at to the hill we had to climb up, and the cliff we had to climb down to get to the beach from which we could swim out to the rock. It would have been much easier to just go back to the bar, drink *four* buffalo milks and kill ourselves by alcohol poisoning. Neither one of us really knew it (or if we did, would admit it) but we had each decided that the other one was going to have to be the one that would call the ridiculous challenge off. Neither of us would.

When we reached the top of the hill I could not imagine how we did it, and I looked down the cliff and could not imagine how we were going to get down it. When we got down to the beach I looked up and could not imagine how we made it down safely (or how we were going to get back up it), and looked out over the water and could not imagine how we were going to make it out that far. There was a lot of imagining that I wasn't able to do that day. I mean, we were truly half dead before we ever left the hotel.

On the beach we discussed how tired we were and was it really a good idea to head out to the rock right away or just stay on the beach and rest a while. While we questioned whether we could make the swim out to the rock, it never dawned on us to question how the flaming hell we were going to get back up the f---in' cliff. "I can make the swim, can you?" "Oh yeah, man, I can make that, no problem." "Well, let's go then…"

Please God, let's not, I thought, hoping some Coast Guard boat would suddenly pull up and cruise the edge of the beach with a guy in a white uniform calling at us through a bullhorn, "Swimming out to the rock is not permitted, even if you both can make it. Oh, and would you like a ride back to the bar for some Buffalo's Milk? We understand you're members of the yacht club. Besides, we're trained expert rescue officials who have seen hundreds of these situations and we can't imagine how the flaming hell you're gonna make it back up that f----in' cliff."

We hit the waves and headed for the rock. About halfway there we both stopped and just relaxed a little bit, floating on the surface and looking around. I had swim goggles on and could see looking straight down that the water seemed to be about sixty or more feet deep, and the swells were about two to three feet. We were out a lot further than folks who swim at the beach typically go and we were only about halfway there. I was a little nervous, but reassured myself that we would rest on the rock as soon as we got there and everything would be fine.

When we did arrive at the rock we were both pretty exhausted and started to approach the rock, which was very steep in most places, so we swam around until we found a slope that was gradual enough for us to climb up on. And then when we were close enough to the rock we saw something that made both of us sick to our stomachs.

From about ten feet below the surface of the ocean to about two feet above it the entire approach and the edge of the rock was covered, completely blanketed in black urchin. There was absolutely no way to climb up on that rock in anything but a Sherman tank. In fact, by the time we were close enough to realize that all that black coloring was actually not the rock itself but thousands of black urchin, we were already in danger and had to muster all our strength to do a backstroke because the swells were big enough and we were close enough to be picked up and washed right into them. Simply treading water in the middle of the ocean until we drowned from exhaustion would have been preferable.

Being impaled on the urchins' two-inch spines is not the only thing that would happen if that were to occur. When excited, the urchins actually eject their spines into (about half an inch) the offender. They have barbs. That means they usually have to be cut out, and a single sting from a single spine is excruciating. Roman soldiers in all their sadistic imagination could not have devised a more painful way to die.

We scooted back about twenty feet from the rock and treaded water while we talked about our options, of which there was one. Swim back to shore.

By the time we made it back to the beach, or at least to water shallow enough to stand, neither of us had any strength left to do it for long. That is the closest I have ever come to drowning. The shore, at that point, was littered with large sometimes sharp stones and there really wasn't much of a beach. There was no easy way to get to the base of the cliff, but we both realized that it didn't matter...there really was no possible way we could make it up that cliff. We could hardly make it stumbling over the rocks in two feet of water to the edge of the cliff, what with the waves crashing. Again, we had only one option. Make it around the point to where we could beach at the little town of Two Harbors. That meant half swimming (which we were too tired to do) and half stumbling over rocks in the surf and cutting ourselves to pieces (which we were too tired to care about). I remember collapsing on the beach within maybe fifty feet of the bar, but just laying there grateful to be alive and that the whole ordeal was over.

A few days later we were in Avalon standing in line to board a twenty-foot inflatable and head back out into the Pacific to ride the swells at top speed bouncing sometimes ten feet into the air straddling the big tube edge of the boat and wrestling against the splash to hang on, like some wild roaring bronc slapping the sea to shake us off.

Still laughing, when we got back we headed straight for Luau Larry's.

My buddy had the inclination to flirt with women in bars hard-wired into him. He was a pick-up dog at the cellular level. And I came to realize that he thrived on waitresses in cheap bars asking him if anyone had ever noticed the color of his eyes.

I was sitting in the window box open air out onto Crescent Avenue watching the light change as the sun went down, enjoying the ice-cold beer and the incredible view, and I noticed that he had disappeared. I looked around (without getting up and risking losing the best seat in the bar) and noticed him standing at the bar, turned to his left and hovering over a young cutie in a tiny little bikini. They were locked into a conversation and every few seconds would both erupt in laughter, like they had been best friends all their lives. He was definitely well on his way to his next...um...should I say, entertainment. I was adjusting to it and kind of planning how I might entertain myself for the remainder of the evening when I noticed that standing immediately to his right at the bar was a guy who seemed to have just as much interest in their conversation as they did.

He was staring at my friend like he was imagining the way he would kill him and I could almost see him wondering if there was a huge wall of black urchin he could throw his ass into. And he was built like one of the pillars at Stonehenge…the guy was massive. He had muscle definition where I didn't even know the human body had muscles. He could smother you by simply sticking his thumb in one ear and his middle finger in the other and pressing that immense palm into and squashing your face. And I wondered if he was thinking that would be his favorite choice in this particular situation. Of all the ways I could spend the evening, I decided I didn't want to spend it being interviewed by police standing next to whatever was left of my friend covered by a sheet. I tried to get his attention to direct it to his left where he could see the guy, while there was still time for him to grab his beer and flee.

He eventually did, and while I was thinking *all is lost, this is the point at which bones are going to be broken,* I observed him make some kind of comment to the guy and within seconds all three were laughing. He eventually did grab his beer, wander back over to where I was sitting, and said, "I love it here; the people are great…"

The whole time I lived in the LA area we had many adventures like that, often going back to Catalina Island and snorkeling the waters there. And I made it to the emergency room of the only hospital not once, but three times on three different visits. The third time the nurse asked me, "Are you a local? You look familiar to me." Like the time I was sitting on the table in the emergency room in Boise, Idaho, and when the doc showed up I complimented him on the set-up. He said, "Oh, are you an ER doc too?" To which I answered that I wasn't but I had seen quite a few ERs in my time.

My worst close call, though, besides the rock thing at Two Harbors, was at the kelp forest across Avalon Bay from the casino. It is a really cool place where the kelp grows in about twenty feet of water right up to the surface. You can swim around in it like you're swimming in a forest. There are plenty of Garibaldi swimming around and if there are no seals in the water you can spend the whole day exploring. Seals happen to be the favorite food of some sharks, and people swimming around with them tend to look to a shark like a wounded (or maybe just a really old and awkward) seal…you can guess the rest.

Well, I was snorkeling along having a grand old time, about maybe fifty yards from shore. I tend to spend most of my time below the surface when

I snorkel and only come up for air occasionally. At one point when I did I was clearing my mask and I heard a strange humming behind me. I was far enough from shore that it didn't make sense initially; there was nothing out there but me. When I turned around I was face front with the bow of a huge boat bearing down right on me at about ten feet distance and closing fast. It was too wide and there was no time for me to make it anywhere near either side. I had just enough time, maybe less than a full second, to duck and swim for the bottom as fast as I could to make sure I got away from the prop. I was in a flat panic and as I headed for the depths in my best spastic old seal stroke, I was bracing myself for the searing pain of the props slicing me like a spiral-cut ham. I kid you not, when we were back at Luau Larry's that night we heard some folks sitting near us laughing about some idiot they saw through the glass bottom of their boat that they must have barely missed, swimming for the bottom so fast he almost left his trunks behind. I shouted at them "That was ME!!" Too quick to stop myself from grabbing the "idiot who can't see a fifty-foot glass bottom boat heading his direction'" honors. The boat was called "Phoenix." Prophetic, huh.

But even though I started these stories saying that this was not about me being secretly overly dependent, the friendship was too strong for me. It just wasn't healthy and I could tell that it wasn't good, but I couldn't do anything about it. Every time I knew we were going to do something like hang out at the beach, or go skating on the sidewalk at Manhattan Beach, slam back some beer at our favorite pool hall in Redondo till we were too drunk to walk...I couldn't wait. There was nothing I wanted to do more. But always, always I had this backdrop of fear. It's a weird sort of insecurity because it makes absolutely no sense, so there is nothing you can do about it. Anything you do, anything you say, would probably initiate the very thing you fear the most: having the other person suddenly see you clearly, and want away.

And what makes it even worse, if that's possible, is being stuck in the situation at the same time that you know you are. It's much easier to just find out after the crash, after the abandonment. Sort of like looking back and thinking to yourself *Wow! Why didn't I see THAT coming, tuck my head and run like a Tom Turkey!* But you did see it coming. You saw it when it arrived.

That makes everything a lie, even if you even know that too! Even if you know you are lying to yourself, it doesn't matter. Even if you start the same lecture every time you are alone with yourself in your car, or washing dishes. Over and over again until you just quote the lines rote.

What are you doing, you KNOW this is not going to end well. But he really does like me, he does care for me, I know it...look what he says, look at the things he does. But he doesn't know who you really are. Yes, he does. HOW? How can he? I don't care; I'm just having a good time with a friend, that's all, no big deal. That's NOT all; you're a liar and you're going to get slammed, bashed and broken to bits, and you <u>know</u> it. You know it.

And the next time we get together I shoot pool, drink until I can't walk, and crack jokes laughing the whole time, like it wasn't anything more than that. I'd tell you how it ended but it doesn't matter...and I am not sure if it ever does end, really. Never a different ocean, just a new beach. But that's some other letter.

It wasn't long before I realized that I wasn't going to be a composer for the movies and I left LA and moved to Phoenix.

I think it was about fifteen years before I began to get involved in men's ministry, which is coming up on twenty years ago now. It seems like a lifetime ago, but like they say, it also seems like it was just a few days ago too.

As you know I've since lost my home in Phoenix but sometimes I can imagine feeling like I can just get in my car and go back home, get out my key and let myself in. The house is still there. We could have our group meetings there like we did for those few years, up until two years ago now.

I could walk back into the house and plop myself down on the living room couch and look around at the walls where for seventeen years my life took place. My piano would still be there, just as would my complacent assumptions that I would never be displaced, never have to give anything up, never have to walk away leaving pretty much everything behind.

Those years in Phoenix started out with so much hope, and not a little bit of excitement. The first weekend I moved into the house I was so excited. I had never really ever expected to be able to buy a house of my own, and there I was unpacking my possessions, all fitted to a one-bedroom apartment, not a regular free-standing home.

That first night, which was a Friday night, I unpacked what I needed to unpack and then went and bought groceries. And a big bottle of Carlo Rossi. I proceeded to get snot-slinging drunk and put on an endless stream of music alternating between Don Henley and the Gypsy Kings...and I danced and spun around on the floor all by myself for the sheer joy of having my own home where I could do whatever I wanted to.

I really didn't have any friends in Phoenix yet, had my sister and brother-in-law, but no friends of my own. Still I was jazzed, stoked, rigged and ready to sail.

I moved into my house the very weekend before I started my new job, working for the State as a bean counter, and I was pretty charged up about that too. I wasn't going to get rich, of course, but I was making enough to be paying for my own home. For the first time things seemed to be under control. I had "made it" in a way, even if that way would be different from what it would have to be today to get me to think like that again.

It wouldn't be long before I did have some new friends, and I did still talk to my friend Ted in LA pretty regularly. Within a few months I was in a relationship with a woman too. Well, I was in something with her; whether it could be called a relationship I'm not sure would be fair to say. I met her at work and within a few weeks we were shooting pool and getting drunk together. Within a few hours of that we were back at my place, laughing and getting naked pretty much as fast as we could. I'm trying to think of a polite way to say "having sex." I could say "making love" but love had nothing to do with it. I was drunk enough not to stop it from happening, but not so drunk that it couldn't. Not too long ago on an afternoon here in the Yucatan as I was walking home my mind wandered to the wild days and it occurred to me to wonder if I had ever had sex when I was sober. Ever. The times when it was forced on me or when I was drugged and knocked out and it happened without my permission don't count. I was appalled to realize that I could not remember a single time. What does that say about me?

"I was drunk enough not to stop it from happening, but not so drunk that it couldn't." That statement is describes pretty much every aspect of my life for those years.

The beer-and-pool girl and I toyed with each other for a few months. Once after I had my sprinkler system installed we got naked and played in the sprinklers late at night when the whole neighborhood was asleep. You know my yard, across the street from the golf course on one side and the park on the other. We were lucky no police cars passed by.

Then after a brief time doing that kind of thing, we just stopped and went back to being friends. I'm not sure why.

There were lots of stories I could tell from that time, but they were all the same thing. Getting drunk, getting laid sometimes, waking up hung over and going to work. There was no humor in it, even looking back from out of that fog…I can't even make some up. Reading the stories would be even more tedious that writing them, and for what purpose?

I went back to LA from time to time to get drunk with Ted, but mostly I stayed home and got drunk with my friends in Phoenix, or I just got drunk alone, put on the Kings and spun around on the floor. Once a year I would head back out to LA and we would go back to Catalina Island for a week to do some more snorkeling, hit Luau Larry's, and wake up the next morning starting the day with the ritual of mining the remnants of each other's memory so we could piece together the story of how we made it home the night before. I was always partying, but there was never a party. I was always celebrating but there was never an occasion.

Working for the state was easy, predictable, and fairly innocuous. I was in a high enough position so that I didn't have direct supervision and pretty much everyone who reported to me also drank and, even if they did recognize a real dialysis candidate of a hangover, didn't seem to care. Or maybe they had one themselves…I wouldn't know and certainly couldn't have cared less. Not all of them, sure. But a few key folks. We knew.

Secretly I knew that I was in trouble. I sensed that I was living in a form of insanity and I needed to do something about it. One time I called 9-1-1 at three in the morning because I thought the street lamp in the park across from my house was a spaceship. But the next day I was at work reviewing forecast comparison reports that I designed to monitor the five hundred million dollar budget for which my staff and I were responsible.

When I inherited the position, the instruments that they had for use in financial management and reporting were so crude that a third grader could have made improvements. They did no forecasting at all other than the simplest straight line…you didn't even need a calculator let alone the occasional appearance in an accounting class in your past. I had implemented methods that threw forecasts with accuracy to within half a percent. I was treated like some kind of bean counting Nostradamus. The perfect job for someone who lives life drunk by the time the sun goes down and hung over pretty much other than that.

Fortunately for me there was another state administrator who was kind of the drunken employee lightning rod guy. He was so obvious that he drew all the attention. He worked for the Attorney General's office and would come into a meeting in his best corporate suit smelling so strongly of Listerine and Paco Rabanne that no one even cared that he was drunk, they were just trying to figure out how to get some fresh air. I never saw him when his eyes weren't bloodshot and his nose red, and I saw him a lot. We were in many meetings together.

But my sense of trouble didn't just come from the drinking. It's harder to explain than that, much more obscure. My life was divided into sections. Sections of sections that completely contradicted each other. I was doing well as a financial administrator of a large program, making innovations that were considered noteworthy accomplishments by my superiors and peers even though I thought really nothing of them, all while I was seeing spaceships land outside my living room window late at night. I was having sex with women I didn't care about who didn't care about me, thinking I was a lady's man but deep inside I knew the lie of that. I was a boheme who woke every morning at seven and put on a coat and tie to be at work promptly at eight, doing the things that need to be done to move money and then watch where it goes. And sometimes late at night unable to sleep I'd make it to the piano where I would play a set or two alone in the dark and then just start crying for no reason whatsoever. I had been raped as a child, yet I had no right to the anger. I was a Christian who had lured away a twenty-dollar porn star, a *male*. But not for the kingdom.

My bible sat in my bookshelf the whole time, a different size than any other book and so easy to notice as I passed. But it stayed unopened as the years passed. And they passed unnoticed. They certainly did. They passed with abject disregard.

I can't remember what year it was, but I do remember an incident where I had kind of a private collapse. I got drunk and stayed that way for about three days, which was not uncommon for me, actually. But this was different. The whole time I barricaded myself in my home and unplugged the phone. I made sure it looked like no one was home, all the drapes were drawn and the windows blocked out so you couldn't see in. I think I spent the entire time that I wasn't passed out drunk crying. I couldn't even play the piano. And when I would wake up I would stay awake only long enough to drink myself unconscious again. And I could not stop crying. I know it lasted for at least three days.

When it finally played itself out and I collected myself the first thing I remember doing was soaking in the shower to wash it all off. Standing in the shower I said to myself, "John, you need help."

That same day I looked for and found a therapist named Marilyn. I'm not sure what made me select her, but unlike the therapist I saw for the year I was suicidal when I was a freshman in college, she was a woman. I had never been to a woman therapist before. The guy who kept me from killing myself when I was eighteen was a kind man, an ex-priest. I remember thinking that maybe it would be good for me to talk to a woman this time.

She was expensive, but I learned that she was very highly regarded and generally had a three-month waiting list. When I first talked to her she told me that it would be three months before she would have an opening and could I wait that long. I explained that I didn't think so, and she agreed to work me in. My first session with her I hardly said a word, as I recall. I was so terrified to tell her. But I did. And I cried like I was seven years old the whole time.

Now I was seeing a therapist once a week. I had yet another secret.

I ended up seeing her for probably about four years. She helped me a lot, and I was able to maintain the life I was living, even though the drinking didn't change, nor did really any aspect of the lifestyle I was living. It just kept me together while it was going on. There were many times when I wondered if counseling was doing anything for me, and was it worth what I was spending. But heading to her office on those Thursday afternoons was like poking your head up out of the water to see if there were any boats bearing down on you, and I needed it.

There was one conversation we had, however, and that one hour alone was probably worth the four-year price of admission.

We were talking about my dad and I was pleading with her to help me understand why he treated me so badly when he found out about the molestation. One of the things that folks learn when they go to counseling for any length of time is that even though you hope for the "magic" to happen in each and every session, it doesn't. Sometimes you go weeks or months before you have the moment I learned much later that psychologists refer to as the "moment of discontiguous change" or, in lay terms, the "aha" moment.

Like so many times I was crying and more talking to myself than to her; I was verbally wrestling with how it could have been my fault and if it was my fault what did I do to make it happen? Maybe that was the ticket. Maybe if I understood what I did wrong, then my dad would make sense. He was long dead so I couldn't ask him, but at least I could understand it and maybe accept my mistakes and move on. Maybe if I could do that, the magic would happen and I would be cured. I wasn't even sure I knew what I would be cured of, but I felt sure there was power in the line of reasoning I was pursuing.

What made me think that after then thirty years of struggling for even the slightest insight into the matter with absolutely not a shred of an answer I would suddenly come to a full understanding of it all because a highly educated and kind-hearted patient professional happened to be sitting in front of me, I am sure I do not know.

She sat patiently and let me stumble and fall through my mental wanderings, crying, sometimes raising my voice in defiant anger, and handing me a fresh Kleenex now and again. Eventually I just gave up and held my face in my hands crying, nothing more to say. I couldn't think of anything. Nothing new.

I looked up and she was just watching me. She said, "John, think about it."

Like I hadn't.

It was obvious to me that she had a thought that I didn't have, that she was beginning to believe that no matter how much time she gave me to grope around for it I wasn't going to stumble on it, and that maybe she was going to let me in on it rather than make me wait another thirty years.

"What?"

"It wasn't about you, John."

At that point I was caught between the purely opposite polar thoughts that either she was an absolute clod and I had completely wasted all the years I spent coming to her, and who knows how many thousands of dollars, or this was a moment I needed. This was one of those moments and I needed it so bad my nose itched, my chest felt weak like it was going to cave in. My arms lay limp in my lap, useless.

"You didn't fail him; he failed you."

"What?"

Even I could hear the sheepishness in my voice. Even I could recognize the sound of the seven year old in the word I had spoken, there, hanging in the room between us like it had just stopped time.

"He didn't protect you and every time he saw you he was reminded of it."

Sometimes the simplest turn of a perspective, the tiniest slant on the smallest particle of thought changes absolutely everything in a way that cannot be changed back. A fraction of an idea that slips in so miniscule as to get past the endlessness of years unnoticed, just quietly appears, so small and simple as to seem like it may yet go unnoticed, changes the positions of the very stars and instantly shifts the universe itself into three dimensions where before it had been flat black. You know in that instant that although you do not understand anything about it, you know it is different than you thought and so maybe it *can* be understood, no matter the decades it may take to plumb those depths. What you couldn't before see through, no matter how desperately you tried to focus, became itself the object you were trying to see. And a tiny seed of forgiveness is sown.

It would, however, be many more years before that forgiveness would begin to take root, all the changes in the universe notwithstanding.

I continued to see Marilyn for years after that but I would admit that I don't recall the conversation of any day as significant as that one. But again, nothing really changed. I did have a lot more to think about, and think about it I surely did.

During those years I still thought my dad was Mexican because he was born in Mexico. I wouldn't find out until much later that he was half Cuban with a little Spanish and French thrown in. But he was Latin through and through no matter how you tossed it, and *he* thought he was Mexican so I guess maybe it stops there.

All kinds of things started to occur to me over the years, all springing out of that one conversation in Marilyn's office. Of COURSE he would act toward me the way he did if every time he looked at me he saw his own failure as a father. Of course that explains it. I was too young for him to reconcile these things, because I did not understand any of them. So on top of facing the fact that I was "damaged goods" he had to deal with the fact that there was no way to intellectually work through the situation with me...and he was nothing if he was not an intellectual man.

Not only was there never going to be a day when I would be the innocent boy full of the beginnings of a real man, a boy destined for the soccer field and episodes of shouting hugs hoisted up in the moments after victory, with him nudging the guy next to him saying "that's my boy" such as Hollywood and Little League have made permanent in the theater of American masculinity. Worse. Signs of femininity were beginning to show up.

His fear of and resistance to all that seemed to be unfolding in his young son became focused on his disdain for me playing the piano just as it had long been obvious in the way he shamed pretty much everything about me. What he didn't know, even I didn't know but I do now, is that the piano was a way that I could get away from him and still be calling him back. It was a way that I could run away and get out of his sight – as he so often told me to do – and yet maybe he would hear the music anyway. Maybe he would hear the story in it and come back.

I began to understand that not only was the attack on me a blow to my masculinity because it was sexual, it was a blow to *his* masculinity because he did nothing to protect his son. A man was nothing to him if he could not provide for and protect his family. My damage was perpetrated upon an innocent; his was not.

The attitude that a man is defined by and that his very masculinity is inseparable from his ability to provide for and protect his family is one of the things I most admired about him. Still do. So in a bizarre sort of way, as I look back on the whole thing, it occurs to me that we did in fact both have things taken from us...we both were robbed of something no police force, judge or jury could restore to us. But not in separate crimes. Although we spun off in completely separate directions just like billiard balls hit simultaneously by a cue ball with a rogue spin, it was the exact same point of contact that sent us spinning. He was a victim too. We were both victims of the same crime.

You might think that all this would result in me thinking *Oh, now I get it*, and I would be able to do the proverbial – move on. But it did not happen that way. My anger and self-hatred, the hatred I had learned from my own father, did not evaporate out of the purity of some obscure epiphany. It grew.

My drinking got even worse.

But something much more insidious happened, something much, much more dangerous. Justification.

At this point I have asked myself if I should tell you some of the stories about those times that reveal to you how depraved I became in the years just after that. But I think you get the message, and it would be easier to tell you what I didn't do. I never molested anyone, let alone a child. I am quite sure I would kill myself if I ever even sensed a desire to do that. I am absolutely sure that I would even enjoy pulling the trigger in that event. And I never committed any crime that I am aware of, other than hiring prostitutes. And I did hire prostitutes.

You know how they say that some men have sex (or try to) with a lot of women just to prove to themselves that they are "real" men? Well, it's true. Or at least, it has been for me.

And the encounters with prostitutes increased in frequency just as the drinking hit a base level where I was as drunk as I could possibly be for the greatest percentage of time possible without getting fired from my job. I was addicted to everything that didn't involve a needle. I did stay away from cocaine, but only because I couldn't afford it.

My sexuality was under the highest-powered microscope that you can possibly imagine. I sought and had sex for a mix of reasons; I wanted to feel the sense that I am okay after all, and to satisfy desires that I could not control. And never, not once, did I ever have sex sober. All the desires I had welled up in me like a stereo turned up as loud as it can possibly go, but the music was all crashing and discordant…cacophony. White noise.

There were women in my life that were not prostitutes but in every single case except for one (that I'll tell you about in a minute) they pursued me; I did not pursue them. But the more sex I had with women the stronger my desires became for men. It was really strange. It was like pulling some massive thorn out of your thigh…the more you pulled it out the more it hurt. The dichotomy was maddening, and I mean "mad" as in "insane," not "angry."

When some woman I knew made advances toward me I felt almost obligated to consent, otherwise she might suspect I was gay or something. *I* might have to conclude that I was gay or something. How crazy is that!? None of them were ever asking me to prove anything to them; they just wanted to have some fun. And according to the definitions in our culture I WAS gay. You can have sex with a thousand women, but one homosexual encounter and you are gay, brother. Have sex with a thousand men and have one instance with a woman and you're just deluding yourself.

I was deceiving everybody (or I thought I was), not the least of which or the least pathetic of whom was myself. And in the darkness and refuge of solitude I drank myself into oblivion to get them all away from me. To get it all away from me.

That's all I'm going to say about my dog days back then, so if you have any questions about it you are just going to have to wonder because I'm not saying anything more.

It went on for a number of years, though. Like I said earlier, I didn't just hit bottom and turn around; I stayed there.

At a point though, something just quietly wore out inside of me. It was 2004. It was different than when I was in the shower and realized that I had to get help. It was way beyond that. It was sort of like not even questioning whether you needed help because you had known *that* for years. You *were* getting help.

It was not like something terrible was happening and you finally noticed so you were alarmed and took action while there was still time. Not like that. It was like you were flat on your face beaten to a pulp and as you tried to lift yourself up you realized that something was already dead. It was already too late.

When I carried what was left of me back to God I did not do so as a repentant saint or even as a prodigal son because I knew about him and I was not that worthy. I certainly had no expectations of a warm reception. I took myself back as a man might take out the garbage and leave it on the curb. If He threw open His arms and called for rings and robes and a fatted calf, I didn't see or hear it. My back was still turned as I moved to walk away.

But I chose to hope.

And that is what started a way back for me; it was the very beginnings. Sitting here now seven years later I can tell you that I haven't yet had the party, and most of the things that have happened in the last seven years are not what I would have predicted. Nothing that seemed like it would change things in a flash – make things all better in the moment they happened – did that. There have been no flashes, no rings and robes. He has not allowed me to walk away from that curb, either. He turned me around so that I could see Him. He did not send me on my way. He grabbed and held me like I was something He wanted and that He would never let anything or anyone take from Him again. And He holds me still.

I decided to go to the Internet and start a search for some kind of group or some kind of chat room where Christians might be. I'm not sure what I was expecting to find, or what I would do when I found it, but it didn't seem to matter. I just didn't have anywhere else that occurred to me to go.

I did find a support group, a chat room. I think it was related to the subject of unwanted same sex attraction. Back at that time I was so terrified that anyone would find out that even being in an Internet chat room with total strangers who might just as well have been in Juneau, Alaska as in my home- town scared me. I have almost always lived alone, and yet I found myself looking over my shoulder as if someone might be outside passing by and glance in the window and be able to read the headers on the chat room web site.

There was a movie years ago about a world where all books were banned and anyone caught reading them could be severely punished (maybe even killed I think). Anyways, there was a guy who still read books secretly, and he was eventually taken to some woods by an underground colleague who he discovered also read books, and there he saw people walking around reading aloud softly to themselves as they were memorizing the book in their hand. The feeling was eerie; it was his moment of discovery that he was not alone.

My Internet search was something like that.

There were men who felt exactly the way I did. There were people who struggled exactly like I did, who were terrified exactly like I was, and who just like me, assumed they were alone.

I learned about a group called "Courage" which is sponsored by the Catholic church. They're men and women who experience same sex attraction but do not want to live life in that way. They have turned from what folks call their "orientation" because of religious conviction. I was still so new to all of this that I didn't even question this concept of "orientation" like I do now. I was fascinated that anyone could have the courage to be part of Courage. That any man could actually face a woman with this issue openly and honestly, at all…even if it was a religious group, and even if the women were feeling exactly the same way! It just didn't seem possible to me. How did they discover each other? Where do they meet so that no one else discovers them? How could they face it?

I found out that there was even a group in Phoenix, where I lived. And I resolved to attend one of their meetings, even though I am not Catholic, or not anymore anyway.

On the night I went to the first meeting as I sat in my car in the parking lot I was almost freaking out at the possibility that someone I knew might drive by, see my car in the parking lot of a Catholic church during hours when there was no mass, *guess* that there was a group of men and women getting together to support each other because of the same sex attraction that they rejected, and conclude that I was part of it. I could not bring myself to get out of the car and walk the thirty feet to the door. I would have to tell the receptionist that I was there for the Courage meeting, which would mean that she would know. It all made me physically sick to my stomach.

But it occurred to me, *that must be why they call the group "Courage," John.* Once inside with the others in the group I wrestled with this idea inside my head...*you may be like this, but I'm really not. I have sex with women.* I was so totally messed up that my own hypocrisy was lost caught up in it. But they were kind, and patient, and they accepted me. I left that meeting that night loving them and they didn't even know it. And my hope grew, even though I had no idea what to hope for.

Now bear in mind the drinking was not going to stop for another five years. These events were the very smallest beginnings.

While in the chat room I learned about a conference that was going to be held in Wilmington, Delaware. The subject of the conference was deliverance. It was described as a three-day series of meetings in which national and international speakers would be leading discussions on the subject of spiritual healing and deliverance from bondage. I knew nothing about this, but I was intrigued and researched the conference further. If anyone needed being delivered from stuff, I did. At that time I had left the state government, was working as a consultant, and I made a lot of money. So flying off to Delaware for a three-day conference was nothing. But I dared not tell anyone why I was going or what it was really about.

When I first arrived in Wilmington I left the hotel, drove my rental to where the conference was so I would know where to go the next morning, and then I came back, parked, and just headed out for a walk. I walked way up the street in the old part of downtown Wilmington and allowed myself to be in the pensive mood I was definitely in. I did not know what to expect. But I had really high hopes that the contents of the weekend would change my life. It really is sad to think about how much of my life I have spent trying to change it, or hoping someone or something else would.

I grabbed a sandwich and headed back to my room. That night I prayed and made a conscious effort to mean it when I said aloud that from that moment forward I was rededicating my life to Christ, come what may.

There were two men I heard speak at the conference who made a huge impact on me (and possibly many others in the room). They were David Kyle Foster and Peter Horrobin.

David Kyle Foster spoke about his life and his incredible struggle as a child movie star, a man given over to his own sin, and then his miraculous redemption and ministry. I was in awe. I had never encountered a person with such courage alive and in front of me. When he spoke I sensed the Holy Spirit in a way I had never really seen it, visible, in another person. Just from what little I know about him I know he would deflect such compliments and redirect attention to that Spirit, but in the moments I heard him speak it was truly amazing to me. And humbling. And encouraging.

I purchased one of his books and gathered the courage to approach him on the break to sign it for me. I had so much I wanted to ask him but I did not know where to begin. As I sat there while he was signing the book I noticed that others were waiting for a signature too, and even if I could think of what to say, there really wasn't any time to say it. I was another of the many who wanted to reach out to him or to have a conversation with him no matter how brief. But one of too many, one I was sure he would never remember anyway.

Peter Horrobin spoke on the subject of deliverance. Not the kind of Hollywood exorcism fantasy you sometimes think when you hear the term, but a levelheaded scripture-based reality. And he clearly knew what he was talking about. He discussed it the way a heart surgeon would discuss cholesterol, and quietly changed my mind about such things. He described a process of deliverance from torment and told us all about the ministry he founded, Ellel Ministries, and I was resolute to find out how I could find out more and maybe even get involved. That first full day of the conference I spoke to no one, I did not stay for the social thing that night, I headed right back to my hotel room only having exchanged the few words with Foster to get his signature.

That night I went for the same walk and my thoughts were racing. I was talking to myself so fast I couldn't stay on subject. One thought clung to the fore just long enough to be identified before another shoved it out of place. And I felt almost giddy. I ended up taking sleeping pills that night just to be able to get some sleep. I had names; I had the identities of organizations I could contact. I had things to do.

But the most amazing thing in the entire conference happened the next and last day.

At the very end of the conference we were all singing some worship music as the conference came to a close. There were about two hundred people in the small auditorium, maybe more. Men and women, young and some older. Who could imagine what torments brought *them* to this conference? But I knew with absolute certainty that no one was aware of mine. Because I had not had a single conversation with a single person there, not at any point of the conference. Apart from my brief exchange to get the signature, I made sure it was almost as if I wasn't even there. I was the American Jew who could speak only cursory German at the Nazi rally.

They announced that there was a dinner thing that night and everyone was invited. They wanted to give everyone a chance to get to know each other and compare notes on their respective experiences with the conference. While they were going through those announcements I planned my escape. I just wanted to take my list of names and the ideas I had harvested and quietly disappear with my loot.

As I headed up the side aisle – this was before we were actually dismissed – I climbed the steps until I got to this guy standing in the middle of the aisle with his hand held out to shake mine, blocking me. No one else had yet left his or her seats.

"Hi, I'm Jack". *Great,* I thought. *Always just one freaken' minute too late.*

"Did you enjoy the conference? I'm here because I really struggle with same sex attraction." I had never heard that term before. I looked at him with an expression that must have revealed my surprise. *Why the hell did you step out into the aisle and block me, Mr. Same Sex Attraction Jack, and how the hell did you know?*

"John, nice to meet you."

In the conversation that ensued with him, as everyone was chatting and filing out, I actually told him that I was there primarily for a drinking problem I had been struggling with for years, oh, and that – the same sex attraction – that too. I have no idea why I told him.

He seemed to burst forth with a wealth of ideas, most of them I cannot even remember, but he gave me an Internet link to a support group for men in the "ex-gay" community. I didn't know there was such a thing. An "ex-gay" community. Man was I wrong.

I never sought out such a thing, really. Even when I figured it was something I needed to look into, somewhere deep inside of me it didn't seem like I fit. But I went into it anyway. That led me to the "Journey" weekend, and eventually to New Warriors, and to the Re-trek weekend.

By the time Jacob Group (a men's accountability group that I helped form started meeting at my house, I was about two years into the whole restorative therapy scene. I had even switched therapists from George to Floyd. I don't think I told you about George.

I started going to George because I saw an ad for his counseling practice in a smut magazine. He listed himself as having a Master's Degree in Divinity, and this was after I had made the decision to return to my faith. So it seemed like a good fit.

Two years later he's still trying to convince me that my drinking is related to my refusal to accept that I am gay, and if I just come out of the closet, trumpets blaring, flags waving and all, and embrace the lifestyle, my problems would be over. We had that particular session repeatedly, but I refused to do it. I didn't want to do it.

I tried to explain to him that I did not want to embrace anything of the sort. I even told him that many years earlier my very first visit to a psychiatrist was because I was seriously thinking of killing myself just about every waking minute of the day. He had told me that my depression resulted from the fact that my sexuality was "diffused." And if I were to un-diffuse my sexuality, my suicidal ideation would go away. Everything would be fine. Now George was telling me that if I just decided to be gay, everything would be fine. Why, I thought, does un-diffused have to equal gay when I have been with women my whole adult life? Why can't I just decide to be straight, consider myself un-diffused and stop spending so much money on therapists and Carlo Rossi?

And to make matters pretty much worse, I had by then finished my own Masters Degree in Counseling and was, in fact, busy as a volunteer trauma therapist.

During my sessions with George I used to glance at the photo he had on his bookshelf of a young man he had identified as his son. It always made me wonder why he would be so adamant about trying to convince me to accept myself (when in fact he was really only trying to get me to accept one small aspect of myself to the exclusion of all others) when he seemed like a family man to me. And he also told me that he was a minister as well as a therapist. After all, he had a Masters in Divinity.

I have spent many hours over a very long period of time sorting out where I stand on the theology of homosexual sex. But you don't trot off to a therapist to get relief from things simply because they chafe against your theological constructs. You go to get relief from torment.

Still, he was a minister and all. His was not the clinical approach I would have expected nor would have divined from the ad.

It turns out that even though he did indeed have a son, he also had another man who was now his significant other, life partner, husband, and soul mate for all eternity and stuff. I know, don't hate the player; hate the game. I couldn't help but feel like I had been deceived.

I finally, after over two years, realized I had been wasting my time and money and confronted him. I politely told him that I didn't have to pay a therapist to know that pursuing sex with other men openly was available as an option. Particularly a therapist that didn't seem to hear me when I repeatedly explained that I didn't want that option. Give me what's behind some *other* door, please. Whatever else he wasn't hearing I'm sure I didn't know. I discontinued the sessions. Some three months later I received a form letter that I assume he sent out to all his clients informing us that he had had a "change in life" opportunity and was moving to Great Britain. I found out from another guy from one of his groups that it turns out that his soul mate was apparently mating with more than one.

I'm not going to talk much about the "Journey" weekend because I know you went on one yourself. You and I have also both been on a "New Warriors" weekend, and as a chance to bond with a bunch of other guys without having any idea what their issues are, it is a pretty cool experience. And you and the other guys in our group know how much the Re-trek weekend helped me. I could write volumes on that experience and only wish that every man who has things to confront could attend one. Each one of them gave me something, Re-trek more than the others, but from "Journey" I did get one good thing – I met a terrific new therapist. And started my sixth formal client/therapist relationship.

I admired and genuinely liked him, and for the two years I saw him I never felt like a single moment was ever wasted. He was as kind and gentle a therapist as you would ever hope to meet. And we all held him up as proof that you can get married and have kids even if you have this other thing going on in your head. He introduced me to the writing of Elizabeth Moberly and the rest, whose books I carefully hid in a drawer in my study often reassuring myself that no one would ever stumble across them unless I was dead, they were packing away my stuff, and it wouldn't matter anyway.

It was during that time that I started a relationship with M. It was when I was seeing the new therapist that I really fell for her, and actually believed it might be possible for me to emerge out of it all into a marriage even like some guys I knew had, even though I was already too old for kids.

Our first date we went to dinner and then to shoot pool.

M is a beautiful woman by any measure, and she has a sexiness that did not seem to be painted the same color as her personality. It was almost like walking up to a Georgian mansion and stepping inside to find the entire thing furnished and decorated in 1960's James Bond. Not at all displeasing but intriguing in its discontiguous sort of way. Or like biting into a chocolate and discovering raspberry rum.

I was most definitely attracted to her, and she let me know she was interested in that too. So early on we talked about sex. I explained to her that I was the leader of our group and that the guys in the group were all pursuing a life of sexual purity, and so I was not free to do otherwise. So we had to remain platonic until we got married. Her reaction was really very simple.

"That's crazy."

Which led me to my explanation that I was really hoping to get married anyway and not looking for a relationship just for casual sex. She wasn't looking for meaningless sex either, but neither was she protecting any virginity, holding herself back for what would otherwise be spouse number three. And she knew damn well neither was I. She took it all very gracefully, as a challenge. There's one story I just can't pass up.

I made what I consider in retrospect the mistake of telling my brother-in-law and very close friend Greg that while, yes, M and I were dating, we had decided not to have sex unless and until we get married. His reaction was really very simple. "That's crazy." On a number of occasions he tried to explain to me that neither of us were children anymore, that we were both adults, and that if we had feelings for each other and had made a commitment to each other what could possibly be wrong with consummating our affection? He didn't understand it any better than she did. But she stayed with me, and we handled the frustrations enjoying each other's company just the same. But we often had evenings at my house where we "watched TV." Well, the TV was on anyway. We didn't have sex in the biblical sense, more like the teenage hope-mom-and-dad-don't-get-home-early kind of way. It was almost ridiculous what I was putting her through.

At around that time I was finishing up writing that children's story (Kitninny Catness - New Dog in the Neighborhood), and there were a few people who had been waiting for the story to be finished and published. My youngest sister Connie asked me where the story was every time she saw me.

It was my fiftieth birthday and my youngest sister had come to town to celebrate with me. M and I went over to my other sister's house (her husband being the brother-in-law I had talked to about M) for dinner and we spent the evening just talking, telling stories, and laughing. As we were just about to leave I was standing in the open car door, M was to my left, my other sister next to her, then the youngest, and finally Greg to her left. We were in a big circle, and everybody had already hugged goodbye, all that was left was to get in the car and drive off.

The youngest leans forward and says to me, "Um…gettin' any?"

I was mortified. I'm sure all the color immediately ran out of my face, and I turned to Greg restraining myself from saying "you son of a b#$@." I could not believe he would have shared such intimate information without my permission just as I was astonished that my sister would blurt something out like that, just like that, as we were getting ready to leave. I could not believe it! Greg stared back at me. He must have thought that what he saw in my face was a question, like I hadn't heard her and was wondering what she said. When it was really a question like *what the hell kind of an a-hole are you?* In a matter-of-fact tone he simply repeated, "Gettin' any." And even I could hear his thoughts…*told you it was crazy.* My sister broke down laughing.

I gasped and looked back at her, assuming she knew the whole story, and said, "She's standing right HERE!" and opened the palm of my lowered hand toward M, in the gesture of *how could you BE so rude?*

My sister's legs seemed to give out from under her she was laughing so hard, and she sat back on the banco trying to catch her breath, waving her hand as though something was wrong, it was too funny, and she couldn't get her breath enough to talk. Finally she slowly spoke the word: "K I T ninny. Where. Is. The. Book?"

And while we all started laughing my other sister calmly said almost more to herself than to the rest of us, "I *thought* that was rather inappropriate."

In the car I asked M what she thought during the whole exchange, certain that she must have been tremendously offended. She said, "Well, I knew you all were close, but I didn't think you discussed *everything* with each other."

More and more she became the subject of conversations with the therapist. And more and more I started to think about her all of the time. But you know, Pretty much every time I dropped her off at her house after we had spent an evening together, the first stop I made on my way home was to the store to buy two bottles of Chardonnay. I could down the first one inside of five minutes, just to get the buzz started, and then relax pouring myself glasses from the other until I passed out. I was in love.

The friends we had in common thought I was crazy. They all thought it would never work.

My work as a consultant had me on the road constantly and I was never home during the week. At that time I was working simultaneously in Florida, Minnesota, Delaware and an occasional trip to Los Angeles. In the type of consulting that I did all those years it was reasonable to have two projects going at the same time, but never a good idea to take on more than two. I was leading five. I was making more money that I ever imagined I would ever make, and that's when I bought my place in Mexico. I still want to get you down here one of these days for a visit, you know.

So the place was under construction in the Yucatan, I was working like a man possessed spending more time in airports than my own living room, seeing a therapist to make me a good prospect for marriage to a girl who didn't want to get married, leading a men's group for support in the pursuit of sexual purity, and getting drunk every free moment I had. And some moments that weren't so free.

I was down in the Yucatan by myself, the place had been finished but had been flooded by some guests that had stayed there and I needed to refurnish it when the call came.

It was a Saturday afternoon.

Like our father before him, my little brother had suffered a heart attack and had died in the seat of his car on the way to the hospital. I had friends arriving the very next day from Minnesota who were going to be there for the week with me, and I had to go back to Austin to be with my family. I couldn't even move. I made it into town to make the phone call to my mom.

My place did not have a phone at that time so I had to go into town to call the US. At that time my favorite place to do that was a little touristy convenience store right on Fifth Avenue. Five dollars, as long as you want anywhere in the US. As I stood there I explained that I couldn't be in Austin until probably Tuesday because I had to get my friends off the plane and explain everything, then catch a flight back to Phoenix, then to Austin.

Tourists were milling around me eyeing the trinkets that hung from the trinket stands and talking about which restaurant they might like tonight. They laughed the laughter of folks who had been there more than three days or so, with just enough of the red blush still fresh from the sun, and the pace already showing slowed in their banter. They were beach town happy as a visitor who measures every moment until they relax and let go, content, loving life and loving the ambiance of everything, while I stood there like disease. Shading my conversation from them and pleading with my mom to know something. What, I couldn't find to tell her. I just couldn't find the words.

She just sounded defeated, ravaged. I walked home, got in the shower and wept bitterly for my brother.

That was the weekend of February 17, 2007. It was when the fog truly began to get thick…and much of the Spring and Summer I don't even recall. I was seeing M a lot, seeing Floyd whenever I could schedule a session, always on a plane or standing in front of people giving presentations and hoping they didn't notice how hung over I was, and struggling against a loosening grip on other key friendships. In fact, my grip on everything was weakening rapidly, but not like you would think of weakening the way you would weaken when you get really tired. More like the way your grip becomes weak when your hands freeze and you cannot control your fingers. You can't move them; you can't feel them. And all you know is that you're scared because if whatever is in your hand slips there will be nothing stopping it from crashing into a million pieces.

In July I was at our office and I noticed as I was walking back from the car I felt sick to my stomach. I hadn't eaten anything so it didn't make sense. I also noticed a pain in my shoulder, and in my jaw. I asked my brother-in-law (a physician) how you knew *exactly* if you were having a heart attack. He refused to discuss it with me and ordered me to the fourth floor of the hospital next to our offices, which is the cardiology unit. Two days later (Saturday) I am the only person lying on the only bed in a cavernous cath lab that my cardiologist ordered the hospital to open, convinced that I would not live to see Monday otherwise.

While I was convalescing in the hospital, three stents in my chest, M told me she couldn't "do this anymore" and it would be better for us to just be friends. I think I asked her if she could have waited until they removed the IV's before she broke the news, but I don't really remember what I said. That is what I was thinking anyway.

Interestingly, it was only a few weeks after I got out of the hospital that I did the New Warriors weekend, still on powerful blood thinners. One of the guys on the weekend noticing the medical alert bracelet told me he was a medic and asked, "Are you CRAZY?!?" He told me that the evening's events the night before (another closely guarded secret about that weekend) could have given me a right ripe bump on the head, and I just might not have woken up that morning. It seemed funny to me.

I made copious notes from that weekend and I thought I had it all figured out. So I went back to M, gradually at first, to win her back. I think I will never know if she was willing to try again with me because she actually did love me, or just because she is such a graceful woman and grace always compels kindness.

One night she was at my house and I played the piano for her. She sat behind me giving me plenty of room on the bench. When I finished the set I turned to look at her and noticed that she was crying softly. I asked her why she was crying and she said, "I don't think any woman can hold the emotions in you."

By then I knew my feelings for her were different than any I had ever felt for any woman before. She often said things I didn't understand. She understood things I didn't think. She bested me when we sparred and her wit was a pure delight to me, even though I was so often the object of her humor. And I loved to just watch her. Even just watching her walk. She would communicate volumes to me by just touching me in passing; here a hand on my shoulder as we looked in a store window, there a glancing rub across the small of my back because she knew I suffer back pain from time to time and she always seemed to know when. I'm pretty sure she never knew how deep my feeling were going and that hers were not headed the same way.

I kept so much from her, but somewhere suspected that it was not she who was deceived by me. I was deceiving myself.

One day she talked to me about going to Mexico, not the Yucatan, but a Pacific coast town where she and her deceased husband had owned property. She felt that she needed to resolve the status of the property since he had died in an accident and it was left to her, but she had never received title or been asked to pay taxes or anything. She does not speak Spanish and asked if I would go along to translate for her, and we could make a little vacation out of it. I happily agreed.

Because of our diligence to my self-imposed mandate, we reserved two rooms at a quaint little hotel on the beach. But when we checked in the lady indicated that we had two rooms reserved and seeing as there were only two of us, asked if we wanted to keep both rooms? I said, "No, one will be fine" before I even had time to give it a thought. We didn't make it fifteen seconds inside the hotel room door.

I don't know what M would think if she knew I was writing this, so I don't plan to tell you anything in the way of details about that day, but let me say that if I were to do so every word would be loving and gentle.

The next morning we woke to an absolutely beautiful day and went down to have breakfast on the deck overlooking the water. While we were at breakfast we began to speculate together what we would do if we were to get married. Would we live in her house or mine? Would we sell her place in

Mexico, or mine, or keep them both? And what would our friends say? We had great fun speculating about *that* one because we both knew that they thought we were as mismatched as you could possibly get. We knew without them saying anything that they suspected that our romance would more likely end in murder than marriage. And we laughed about it.

We planned the day and while we were up at a point – a high rock sort of thing – where we could look out over the ocean I had a sick feeling in my stomach because I knew I had to tell her. I could not let her love me anymore, or for a single moment longer, without her knowing. I asked her if we could go for a walk on the beach, that there was something I had to tell her about.

For the whole drive to the beach I felt like I was going to throw up I was so scared, but I couldn't back out. My thoughts were racing and all the demons inside me were casting their suggestions into the ring for what I would say, just as were the angels, but who could tell them apart? I was stuck dreading her rejection, certain of it, but loving her too much to hide from her.

I started by saying that I was absolutely terrified. She held my hand and asked me what it was that could be so bad? I began slowly, but told her about the sexual abuse, and the same sex attraction. I explained that that was at the heart of my ministry with men – helping other guys get past it without giving into it – and that I loved her. I told her that I didn't expect that she would want anything more to do with me, but that I respected her too much to keep her from making that decision, no matter how badly that decision might hurt me. Her answer left me stunned.

I've heard a lot of guys in these groups wrestle with the question of whether or not you tell a girl about it. "That's the past and what's in the past doesn't matter; it's over and you aren't obligated to talk about it," they often say. I could not disagree more strongly.

The truth is that it is not in the past. Even if you have made a solid decision never to ever engage in anything like that any more if you ever did, even if you never did, and even if you don't ever even have the most fleeting thoughts about it, the fact that you did think about it has everything to do with you – now. That very conviction is part of who you are today, brother, even if those actions are not. Keeping the truth a secret does not make it not exist. The truth exerts its own existence, whether it is known to others or not, and it will not be denied.

Ask yourself, *Were the tables turned and she struggled with same sex attraction, would I want to know? Should I know?* And I think you would realize that if she told you, then it meant that she loved you enough to choose you over those desires. And how could you then not love her even more? She would only tell you for one of two reasons: she wants you in on the struggle because the truth of it is that it is not her struggle alone, it's yours too. It's both of yours. And the second reason she would be telling you something like that is because she is NOT choosing you any longer but wants out. And if that is the case, she is already out. She is already gone.

And the exact same conditions apply when you ask yourself if you should tell her. I submit, and I feel very strongly about this, that if you don't you are lying to her. You are deceiving the very person you profess to love more than anyone else in the world. Your cowardice is stronger than your love.

But know something. If you tell her, she may reject you and leave you. I know more than a few who have. I mourn each time I know it to have happened in the past. I know of one guy who had never so much as touched another man and he was doing everything he could to manage his attractions toward men, and they were very strong. When he felt he had to tell his wife because hers was the support he needed more than anyone else's in the world, he loved her, and felt that she was owed the truth, she took their two toddler boys and left. Who failed whom? She failed those boys. He was destroyed, but his devastation is academic, in the end. Tragic, but of little consequence.

It is of little consequence because his fear of her rejection and his pain when it happened is not what matters. What matters is that he showed himself a man. He stood up to his fears and gave her the honesty that his love compelled him to give even knowing that it may well cost him everything. And it did. Her reaction did not diminish his choice, and never will.

Courage is not the absence of fear; it is the willingness to act in spite of it. When those boys are men themselves and they have the chance to hear from him what happened, and his motives, his fears, and his loss, they will know the integrity he exhibited because every boy searches for it in their father. And knows it when they see it. And the details will be lost. Never again will they be able to themselves cower, at least not without a moment's pause. And that is what all fathers strive to bequeath to their sons, but few ever really can; all sons long to get from their fathers, and too few ever do.

When the day comes for you to be in this situation, be mindful, be clear headed. Above all make sure you are truthful with yourself, particularly about your motives. Do not do it instead of telling her you want out (but you want her to swing the ax). That is just another form of cowardice. Do it for no other reason than love for her that respects the truth. And know that you may well lose everything. But show yourself the man anyway…or if you ask me, you already have.

Okay, I'll stop the rant.

She said simply, "It couldn't matter less."

But my greatest mistake with her was yet to be made.

When we got back to the hotel room we decided to watch the sunset, and I opened a bottle of wine. To make a long ugly story short, I treated her like a man with something to prove that night, something that didn't even involve her. Rather than celebrate with her a new, deeper, even more loving intimacy, I trashed the whole situation, thrashing about like a sixteen year old in his first encounter, like all the stuff I told her wasn't true, or wasn't going to make a difference. It was beyond stupidity; it was beneath selfishness. And it was in flat disregard for her kindness to me. The moon was full.

That was the end of our romance, and the end of any possibility that we would ever end up together. It wasn't my past that ruined it; I did it all by myself.

As much as I slipped into even deeper depression I had no one else to blame, and I never lost sense of that. I grieved painfully for a solid three months but I could not openly talk about it. It was too fraught with secrets, too pregnant with shame. I scheduled a time to talk with my pastor Forrest, and like he always did, he coached me and lovingly listened to me. He was my coach, my older brother in Christ, my role model, and my very close friend all rolled into one.

Months later, even after I stopped being so depressed and even stopped thinking about M every day, I noticed that I could not function because I kept getting angry. Anything, the slightest remark, the most innocent turn of events would set me off. Since I had stopped thinking about M all the time like I did the first three months after the break-up, I was clueless about what was going on. I suspected that all the group stuff, all the weekends, all the sessions with my therapist were bringing the anger of the decades to the surface. I started believing that it was a *righteous* anger.

I remember that while driving around town I would catch myself thinking about it and saying to myself, "*You're an angry man, John.*" And when I tried to figure out what I was so angry about I justified myself by thinking about all that had happened to me and how I had a right to anger, even if it wasn't because of anything happening now. It was a bodacious arrogance, with nothing righteous about it.

In the meeting with Forrest after patiently listening to me rattle on about how angry I was and how I couldn't figure out why, and I was losing control so much that it could start having a pretty serious effect on me…he simply sat there quietly listening. When I was finished he calmly said, "Tell me about the weekend in Mexico with M."

"That was MONTHS ago. We're done. You know that. Why are you asking about that?" *You idiot.*

He told me to tell him everything. I said "Everything?" and he said, "Yes." "Even all the details?" "Yes, all the details." I couldn't believe that he wanted to hear details about such private things, but I knew that he wasn't voyeuristic or anything and could only want to hear them because he knew I needed to think them through. He didn't need to know them but I needed to speak them.

In that hour I realized what I had done when we got back to the hotel. I saw my selfishness and abject stupidity and realized that I owed M one hell of an apology. I was angry at myself. And the identity of the idiot in the room became perfectly obvious. Forrest had dealt with me as a loving older brother, but in a way that I can only describe as masterful. I am one of the many men he has blessed that way. I am one of the many men who will go to my grave thanking God for the blessing he has been.

As quickly as I could, I wrote M an email spelling it all out and asking for her forgiveness. I told her I did not expect anything from her, but only needed her to know that I realized my mistake, and how badly I acted, how undeserved it all was. Ever the better person she accepted my apology but I knew she had already left both behind, the good and the bad.

Things continued their downhill slide, and I was coursing toward a series of catastrophic blows that would leave everything shattered. I knew it, too. But I couldn't stop it. I could not figure out how to stop it.

I did contact Ellel Ministries (the organization I learned about from the Wilmington conference where I heard Peter Horrobin speak). I made arrangements with them to attend a training on addictions and deliverance ministry in that area. While at that training I learned that I could apply for a weeklong deliverance retreat for people who are seeking deliverance in their own lives. The waiting list to be able to attend one was as much as a year or more, but I signed up anyway.

Much to my surprise an opening came up within a month and I grabbed it and headed out to Florida to be delivered.

The first thing they told us at the meeting was to not put demands on God or the Holy Spirit with specific expectations about what may or may not be healed. There were six of us there, and we each most surely came with hopes about a specific healing we needed, or hoped for. I knew exactly what I wanted healed. Exactly.

I told my prayer group everything and they prayed over me day after day. I fell in love with them and with their organization. I felt a peace I had never felt at any point in my life when I was there. I knew they were godly. I knew it so well that it didn't matter that I might not get the healing I came for, that I probably never would. And that week I didn't.

But the last day the entire group all got together to pray together and to talk about our experience during the week. None of the six of us knew any of the details about each other's weeks or the meetings we had had. There were twice as many staffers as folks seeking healing so we numbered over twenty people in the meeting.

As I sat there and listened to each person pour out their suffering and their hopes and the amazing grace they had experienced…as I witnessed the love the staff had for people they didn't even know, there was only one thought that burned in my head: *I have to be part of this. I have to spend the rest of my life loving people like this or how could it possibly matter?*

God didn't heal what I went there to have healed. He gave me something I didn't know enough to ask for.

I got back to Phoenix and struggled to keep my business alive. As you know, my arthritis was getting worse by then. Or my tendinitis, or whatever it was. Greg always told me it was all psychosomatic or stress related. Whatever it was it left me permanently on a cane and always in pain. I always suspected that it was alcohol related because I was drinking enough to kill a person pretty much every night by then.

I'm going to speed up a little and just get these last two stories on the page so I can wrap this up.

By then I knew that the business was failing and it wouldn't be long before it was over and I would have to let my employees go. I had become seriously attached to one of them, a young man who was like a son to me, and I dreaded the idea of failing him. All he wanted was to get married and have a family and he needed a good career to do that, and I wanted to be the person who would make that happen. But I knew that I wouldn't be, that he would move on to better things and to whomever could make it happen, leaving me behind, and I could not stop that either.

I could see that eventually I would end up at my home in the Yucatan, mostly because I wanted to end up there. I wanted to escape to the beach and never come back.

I researched churches in Playa del Carmen and found one called House of Hope. I contacted the pastor and made arrangements to meet him when I visited next time. Which was in April, with three of my friends.

When I met Ron and his wife for lunch I approached the couple hobbling on my cane. It was my favorite, hand crafted of poison sumac that I had bought while on a visit to the Oregon coast with my buddy who worked for me. We were doing some work for Oregon and took a trip along the coast. I bought the cane at Cape Foulweather.

Ron asked me to tell him about my faith and such. I told him what he wanted to know and explained that I had a strong interest in healing ministry, and I told him about Ellel. He then gave me the history about how House of Hope was begun, and explained all about how the church was founded on healing ministry. I knew at once that I had found my church; that providence had prevailed and led me directly to him. I knew God was at work.

At the end of lunch Ron asked me if I would like to come by his house before I left on Saturday morning. He said he would like to pray for me.

I did not know when he invited me what he had in mind. I thought he just wanted to give me a blessing and send me on my way. As we sat together above his house, above the tree tops of the Yucatan, he gently but with authority led me into what was to be a prayer of healing. He had noticed my cane.

He said, "John, I suspect that you are a man who harbors hatred for himself." Just like that. "Is that true?"

I told him that I would not deny that, but that I didn't think it defined me. I didn't even know this guy and he was already all up in my stuff. I told him as much as I thought he needed to know about my past.

"Do you know the name of the man?"

"Yes, pastor, I do."

"Pray with me and repeat what I say..."

He then spoke words I was to repeat, with which I was to forgive that specific person for that specific event in my earlier life. My eyes were closed, he spoke the words...and there was silence.

"I can't say the words."

"Say them."

My eyes were closed tight, and my jaw tensed to the point where I could feel it begin to ache.

"Pastor, I can't say the words."

"Say them, John. 'Father, I forgive...'"

But I stopped short. I wanted to bite something; I wanted to spit or choke or just sit with my body locked up tight in a very old and very bitter defiance. I wanted him to leave me alone.

"But pastor, they would not be true. I cannot say those words and mean them...I would be lying."

"It doesn't matter, John, say them. There is power in the spoken word. Repeat after me... 'Father I forgive...'"

I couldn't and didn't, and my pastor, although loving and tolerant, after a time set aside his patience, shifted his weight to duty, and became resolute.

"This is not about your feelings, John. This is about obedience. You are at a point where you make a choice; you either obey, or you don't. Are you going to be obedient? Are you going to obey?"

That was in April of 2009. I left the roof of his house holding my cane in my hand. The pain in my left leg was completely gone and from that day to this it has never come back.

That summer my financial situation reached bottom. My friend and employee resigned from the company realizing what was happening. He also distanced himself from me personally in a way that stung me deeply, and I began the proceedings of bankruptcy.

During the fist days of July I had to make arrangements for my possessions to be removed from my house because I was losing it to foreclosure. I really didn't care about any of it all that much, except for the day that they came to get my piano. I did not know I would ever suffer like that again. It gutted me. Seeing them take it apart and strap it to the dolly and wheel it away from me was simply more than I could bear. The piano had been my oldest and best friend, my anchor, and my hiding place. That night not only did I drink so much as to be knocked unconscious, but before I passed out I also managed to swallow fifteen Zanax.

The only thing that suggests to me that I did not want to actually commit suicide was the fact that I had sixty. But there are those who considered it a suicide attempt and very nearly had me taken away. I'm not so sure it wasn't.

I left Phoenix for good and after spending the summer with family sort of convalescing in New Mexico I headed down to the Yucatan and planned to get involved in the church. I did not know what the future was going to have for me, and I was just too weak to care.

One more story and we'll be done.

Life in Playa was good. It is one of the most beautiful places I have ever seen, and I love it down here. I did get involved in Ron's church and I did make new friends. While I was down there my friend who worked for me contacted me and wanted to reconcile. He asked me to forgive him for not being able to help me and for what seemed to me to be turning his back on me. I did, and we decided to remain friends. I know I can't make his life what he wants it to be, but I know God can, and I can pray for that.

And I started to depend on God while I was down in Playa. I started to think that all the losses and all the things He had taken away were not punishment, but a plan. I told my pastor that I used to think that God always went behind me repairing the walls where I smashed them, but now He was tearing them down. My sister (the one at the window with me) who has always shown me a greater love than I could ever deserve said, "He's got to, John. He's building a *new* house."

Everything in Playa seemed to be going great, except for money of course. I didn't have any and I was always worrying about it.

But the drinking did not let up. It got even worse, if you can imagine that. Before long I was drinking a fifth of rum every single day, and hiding it from everyone.

Something in me just couldn't stay in that state. Something in me just wouldn't die no matter how hard I tried to kill it. And one morning while desperately hung over I prayed the most fervent prayer I think I have ever prayed.

I was pleading. I was begging. I was at my very end and I told God these exact words: "I don't care what you have to do, whatever it is; just DO IT. But get me free of this. I can't stand it anymore." When I stopped praying I knew what I had to do. I needed my brother from church, Daniel, and my pastor Ron to pray with me. So I went to the living room and fired off an email telling them that I needed to meet with them. I needed their prayer; I was in desperate shape. Then I went to the Oxxo to buy another bottle of rum. That was a Friday.

The next day Daniel stopped by to check on me because he had texted me on my phone and did not get a response. He didn't realize it was a landline.

I told him that things were not good.

We all three made arrangements to meet at Daniel's apartment the next Tuesday afternoon.

We met that day and they prayed with me for four hours. Four hours. The whole afternoon was one long prayer of forgiveness. Ron started with events when I was seven years old and took each and every one of them one at a time. Daniel would stop and intercede in prayer for me, Ron would lay hands on me and pray over me and we would move on to the next. I was forced to examine every person, every event, and every injury whether I thought I had forgiven it or not. Then I had to face myself.

I had no idea how hard it can be to forgive yourself. I had no idea how dark it can be to be your own worst offender. I had no idea how ugly and difficult it can be to hold hatred for yourself when you really do have nothing but disgust in your gut for who you are. And how hard it can be to even consider letting that go.

Then I had to forgive God. Omnipotence is a pretty big thing. No excuse is available when nothing is beyond your ability. There is no forgiveness for the all-powerful. Theirs is a culpability that is absolute. I had to reconsider that as well.

We only stopped because all three of us were exhausted and Ron was so hungry I think I caught him looking at the wall paper kind of funny. But we were also done. We had covered everything.

I tearfully thanked both of them, trying to hold in the overwhelming sense of love and gratitude for them. And stopped at the Oxxo on my way home to buy another bottle of rum.

Sometimes events create a border in time, a wall through the middle of our history that both shields us from it and prevents our return. Indifferent to whether we laugh or cry, standing there…

Three evenings and three bottles of rum later it was Friday morning and I woke still drunk, but sober enough to head out to Oxxo for that day's bottle of rum.

I remember seeing the street going by on my bicycle; I remember the drizzling rain and fog. It was about ten in the morning. One minute I was looking at the street as I went to turn right onto one of the major streets and the next second it was coming up at me and I mean fast.

I opened my eyes and there were four people leaning over me talking to each other, asking each other questions. An ambulance pulled up behind me and three guys (I think) scrambled over to me and knelt down beside me strapping things to things. Asking me which hospital I wanted to go to. The left side of my body was numb and I couldn't move my arm. My head felt like it was broken. I don't know how else to describe it. I knew I was hurt, and I knew it was bad. I lost consciousness. I felt the gurney get hoisted up into the ambulance and everything went black.

I went in and out of consciousness in the ambulance and didn't really wake up completely until they were wheeling me out of the emergency room and parking my gurney in the hall.

I had a badly broken collarbone, torn ligaments in my neck and shoulder but thankfully the shoulder was not broken. I had had a concussion and was pretty severely bruised along my leg and side. Apparently I had hit the street at an almost perfectly perpendicular angle with my shoulder taking the full impact. Had I been slanted more to one side or the other I would have slammed into the street head-first and the injuries would have certainly been considerably more severe.

When I got home from the hospital it took me ten full minutes to maneuver myself into bed. They had strapped me and cabled me and wrapped me into slings under slings. It was an engineering project just to figure out how I was going to get myself into bed and how I would provide for the necessary straps and things waiting for me when I would need to get back up. I had the use of my right arm but that was about it. My whole left side was immobile and what wasn't strapped down was in pain.

After I eased myself flat in the bed, I was staring up at the ceiling and a new wave of emotion came over me. A new calm settled on me. A single thought...

It's over. I'm free.

PART TWO

A GOOD FRIEND ONCE MENTIONED THAT he wondered if God answers me when I talk to Him. I told him that He does sometimes give me answers, but only rarely to the questions I ask.

Well, it's been over a year since the bike accident and I haven't had a drink since that day. Pretty remarkable when you consider that in forty years I only had more than three days sober in a row three times (that I know of). And for the last ten years I am absolutely sure I didn't, because I spent those ten years trying, But what's really remarkable is that I haven't wanted one either. As they say, I don't know if I will ever get drunk again in the future, but I know it won't be today.

I was talking to one of my sisters about finally being free and I told her it was like waking up in a room I don't recognize. But it feels good, man. No struggle anymore.

My shoulder is mostly recovered although I have a little bit of deformity and I still wake up in pain from time to time if I sleep in the wrong position.

I'm living a lifestyle that doesn't include sex, and although I still have those feelings, they don't drive me crazy anymore. Obedience is a comfort to me.

I have had all this time to think about things. I stopped going to any therapist. Don't go to AA, and I'm not on medications of any sort. I have stopped trying to change things altogether. Nowadays I wake up every morning and I spend a little time in prayer because the only thing I try to do now is to love God the best I can, with everything I've got. There just doesn't seem to be anything else in this whole experience of being alive worth a minute of time, by comparison. I'm not perfect by any stretch, but neither am I tormented. By anything.

And after all those years in therapy, after all those years in school to *become* a therapist, and all those years being one, after all the years as a man given over to addiction trying every single method to get clean and sober known on the planet, two suicide attempts and all the rest…after all the stories I just finished telling you, I realize one thing at the top of the list.

All this time I've been wrong about pretty much everything.

6. About Being Crazy

Maybe I should start by saying that I mean, "about *thinking* you're crazy." But I'm not sure if that is quite right either. I wanted to say a few things about something related to the whole mental health aspect of life in general, but as I started to set my thoughts down they just kept coming.

And from what perspective would you want me to even talk about it – a guy who has lived most of my adult life as a patient or as a therapist? Sometimes the only difference I can think of is that one is the talker, the other is the listener, but even that doesn't work, really. Then I hit on the idea that one is paid, the other is doing the paying. Usually.

One time a good friend called me up pretty late at night. He was in considerable distress over events related to his son. We had a lengthy phone call and I was doing my best to navigate through the conversation, careful to reflect back to him the complexity of the thoughts he was describing to me. I definitely had my counselor hat on and I was using every technique I thought would help him. At one point I felt guilty about it. I thought, *this guy calls me as a friend and wants to unburden himself on me like friends often do, and here I am treating this call like it was a session.* I felt guilty enough to say something as the conversation was winding down.

I said, "I think I owe you an apology. For this whole conversation I have been responding to you as a therapist. In fact, I even used a technique called 'cognitive restructuring' that we sometimes use in anxiety situations. But I know you called me as a friend and I just think I haven't been exactly honest about my side of the conversation." I expected him to be mad, or at least a little offended.

He said, "Are you kidding? I have plenty of friends; you're the only therapist I know."

The lines are so hard to see sometimes: therapist, friend, patient...you *are* crazy, you only *think* you're crazy (like there's a whole lot of difference there!) And then once you actually get into the subject of mental illness there are maybe hundreds of disorders you can decide from in the Diagnostic and Statistical Manual (the bible of diagnosing mental and emotional disorders). There is something in there for everyone.

So whether it is because I have been a person who needed to talk to a mental health professional or because I ended up becoming one, I have long believed that it's all legitimate. But I'm not so sure anymore.

I do know that it seems to be all about labels.

So let's start with the first label that comes to mind based on all the stories I have just finished telling you: "attachment disorder." Here's where I was going with that one:

I think we are all born a little attachment-disordered but most grow out of it. Some of us, however, end up wearing it like mirrors facing back at us. For me, it was that I suffered something, but I never really understood what it was or why I was in trouble. I was also aware that no one else seemed to be suffering much at all. Everyone else seemed to be living life and enjoying it, no worries. For me it was always an effort.

It's funny that up until just a few years ago I never thought about attachment issues when I thought about other mental disorders in our course work on diagnosis. Of course, in school we learned about attachment disorders, but it was always in the context of very young children who get traumatically separated from their parents at a young age and then get adopted. We know there turns out to be a problem when the child shows no interest in their new adopted parents, and someone gets a call from them.

As a therapist I even gave trainings under a contract with a state agency to teach case managers how to differentiate between behaviors in young children that indicate attachment disorder, situational or clinical depression, and critical incident or traumatic stress. It is a very important distinction. Critical incident stress response can *look* just like a passing depression (situational) but could easily be a response to molestation. And that, brother, is a totally different situation. You don't want to be talking about selective seratonin reuptake inhibitors when the problem is not in Johnny's head; it's what's going on behind the garage. And time is precious.

But I never really gave any thought to attachment as a process without thinking about it in the context of some kind of disorder. I always thought it was a yes or no thing...the young kid attaches easily and painlessly to others, or doesn't. And if he or she doesn't, there are problems that we can easily see.

In other words, I thought that there really is no such thing as attachment; there is only attachment *disorder*. And at some unspecified age even the legitimately disordered child (because no adult is so disordered) either grows out of it and becomes normal or just ends up a jerk that people don't like. That's a natural thing, isn't it?

I thought that attachment disorder was a condition that a person might have, or not have. They either had it or they didn't; yes or no. I never thought about attachment in any other terms. Once we're all grown up it is no longer an issue. We might be wracked with issues, but they are all related to specific events, just like a broken arm might be related to a fall. But what if it isn't yes or no? What if it isn't even yes, no, or maybe?

There's another thing that I somehow ended up believing that I never even realized that I believed. Funny how you can live so much of your life holding some pretty important beliefs you didn't even know you had! I had come to conclusions, or maybe I had these assumptions but I don't remember getting them. I don't remember anyone telling me these things or explaining them to me as if they were true, and yet I ended up just assuming they are true.

But what if attachment is really something more like a *skill?* What if it is a skill that every person learns, even if they are never taught? If everyone grows up with an inborn necessity to learn to attach but we are not aware of that as parents, and no one is teaching them, then what they might learn could be worse than if they learn nothing at all. And they <u>will</u> learn *something*.

If this is an accurate way to think of it, then a lot of things begin to make sense. I need to ask you to hold this thought – the idea that attachment might be really more like a skill and everyone uses it, whether they are any good at it or not.

I have to interrupt myself here but I will get right back to this thought in a minute. I realize that I have to preface everything else I'll say about disorders with the following story.

When I was a trauma therapist with the Veteran's Administration we used to have staffing sessions with a prominent psychiatrist about once a month. He was very expensive so we could only have him for a couple of hours and we were encouraged to bring to the teaming only our toughest cases.

One day I saved up the case of an individual I was working with who absolutely refused to talk about his "in country'" experiences. He would not discuss the events that traumatized him in Viet Nam. Not. At. All.

It was very frustrating for me, because even though I recognized his refusal to talk about it as a form of hyper-vigilance (common in Post Traumatic Stress), I believed that if we did not talk about it he would never heal. So I planned to bring it up with the doc.

When I had my turn I laid out the entire case to him. He sat pensively for a moment and then asked, "Why do you want him to talk about it?"

"Well, so that he can process it."

"Why does he need to do that?"

"Because he needs to deal with it."

"Why?"

His line of questioning continued and I never could come up with a good answer. When he saw that he was frustrating me and that I would likely never be able to come up with a good answer he calmly said, "John, talking about the shipwreck doesn't get you off the island."

It sent me off on a new direction, and it was the first time that I ever realized that when it comes to mental health stuff, not everything we think is true is always true. I heard it another way sometime after that, but I don't remember who said it: "There are three things that are vastly over-rated: sex, whiskey, and insight."

As I started to talk about attachment concepts and how thinking about it always just in terms of a disorder might be making it hard to understand the reality of it, my thoughts flashed on *that would be insight, wouldn't it? You remember what the doc told you about insight?* See how convoluted it can get?

But let's go back to it, anyway.

It helps me to suppose that attachment is a process that we learn, but we don't know we're learning it. Now, of course, we don't have to learn to attach to our moms when we are just born. It's kind of fatal not to, in most cases. But fast forward ten years and now you're in Catholic school and a black-and-white-upholstered nun is coming at you Mach 5 with her habit on fire, rosary swinging out - of - control, and how are you going to attach to *that*, exactly? I know the exaggeration might seem a little ridiculous, but there is a point here. The point is degrees.

What if since we don't really know we are learning to attach (when we are young children) and no one else seems to realize it either, neither we nor anyone else can monitor whether or not we are learning it in a way that will work for us? So we become adults who need a skill we just don't really have.

Imagine asking a really wealthy person who is always lavishing presents on folks, always buying dinner, why he or she does that. Usually we would just conclude that they are really nice people and we label them "generous" and admire them for it. Now mind you, most people who are like that really *are* generous and there is nothing more complicated about it than that.

But imagine asking one why they were always doing that and they calmly answered, "Well, I don't trust that people will like me, and I want them to like me, so I buy them. And it's ridiculous what with inflation, I mean. Just not cheap anymore."

Would that not be true? Is that not true for some people? I can tell you that in the past it has been true for me. What for me was considered by others to be generosity was really not that. It was a stop-gap for a skill I didn't really have.

What's really amazing is that I even understood that and I still could not muster the courage to keep my credit card in my wallet and let folks either like me or not regardless of whether I paid for the tacos. That insight thing.

But if this line of reasoning is worth it – thinking of attachment as a skill we either learn or not – then it opens the doors for a lot of other things to possibly be true. For instance, it dawned on me to consider that maybe we all do learn to attach, some of us just might learn ways to do it that are more successful than others. My method, the VISA card approach, worked fine until I ran out of money. Then I really paid. But it was never anyone's problem other than my own. No one else was ever at fault.

And what if instead of learning that people are good and kind and fun to be around, we learn that there is something in us that is messed up. What if we learn that we are damaged goods? And what if for whatever reason at some point in the past we learned that everyone – everyone – will toss us aside if given the chance, no matter how much we love them. What if we learn to hate ourselves, even though whoever taught us to do that would never in a million years have done it intentionally. And then we confirm that we are detestable by our own actions…in effect, pick up with the lesson where our initial teachers of self-hatred left off. What if we carry that around deep inside ourselves hidden? Hidden so well that we don't even realize we're carrying it? How much do you have to pay someone to ignore something like that?

Let's move on to label number two. I want to talk about same sex attraction for a minute. I know it has been an issue for you and me both, as it has with a lot of guys we both know. I have been very wrong about that one, too.

I think the whole issue of same sex attraction is the single biggest example of a straw tiger I can possibly imagine. I cringe when I think of the massive amounts of grief that that one has caused. Now, of course, the pendulum is swinging the other direction and "being gay" is popular in some circles.

But to make sense of what I suspect now, I'd like to set aside the vernacular of "gay" or "straight" because I think they are labels that don't belong anywhere. Like printing up an adhesive label with the word "funny" on it and wandering around the house trying to find a piece of furniture to stick it on.

When I first realized, back when I was dating a woman I was having great sex with and with whom I was engaged to be married, that I had these sexual curiosities toward men…I immediately slapped that label on my forehead and lived in fear that anyone would see it.

So rather than talking about being "gay" or "straight" and rather, even, than talking about experiencing same sex attraction which can be transitory, fleeting, or all-consuming, let's use the concept of <u>unwanted</u> feelings of sexual attraction. A lot of people, and more and more every day, are rejecting the idea that there should be any reason for them not to want to have same sex attractions. But you're not one of them, neither was I, and neither are a whole lot of other people. No matter what, there will always be people who want their sexuality to be lined up with their desire to marry and have children, and to live life in an intimate relationship with the other biological parent of their children.

I was wrong in thinking that same sex attraction is an identity. It is never an identity any more than craving Fritos is an identity. Now we all know that I cannot "will" my unwanted attractions away. But neither is it truthful to say that because I have experienced them, even if I continue to experience them, all the other desires that conflict with them are lesser or don't mater at all.

None of the other desires that I have, which run completely contrary to the idea of acting on sexual urges I do not want and didn't ask for, are in any way diminished. So what is the truth? Is it true to say that I am gay and just won't face the reality of it and won't be happy until I do? Of course not. Is it true to say that I am at least a little conflicted? You betcha.

But here's the clincher. No matter what else has ever happened, no matter what I have ever done, ever, or ever will do, I desire to live a life that I believe pleases a God I love, and I believe He wants me to remain celibate until and unless I am married and to never be sexual with anyone other than my wife. And that desire, at least for the moment, is the one I choose to satisfy.

The lifestyle I used to want to live is a lifestyle that included satisfying my appetite for whatever I wanted, no matter how much it ended up hurting others or me.

But now the lifestyle that I want to live is one that is reconciled to my faith. My faith is rooted in scripture. And scripture is clear on this subject.

It's simple, really. I wish it were different, but it isn't. Nor is it complicated.

If you were to ask me if I judge those who do things that scripture condemns (whether it is have sex outside of biblical marriage, abuse drugs and alcohol, lie on the internet, or steal a candy bar) my response is, "What would be the point?" Would that bring me closer to the God I love? Hell no. All I know is this: I did those things. And I don't want to do them anymore.

God will not let me forget that He loved me back when I hated Him. And He loved me then as much as He does now. I'd have to turn away from Him to show scorn for someone else, and I'm just not sure how I would explain myself when I turn back, afterwards.

But there is something else that occurred to me about how I have been wrong about this sexuality thing.

It didn't have to torture me.

As you well know there is an entire area of the mental health profession dedicated to re-orienting people's sexuality (reparative therapy). Whether it works or not, who can say. There are guys who say they have been "healed" and are living lives as husbands and fathers. And I know just as many or more for whom it did not work and out of frustration and resignation have entered the gay community and are having sex with men. Are they still "sick"? Are they "un-healed"? I think not.

But for me, and I think for a lot of folks, whether it is a disorder or an illness to heal ends up all being academic. It doesn't matter.

There are organizations that set themselves out there as being able to "heal" same sex attraction. There are weekends that you can go on and come back a new man. Be careful about them. I'm pretty sure I have done them all, and when I was counting on them, when I placed my hope in them, I was disappointed. In my case, it came to more hurt than good. After the events of the last two years of my life I am now convinced that my time would have been much better spent just sitting alone with God and asking him what He thinks. I am sure He would have said to me then what He says to me now, "I love you more than you can imagine," and nothing more.

How much pain I could have missed had I ever just considered that.

And I'd like to briefly mention a bit about another big area related to this sexuality thing that I have been completely wrong about: Same sex attraction is about sex.

Not three nights ago I had dinner with a friend and I need to leave his name out of this because he asked me to keep it confidential. He is a wonderful man, married and dedicated to his family. He also experiences what we all refer to as same sex attraction.

While at dinner he asked me if he could unburden himself of something that has been weighing heavily on his mind and heart. I told him that of course he could. He told me that there is another young man who is also married, with whom he has become very close friends. What he then told me is that the friendship is causing him a considerable amount of pain.

From everything he told me, and speaking as a therapist, I find absolutely nothing in the characteristics of that friendship that anyone I know would consider unhealthy. They are good male friends who have bonded and share many life circumstances in common; they care very much for each other and for each other's families. He described absolutely no inappropriate contact or even inappropriate conversation whatsoever. And yet for almost an hour I listened as he tearfully told me that he is "not free," and it was very obvious that he was in a good amount of distress.

I explored with him the obvious question – *free from what?*

He not only sensed but he knew that he was overly entangled emotionally with this other guy, who had no idea at all about it, and that each moment was overshadowed by a fear of rejection. He said that when he leaves a text message and does not get a response, his feelings get hurt. When he got no special greeting for a major holiday, he was hurt by it. And it all spelled that he was overly dependent. And the truth is, he has been.

I asked him if he wanted to have sex with the guy, and he assured me that not only did he not want that, but if the other guy were to suddenly and inexplicably turn out to have sexual feelings toward him and propose the idea, he would be turned off. He went so far as to say he would likely lose respect for him, and that would be enough to turn him away – ironically that if that were to happen it would be over; he would be free.

He was talking to me about it because he knew I would understand his experience perfectly, and I definitely do.

And not two weeks ago I had dinner with another friend, married with children, who is currently going through the very exact same situation.

Because all of us have experienced same sex attraction we immediately chalk this bizarre emotional over-dependence situation when we get tangled up with some other guy as being "gay." But think about it. Sex has nothing to do with it. And in not one of the situations was sex what was even wanted.

Something else was wanted, so much so that there was pain involved in an otherwise completely healthy and wonderful friendship. What is that *about?*

But there is something in scripture that we can't ignore while we are on this subject...It is the relationship between David and Jonathon. David loved Jonathon with a love that is said to have exceeded any he could ever know with a woman. And yet there are few men in scripture who could be considered *less* of a homosexual than David. He murdered an innocent man to cover up having sex with the guy's wife and was thrown into such deep remorse about it (once he was busted) that he spilled his heart out to God and now we have Psalm 51.

But in our psychological framework we don't really have the means to deal with love like that. Floyd told me that there is such a thing as homo-*emotionality* as distinct from homo-*sexuality*. Okay. So we have a new label.

A lot of us dealing with the issues of same sex attraction have all read the same books. We know the writers who theorize that homosexuality is actually an attachment disorder, and we are right back to that again. I think the idea that homosexuality is really just an inability for a man to attach correctly to other men becoming sexualized is very interesting, really. I know a lot of guys who have struggled with this, and every one of them, to a person, perceives himself to be less a man than other men, or he is fascinated with some aspect of the masculine persona that he believes is lacking in himself. If you complete the aspect of masculinity that you perceive yourself to be missing, the attraction should go away, right?

I even had this epiphany once that it seemed like when I noticed a guy who I found to be attractive, he was usually wearing a baseball cap. I had this whole thing reasoned out that it went back to me being kicked out of baseball games by my dad and how that not only devastated me in the moment but convinced me that I wasn't like other boys. And my friend Mike was always a good baseball player in the sixth grade; he was the first guy that I ever became overly attached to and he always wore a baseball cap. But then I remembered that I was never interested in having sex with him and the whole thing just kind of fell apart. And besides, I started wearing baseball caps myself and nothing happened. No magic cure. Maybe if I had learned to play baseball...

Now don't get me wrong, I think it is a great thing to pursue doing whatever you think you need to do to feel more comfortable with yourself, or to be the man you want to be. In fact, I think it is critical that all men at some point face the issue of their own authenticity. Some of us need help, however. That's why I so strongly recommended the organization "In His

Fullness" and their weekend "Retrek" to you guys. Lance and Jared helped draw me out and really helped me.

But I think it is also important to know what really matters, and what doesn't.

One last thought and I will tie it all together.

The last big thing I have been wrong about that I am going to talk about, number three, but this one isn't a label: the idea that every individual problem that a person might have or every single emotional struggle that they might be going through is a unique thing. It is unconnected to anything other than its own causes and effects. A person might be codependent, but that's because they have low self-esteem. Like co-dependency is related to low self-esteem the way that fluffy bread is related to yeast. And that these kinds of things can be linked in chains. They have low self-esteem because their mom used to tell them they were stupid. Their mom used to tell them they were stupid because she had low self-esteem herself. And if only HER mom were still alive someone could go slap her and get the whole thing cleared up. I'll call this the <u>vertical</u> dimension of craziness: it has an origin, a festering or developing stage, and then it blooms into a hefty percentage of your disposable income being paid to a stranger because he or she won't gasp when you tell them things. Or is really good at hiding it when they want to.

And in addition to having sequential chains of disorder at play, a person could have multiple disorders at the same time. A collection. Each unique, with its own presentation, its own cause, its own influences, and often its own prescription.

When I was a therapist at the residential treatment center in Hawaii, we took care of teenagers who came to us through the court system and lived on campus. There was one story – for every therapist there is always one story – that will go with me to my grave.

I'll call him Bill (not his real name). He came to us at the age of fourteen having been arrested for dealing heroin. He was himself a heroin addict at fourteen years old and had also been diagnosed in some hospital somewhere, most likely during an over dose, with bipolar disorder. At the time he came to us he was drinking almost a fifth of hard liquor a day as well. And he smoked pot, but we didn't much care about that (in his case). At intake with us our clinical director added the diagnosis of clinical depression. Why, I have no idea. My thinking was *the kid's just been locked in a treatment facility where he can't have any drugs, alcohol, or contact with girls. Howdie Doodie would be depressed.*

As I got to know him in the first days, I immediately liked him and I had to consciously keep my boundaries in place and not treat him with any favor over the others. But he simply could not function. Yet. He was in withdrawal, and the treatment plan that everyone got – two group sessions a day and one individual session a week – did not work for him. He could not manage being in group. I was constantly having to throw him out.

I asked for a staffing on him and proposed to the clinical director that I give him two or three one-on-one sessions a day to ease him into group. As soon as he was stable I would back off on that. She flatly refused. No argument I could make could justify to her me giving that boy what he needed. I even offered to stay late and do the sessions on my own time because I knew he wouldn't make it any other way. She told me I would only wear myself out and she couldn't permit it. She ordered me to assess him for attention deficit disorder.

I said, "WHAT!? The kid already thinks he's worthless and crazy, and you want to stamp A-D-D on his forehead too?" He already had a collection and he knew it. He knew it very well.

Every time a kid got thrown out of group he was one step closer to involuntary discharge. That was pretty serious stuff for these kids because most of them came to us through the courts or some other aspect of the criminal system. If we discharged them rather than released them with the assessment that they had completed their treatment successfully, they usually went to jail, and from there who knew where. When I flat refused to assess him for attention deficit disorder I made the clinical director angry, and one day she called me on her day off and ordered me to discharge him. He had been thrown out of group one too many times. She always ordered someone kicked out by other therapists on her days off. It was just too unpleasant for her to be there when it happened.

I will never forget the sound of his mother's voice as she begged me to give him another chance. Sobbing, she exclaimed, "If you can't help him, how do you expect us to? Who WILL help him?"

And I knew I could have helped him. At least I could have given it a shot. But I wasn't permitted to try.

His father told me that he had had it with the little "S.O.B." and would not pick him up at the airport. I took the phone off speaker so that Bill would not hear any more of his own father's abuse. I told him that in the State of Hawaii we call that "abandonment of a minor" and that if he did not take care of his son, if this boy spent the night in the airport, I would personally make damn sure his father would spend the night in jail. And my heart broke to have to tell Bill that I could not stop the fact that he was being returned to his parents.

It is a serious ethical violation for a therapist to follow up with someone after the counseling relationship has been severed in such a situation, but I lost sleep more times than I could count worrying about him.

I digress a little but the point I'm making is that I thought he had a collection too. I bought into that nonsense. I believed that a person could have a list of disorders and each one could be uniquely present and unrelated to any of the others.

And the truth is, I had always sort of ended up believing that I had my *own* collection.

I look back at my evolution as a mental health patient and I can see these huge hallmarks of *progress*, so to speak. I started out the nineteen year old about to kill myself (suicidal) because I was gay. I learned that I was not gay, but that my sexuality was just diffused. I lived through the year of being suicidal and emerged alive, but still diffused. Apparently the psychological community could label me but not fuse me. Fast-forward twenty years and by then I was very mature about it. I was very enlightened and I was able to set aside the label of being depressed because I got past that, and through many years of therapy and some kick-ass weekends with a bunch of other guys I now understand that I am not gay and never was; I only experience same sex attraction.

But then I found out that even that label was not correct. Now there was a nicer label: gender attachment disordered. I knew well that I was a drinking alcoholic and struggling against that, so I had in my collection the following mental health identity labels past and present (by issue):

Issue number 1: "Clinically depressed and Suicidal"

Issue number 2: "Gay" which evolved into "Sexually diffused" which evolved into "Experiencing Same Sex Attraction but not permanently or constantly" which evolved into "Gender Attachment Disordered"

Issue Number 3: "Alcoholic" which includes "Diseased" and "Helpless" (I'll talk about this one later)

The main thing that having all these labels did for me was it helped me to keep from beating the crap out of myself for spending so much money on therapists. But one day I even got another one.

I was in the therapist's office and I can't remember what the subject of the session was about exactly. I can't even remember what I had wanted to talk to him about that day. Some days I had to hunt for something to talk about on my way to his office because I was seeing him every other week (for about two years) and some days just weren't bad days.

But that day we were talking about something and he interrupted me saying, "John, you know what? I don't think your problem is same sex attraction; it's not even alcohol…"

I urged him to continue and he said, "You are suffering post traumatic stress. Well…PTSD along with some serious abandonment issues and the attachment disorder."

"What!!" I answered. I had not had time to really get a handle on my previous three labels and he was handing me at least two new ones.

"PTSD! I'm a trauma therapist myself, remember? I've been working with PTSD for years. You know that! I KNOW PTSD when I see it, and I do not have it. That's ridiculous." I protested. In his loving, inimitable way he just said, "You're the poster child for PTSD."

And we talked about being too close to the trees to see the forest. It *felt* like a moment of discontiguous change – the fabled "aha" moment – I mean it almost seemed like there was magic in the new epiphany, but I just went home and got drunk anyway.

In the days and weeks that followed, however, I started trying to patch together all kinds of different disparate things, experiences, accusations, assessments made of me by others, and conclusions I had adopted. I started searching for connections based on this new bit of information and began behaving according to an as yet undiscovered and unapplied label – obsessively analytical nut case.

Like, for instance, that was not the first time I was called a poster child for something. Some years earlier I was involved with this woman who really fell in love with me. I never loved her the way she loved me, but it seemed to her that I *should* and that I would, if I just stopped to realize how compatible we were. One night we were with a bunch of friends and she and I had ended up in the kitchen together. Everyone was drinking and having a good time.

Out of the blue she pops up with the comment, "I think we should get married!" I didn't want to get pulled into anything remotely resembling a conversation on that subject with her, at that time, in that kitchen or anywhere else on this planet…so I responded, "To whom?" And I tried to figure out a way to get back as quickly as possible to our friends in the living room. It went over like the proverbial turd in a punch bowl. By the time she had finished ripping into my insensitivity with the remark, she announced that I was suffering from "Peter Pan Syndrome." I scoffed. "You don't only HAVE 'Peter Pan Syndrome' but you're the POSTER child for it."

I commented that I felt sure that even if there *were* such a thing as "Peter Pan Syndrome" (which I insisted that there wasn't), no one afflicted with it would ever actually be suffering. "Damn right!! Just everyone ELSE!!" It was one of those many occasions when there is no intelligent thing you can say. The only intelligent thing is to keep your mouth shut even if you have to wrap your head in a Glad Bag to do it. And situations like that make the idea sound pretty good.

I decided not to trot that new label off to the therapist to discuss it. I didn't keep it in my collection at all, but I do admit that I kind of like it.

So here's where it all comes together for me. I'm pretty sure I have been wrong about all of this stuff, just like I have just described to you. What if, rather than having collections of discrete issues that each have their own causes, histories, present effects and past...

What if they are all the same thing?

And what if that one thing is not about a *disorder* at all, no matter how much disorder it introduces into our life?

What if it is <u>all</u> about attachment?

And what if it is <u>only</u> about how we attach *now*; not when we were seven, or nineteen, or fifty-four?

You're probably thinking that there are a lot of mental diseases that are related to chemical imbalances in the brain. They are serious illnesses with biological characteristics and they can't be grouped with things like attachment disorders and Peter Pan syndromes. And you're right. They are different. I'm not talking about those. Medical doctors are needed to diagnose and treat those illnesses and no one else should even be trying to, in my opinion.

But what if the rest of it is so much simpler than we think?

I really like what Atlanta Joe said he thinks Jesus will say when we die and ask Him why we had to be cursed with same sex attraction – "Don't you have anything more interesting to talk about?"

What if some of us don't learn what we need to learn in order to be able to attach to others in a way that confirms our worth to ourselves and to the rest of the people we live around? We learn something else.

We learn <u>not</u> that there will always be some people that we will love deeply who will love us just as deeply, and others who we really don't like and can't get along with easily, but instead that none of that is really possible. What if we learn that it's all bad? It's all ruined, and if we could fold this hand and wait for the next one we would do that, but we can't. And what if we learn that there is nothing that can *ever* change it?

You can learn things that aren't true.

But it would only take learning that little bit of information that over the years would compound and compound and complicate. It would start to weave itself into everything. It would become true.

What if it is not only all about how we attach to people, and how we attach to them right now in this minute and no other, but also that we only need to learn one way of doing it? The way He does. What if all we ever had to do to be fully equipped to live life without any emotional problems is to have grown up being taught to attach to people the way God does? What if it is really just that simple?

But I didn't learn that. Many of us didn't. So what do we do now?

I think there is a way out of it. There is something that I have been shown that can change it; that can collapse all the history and horizontal causes behind causes into this very moment, this moment as I sit here and write this, this moment as you read it.

There is something that can melt all the individual labels no matter how many there are in your collection into a single blob, and then melt that away too. I know you think I am going to say Jesus. But I'm not. That would be true, yes. But there are details. There are details that as a Christian who lived a life given over to sin, snot-slinging drunk more often than not for twenty-seven years _after_ being redeemed by Him, I just didn't have...something I just didn't know.

7. About Addiction

WELL, THERE IS CERTAINLY A LOT to say about this subject. The hard part about writing this is making sure I don't tell you the same stories over again. There are so many stories, I guess I could write pages and pages filled with nothing but the escapades that happened in all those years when I was drinking and drugging. I know I have already told you a lot of them, and when I was telling them to you earlier I pretty much described them in ways that suggested that most of them were pretty funny.

But I don't know if that is really fair. The truth of it is that none of it is funny.

It's important that I mention that for the forty some-odd years that I was getting drunk I really only wanted to *stop* getting drunk for about the last fifteen years. From the age of fourteen to about forty I was quite fine with drinking all the time. There were periods of time early on (usually very brief, of a month or two) where I would stay sober and stop using drugs. But I can only think of two. My life then was a lot like the T-Shirt that read "I don't have a drinking problem; I drink, get drunk, fall down…no problem."

Living in the Yucatan I am often around the tourist shops where they sell T-shirts to the Americans and Europeans who wander Fifth Avenue and the Paseo del Carmen. So many of them are about how funny it is to get drunk. "One tequila, two tequila, three tequila, floor." "I'm home take me drunk." I used to pass them on my way back from the beach, on my way to the Oxxo where I usually bought my fifth of rum for the day. I often would read them and think, *how stupid.*

I can remember so many days I'd park myself on the beach and let the sun cook my hangover away and notice the vacationers wander onto the beach, stumbling and laughing. I got to where I could almost tell you the exact amount of time they had been drinking just by how loud they were baiting each other into arguments or proclaiming that the other is "hot." There was always a certain type, and you knew that they had gotten their buzz at "Frog's" or "Charley's" on the strand up from the peer where the boats take you to Cozumel. Not like those of us with class, who quietly drink ourselves into oblivion sipping rum at "Piñatas" at a table overlooking the beach, imagining ourselves to be Hemingway, or something.

It wasn't until about the mid nineties that it occurred to me that I probably needed to stop.

As I have begun to tell my family and some close friends about all of this, they are usually surprised to hear. They usually say something like "We had no idea." I was what you call a "high functioning" drunk. I once even confessed it to my boss when I worked at state because I felt that he had become a good friend and I needed to be honest. I was beginning to know I needed it to be over and that I might need help. He said that he had not noticed any detriment to my performance but appreciated my honesty. Nothing more was ever said. I was relieved.

Now it is true that I was going to therapists for years prior to the mid nineties (I think it was about 1995) when I was beginning to suspect that drinking was going to end poorly, that it was only a matter of time. But that was for depression or suicidal thoughts. It had nothing to do with drinking.

It wasn't long after I thought it would be better for me to stop drinking that, like so many other people, I began to learn that I couldn't. For someone who does not know what that is like, there is no way to describe it. There is no way to explain it. How do you explain to someone that you can desperately want to be sober while you are driving to the store to buy alcohol, and that you open the bottle in a rush to drink a few gulps just to get things started? Just to end the conflict of not wanting to do it, but doing it anyway. I couldn't even explain it to myself.

I was in a lull where I wasn't getting any counseling when I found out that alcohol was a more serious problem for me than I thought. So I decided to go back into counseling to get sober. That was when I started with Marilyn. But in the very first session the alcohol thing got put aside because I found myself confessing to her all about the same sex attraction, the depression, my utter hatred for myself, and all the rest, that by now you must be sick of hearing about.

In the years that followed with her, I reasoned to myself that if these other things were cleared up, the drinking would just go away; I would just stop naturally like a car that runs out of gas. I was so wrong.

Now I have to say that Marilyn helped me immensely. But I never got sober; I never stopped hating myself, and the same sex attractions didn't stop. She helped me bear it all and may well have kept me from suicide. But nothing changed. Was it worth it to be seeing her? Sure. Was I healed? Nope.

So I'd like to take the four ways I tried to stop drinking one at a time and talk a little about each one: counseling, change in lifestyle, addiction medication, and twelve-step programs. As far as I know, these are the only four generally accepted methods, or possibilities, for recovery available. Not one of them worked for me.

I am not including being shipped off to a residential treatment center because I could never afford it. I never had the time to take off from work either. But if I had had the time and money, you can bet I would have tried that, too.

I think that the intensity of residential treatment centers is probably a good and useful thing because it *does* interrupt the abuse. Having worked in one as a therapist I think it did do some good for the folks who were there. The problem is in returning them back to the environment they came from. Something seems to go wrong at that point.

Unfortunately I do not personally know anyone that has not relapsed and gone right back to their addiction after being discharged from a treatment center, although I am sure they exist. So if I were to speculate, I'd guess that it would not have worked for me any better. I know of one friend who was away in one for a full year. Now he's out, divorced, and as far as I know drinking and drugging again.

But please know something. Some of these things work for some people, or seem to. And I would never want to take anything away from somebody if it is working for him or her. My most sincere hope for *anyone* caught in the tragedy of addiction is that they get free, no matter how it happens. They can paint themselves purple and walk on their hands; and if that keeps them sober, hey, I'm happy for them. I can only tell you what I experienced.

As for counseling, there were a total of three professional counselors (consecutively) and a pastor who worked in pastoral counseling, spanning a period of about fifteen years.

Between the counseling that I had as a patient and the education I got as a therapist I came to think that you can divide the whole mental health community into two camps on the subject of addiction: those who believe that addiction is caused by something else (some other disturbance), and those who think that addiction is its own disturbance and exists completely independent of anything else.

Those that think it is the result of some other disturbance are likely to tell you that the other disturbance is (drum roll...) shame. Addiction is a shame-based disease. Man I wish I had a dollar for every time I heard that.

The reasoning goes sort of along the lines that all addiction is caused by shame. Something else caused the shame and, so the reasoning continues, if you find out what it is, you can deal with the shame and the addiction will die just like a plant whose roots you cut. There is also the sort of parallel idea that when you drink, you do shameful things, which feed what they call the "cycle of shame" and keep you drinking. And it becomes a never-ending cycle unless you interrupt it. And for anywhere from free to a thousand dollars a day there are places that will interrupt it for you. Once you are sober for a while and you are thinking clearly, all the things that caused you shame in the first place can be resolved. Problem solved.

Well, it didn't work for me.

First, I always knew what started the whole thing. There was really never a need to understand *what* happened to me, even though I did spend decades trying to understand *why*. Eventually there seemed to be an explanation as to why the events all occurred and that maybe it wasn't my fault after all. And trust me, it is no small task to live most of your entire sentient life believing that you are garbage and then convince yourself that regardless of why you are feeling that way, it wasn't your fault. You can fully understand that your house burned down because lightening struck it, and lightening struck it because that is what lightening does: you had nothing to do with it. But you're still sleeping in the ashes.

So okay, I thought. *None of it was my fault. I have no reason to be ashamed.*

But the problem is that there is a thought that kept coming back to me. It was the weed whose root I could not cut. *My father and the others did not reject and abandon me because of what happened; they did it because of who I <u>am</u>.*

And I can't change that.

And I can't go back and talk him into changing his mind about it once *he* realizes that it wasn't my fault, because he's dead. And the others who aren't dead are gone somewhere or simply uninterested.

The truth is that there are personality traits or characteristics about me for which I have no respect, things I condemn. Right or wrong, reasonable or not, there are things about me which I hate.

And what about the things I DID do?

I've done things that no reasonably sane person would have any response to BUT shame. I've let you in on a few, but there are many. In my case, shame is a perfectly reasonable, rational emotion to have. And coming to the epiphany that it is causing my addiction or that I am trapped in some cycle of it is of absolutely no use to me.

And while I am on the subject of the cycle of shame caused by the drunken binges, many of the things I did while on those binges I can't even remember. So no shame there. I'm talking about the things I CAN remember.

The whole structure of this approach, understanding addiction as a shame-based disease that can be cured by resolving the shame, just didn't help me. And it wasn't for lack of exploring it.

I also went through the whole process of learning the difference between "guilt" and "shame." If I remember correctly, guilt is the emotion related to things you have done that you wish you hadn't done.

"Shame is the emotion related to who you think you are. Guilt is connected to events; shame is connected to identity."

"Got it. Now what?"

"You take the shame you are feeling and start calling it guilt."

I know I am making this sound a little ridiculous and I truly don't mean to be disrespectful, but it *is* a little ridiculous to me. In any event, it got me nowhere.

And as for the counseling related to the other things that could be causing the drinking – depression, conflicts over my sexual identity, massive insecurities related to abandonment and rejection – well, the efforts there weren't a whole lot more successful. I mean, shame is kind of an easy project compared to the others. After the years and years of counseling it started to feel like someone telling me that all we have to do is to dig a pass through the Rocky Mountains to get me to the west coast where I want to go, and handing me a spoon.

That's when it started to sound hopeful that the trick is not to figure out the root cause and try to clear that all up, but just to consider that the root cause didn't matter because addiction is its *own* problem. It doesn't matter what caused the house to burn; you just have to build a new one. You don't have to talk about the shipwreck, just build the raft. Find yourself a new lifestyle.

There is a lot of appeal to this idea. But like alcoholics are so often wont to say, "The brain I am trying to use to get sober is the one that wants to drink" (or something like that). The instrument with which I am to make the repairs is what is in need of repair. You get the idea.

So if you agree that addiction is the problem and is not related to or dependent on any other problem, then all you have to do is find something to replace it.

I'm going to go back to something else that psychiatrist at the Veteran's Administration said. You remember me telling you about him. He's the one that first caused me to doubt the value of insight and like I just explained in the context of plumbing the mines of shame-based addiction, insight sure turned out to be of little value. So much of what he said made so much sense, even if it was years later.

Well, on another occasion I did a staffing with him about a guy I was seeing at the VA who came in for sessions once a week. He almost never missed a session in probably two years. But the only thing he *ever* talked about was the nights he spent staying up the entire night viewing Internet pornography.

He was a man in his fifties who had been given a full disability status for Post Traumatic Stress Disorder and who lived at home with his elderly parents (who were taking care of him). His parents had given him a room above the garage and he slept during the day and spent the entire evening viewing pornography. The only time he ever left the house, that I could ever discern, was to come to the vet center for our session once a week.

No matter how hard I tried, I could not get him off the subject of his porn escapades, and they really were wearing on me. I hated listening to him talk about his sexual behavior and I came to dread his sessions. I kept trying to get him to see that it was not helping him recover from anything, and that it was actually keeping him from ever having a relationship with a real person. But he didn't care. I came to believe that he enjoyed trying to shock me.

When I explained it all to the doc in our staffing meeting he asked me what I wanted to know. I answered that I wanted to know how to get him to stop doing it, or if he couldn't stop doing it, at least to stop talking about it. His answer was another classic: "Don't try to take away someone's pathology unless you have something better to offer."

I decided to apply the wisdom to my own situation, and this leads me to the second manner in which I tried to quit drinking (the first being counseling), endurance athletics.

Actually I was working in Washington DC and living in a three-story house that my company had rented for all the consultants busy on projects there. One weekend while I was there alone I became very sick. It was a Friday night and it started with a sore throat but by Saturday afternoon my chest was on fire, my body ached like I had been hit by a truck, and I started coughing up blood. I was in real trouble.

No other consultants were expected to be at the house for at least a week so the option of waiting until someone came to the house to discover me was not available. To make matters worse, I was staying in a room on the third floor where there was no telephone, so I could not just call for an ambulance.

Somehow I managed to get downstairs and to drive myself to the emergency room at a clinic that was not too far away. I was diagnosed with a "walking" pneumonia and given some antibiotics. It wasn't long before I was released and told to go home and get in bed and stay there.

But while I was there my blood pressure measured 210 over 120. Among the meds I was given were meds for high blood pressure.

I recovered from the pneumonia within a week or so, but the blood pressure medicine was really difficult for me to take. It gave me pounding headaches and I couldn't sleep. When I went back to the clinic for a recheck I told the doctor that I was really having a hard time with the blood pressure medicine and asked her if there was anything else I could do to lower my blood pressure. She answered facetiously, "You could start doing triathlons."

Well, there was a wonderful lady named Betty who was staying at the house with me by then, another consultant, who was in her sixties but who ran marathons. When I got back to the house she asked me what they said and I answered, not attempting to disguise my disdain, "She told me I could do triathlons." Betty said, "I can help you with that."

So I started training.

By 2001 I did my first one: The Pacific Coast Triathlon at Crystal Cove California. Good story.

I researched all about the races, the distances, which races were where and when, and I started by running each day. Then I added swimming laps and working out with weights. It was great.

On the race day I was really excited, but for some reason I was there alone. I stayed at a hotel by myself and there were no friends at the race to cheer me on, even though it was close to LA where my ocean-swimming friend of Catalina fame lived.

Anyway, I was in the transition area before the race getting everything all set up. There was a married couple next to me and the husband asked me, "Is this your first time to do the Pac Coast?" To which I answered, "It's my first time to do *any* triathlon."

They were incredulous. "You're doing the Pac Coast FIRST!?"

Apparently it turns out to be the second or third hardest race in the California series and most people do not start with a race that hard. They start with something like San Bernardino. They took pity on me and decided to take me under their wing, you know, show me the ropes.

At one point as I was laying out my Spring suit to put it on they asked if I would like them to spray me with Pam before I put on my wet suit. "Helps you get out of it."

I was grateful and thanked them, and then got sprayed head to toe with the stuff. While my goggles were around my neck.

There were about two thousand people doing the race that year and the four hundred (or so) men in my age group all gathered at the water's edge and waited for the gun.

As soon as the start gun was fired we all charged into the waves high-stepping over the little ones and the guys in front systematically diving into the surf in front of me like penguins off an iceberg. As I was charging the waves I was also pulling my goggles up from my neck and onto my head. Which was when I saw the nose bridge pop and fly off into the surf and the band go slack in my hands.

Great. I just hope the eyepieces get enough suction in my eye sockets to stay on without the nose bridge.

Then I noticed that the eyepieces were so well coated with Pam that I couldn't see through them. But it didn't matter anyway, because as soon as I hit the water the goggles were gone too.

How am I going to swim a half-mile in the ocean without goggles? Well, not everyone is going to finish the race. You can stop and head back to shore. Yeah, but none of the people who don't finish the race quit in the first fifty feet of it! Have you seen how many people are standing on that shore? What, are you going to just walk through the crowd and say "never mind…"

I did finish the race, but my eyes watered for a week after all that salt water. The last part of that race is a run on the beach leading up to a hill. You have to run up that hill to finish the race and it is a considerably steep and long one. The others told me that most people named the hill after a woman they didn't like. They said it helped.

Well, when I got to the hill, after swimming without goggles and riding my eighteen-pound bicycle up and down the Pacific Coast Highway reaching speeds of forty miles per hour terrified for my very life, I could not possibly run up it. I could barely walk. One of the guys in the small group of folks I had met in the transition area before the race, a guy we called "Big Joe" (because there was a "Little Joe") came up behind me. When he came up alongside of me he stopped running and walked with me.

"You okay?"

"I can't make it up that hill, Joe. I can't even run at all."

"No one said you had to *run* up the hill, John. Just make it up there even if you have to do it on your hands and knees."

Think about it for a second. He stopped running when he didn't have to, ruining his chances for a personal best for that race for a full year until the next one came around, to encourage me – a guy he had just met a couple of hours before. And then he picked up his pace and jogged on.

I was hooked on triathlons from that moment on. Any sport with people like that in it is the sport for me, I decided. Those people are truly awesome.

The next time I did the Pac Coast (2003) I did something I will go to my grave thinking was among the stupidest things I have ever done. I cannot even pretend to have an explanation for why I did this and can't even begin to imagine what I was thinking.

I was very careful not to get Pam on my goggles that time. The Pac Coast had become the Regional USAT Championship race that year so the number of competitors went to 2,500.

As my age group, now numbering about 500, charged into the surf and I successfully got my Pam-free goggles to my head and secured on my face, I was about twenty feet into the surf when I realized that I had headed out at the *front* of the group. I was in the leading edge.

Now, I am a pretty strong swimmer in that, like you know, I sometimes swim long distances. I've been swimming since I was a toddler. But I am not that fast. So approximately 480 men proceeded to swim right over the top of me. Big Joe, it would seem, was the exception, not the norm.

For that race there were two friends who were there to cheer me on. By the end of the race when we were back in the car and they asked me why I didn't acknowledge them as I was walking onto shore from the swim, I asked, "Where were you?" And they answered, "A foot to your right as you walked by…" I tried to explain that I was so beat up and dizzy I wouldn't have noticed the Lock Ness monster dead and washed up on that beach if I had to step over its tail. Not that there's a resemblance.

The point of me telling you about the triathlon hobby is that I figured I had found my "something better." If I wanted to take away my own pathology and I needed to offer myself something better, I had something.

But it didn't work either. In fact, for both of those races I had only managed to be sober for two days in a row before the race. And by 2004 my joint pain flared up with so much regularity and for such long periods of time (usually two to four months during which I walked with a cane) that I couldn't train anymore, and never did another race.

And there never was a "something better" that I could find. Considering addiction as a problem in its own right and replacing it with something else ended up being a dead end, just as trying to get rid of it by solving some other root problem had been.

So the first method (counseling) and the second method some suggest to stop drinking (change to a healthy lifestyle) had not worked.

Now I have to tell you that in 2007 when I was hospitalized for my heart problems, having had my own heart attack, the cardiologist did tell me that had I not had the hobby of endurance athletics the heart attack might have been much more serious and could well have killed me. So there are some really good reasons to change your lifestyle and become health conscious, or at least there were for me. But it did not heal my addiction.

And today, now that my joint pain is healed, I'm back to training. Funny how things come full circle.

The third method (addiction medication) is really simple and I won't go into a lot of detail on it. I had my doctor prescribe Naltrexone. Now actually before I tried that I was taking kudzu because I heard it would take away cravings for alcohol. And I tried kavakava too. Eventually I was taking enough kavakava to put me to sleep. I was getting to the point where I would end the night after drinking my two bottles of wine, or my fifth of rum, with ten or so kavakava pills. Since they were natural (not prescription) I didn't think it could hurt.

But later I got serious about it, realized that neither the kavakava nor the kudzu were having any effect on me other than augmenting the effects of the alcohol, so I asked for a prescription for Naltrexone and started using it.

Naltrexone is what is called an "Opioid Receptor Antagonist" and seems to work for some people. It works in a way similar to the way some anti-depressants work. Anti-depressants that are in the group called "Selective Seratonin Reuptake Inhibitors" work by clogging the points in the brain where the neurotransmitter seratonin is reabsorbed. That causes seratonin levels to increase, which makes electric currents travel more efficiently in the brain, and gives you a generally better sense of well-being.

As I understand it, they know that the opioid receptors have something to do with the neurotransmitters that communicate pleasure and reward to the brain and have a lot to do with addiction. But they don't fully understand how antagonizing them makes you not want to get drunk.

And I wouldn't be a good person to ask, because it didn't work for me. I guess my opioid receptors were antagonized a long time ago and think nothing of it. Don't notice the difference. So on to method number four.

Before I get to number four, however, I do want to mention the one I couldn't try: Antabuse (Disulfiram). From what I've read, this is a very effective method to stop drinking. You take the medicine and then if you drink after it you get really sick. From what I've read it works by preventing the breakdown of dopamine, the neurotransmitter that is also related to feelings of pleasure and well-being that I just mentioned.

The problem is how it makes you sick. If you drink any alcohol after taking the medicine you start to experience the same symptoms of a hangover but much worse. One of the symptoms is that your heart races. I read that it can be very dangerous for a person with a heart condition. Since it could cause a heart attack, that drug was off the menu. Method three (addiction medication) was down for the count.

Which brings us to the fourth, biggest, most widely employed method for the treatment of alcoholism in the world: twelve-step programs.

There were all together three different times I joined Alcoholics Anonymous groups: once before moving to Hawaii, once again after coming back from Hawaii, and once in the Yucatan. And I was also part of Celebrate Recovery (a Christian Twelve Step program based on Alcoholics Anonymous).

The first time I ever attended a meeting it was pretty difficult. I can't say that it was something I did happily, but neither was it something I was ordered to do by a judge. I think I had a sense that it was the last resort and that if it didn't work, nothing would.

I have to admit I really enjoyed the first meeting, after I got over my fear and self-consciousness. Everyone seemed so genuinely caring and receptive to me. It was the first time I had ever been to a meeting of complete strangers and had people welcome me and truly make me *feel* welcomed. I have to tell you, it was my experience in that first group that the sense of camaraderie and shared burden among the folks there was genuine.

Something new happened to me. I looked around and saw these people who were all so flawed, who had lived lives that all seemed so full of problems, and they themselves were so riddled with imperfections. And at the same time I realized that I fit right in. I didn't feel shame like you might think, but rather I felt a sense of belonging. My own self-righteousness was pierced, and I felt the joy of being free to not have to pretend anymore.

As a brief aside, years later I attended a non-denominational church in Phoenix that a friend of mine had taken me to while he was in rehab. The church was small and a lot of drug rehab programs strongly recommended their residents go there and some even provided vans to take them there. It's called "Fire and Water."

The first time I attended the service, there were about a hundred people in the room and I looked around thinking to myself *these people are all druggies and alcoholics, prostitutes and pimps. I fit IN here.* Every time I have been back to that church I get the same strong sense of love from those folks: love for God, love for each other, and love for any stranger that walks in the door. Every time I spend a couple of hours there I am blessed just to be in their presence. It becomes easy to imagine Jesus, and why He hung out with the poor, the sinners and tax collectors. I often thought to myself *if Jesus were walking the earth today, this is where He would be.*

There is a lot to be said for that. And that is what my first experience with Alcoholics Anonymous (AA) gave me, and I remained sober while I was attending the meetings. But a few weeks later I moved to Hawaii and relapsed the very same night I arrived in Honolulu. It would be years before I would join another AA group, and never again would going to the meetings become a means of sobriety for me. After I returned from Hawaii and when I was in the Yucatan and sought out an AA group and attended their meetings, I never again felt the kind of community I felt the first time. No matter how many different groups I tried, I always just ran into this special kind of cliquishness that is all too common in those groups.

When I first moved down to Playa after I lost my house I knew I needed to be part of an AA group or I would end up doing nothing but getting drunk down there.

I had bought my home in the Yucatan as a vacation spot, a retirement option, and an investment. But it really became just a place I could retreat to, to engage in episodes of debauchery lasting weeks on end. It was down in Playa that I developed a taste for the expensive girls, and it became clear that added to my addiction to alcohol was a newly developing addiction to prostitutes. But this was a much more costly habit than rum.

So when I was actually moving down there I had to figure out how to keep that from happening on a more permanent basis. At the time there was one AA group that met and I started attending the meetings. On about the third meeting it was one of the folk's birthdays and everyone was congratulating him. He was a young guy, maybe in his mid twenties. He indicated that he had been a drinker and drug addict for about five years, clean and sober for about three. Everyone loved him and thought he was the greatest thing since flushing toilets. I don't remember what I said, but he disagreed with me and proceeded to give me this huge lecture, while his groupies were chiming in. I was repulsed.

I left there and never went back.

Now the AA folks would legitimately say something to the effect that my fatal uniqueness (or something like that) was the problem, not sweet cheeks Billy perfect's perfection. I think the more accurate assessment would be that it was my pride that slapped me on the ass and shuffled it out that door. But in the long run it doesn't matter.

When I returned to the US I tried again. The next time I decided it could not be an AA group because I didn't want to repeat another experience like the one I had in Playa. And I blamed it on the fact that they do not have God in their belief system; they have a "higher power" and by their own admission your own special "higher power" can be a doorknob if you want it to be. I needed a group with the real God. The actual one.

I was looking and hoping for another experience like the very first one I had with AA, like the one I had at that church in Phoenix where the drug addicts went. I was searching for a room full of broken and flawed people who are in the same room at the same time because they love God with every fiber of their being, and that love just spills out all over the place, swamping everyone and everything in the room. The same experience I had in the room with Ellel in Florida when those people poured out a kindness that was purely other-worldly and I knew I had to be part of it; the first time I ever experienced it in any situation.

It's the Holy Spirit filling people up and spilling over. And it is worth searching for. I'm here to tell you.

I found out about a ministry called Celebrate Recovery which is Christian, and otherwise similar to AA. So I went to the meeting and started attending it as well.

Let me just say this. God had a plan for my deliverance from alcohol, a plan that He would bring to pass after a few more years, and it did not include Celebrate Recovery.

All of this transpired between the years 1995 (or thereabouts) and 2009. It was in 2005 that in addition to having been struggling against alcohol for ten years already I had decided to rededicate my life to my faith in Christ at the conference in Wilmington, Delaware.

I had spent those years pursuing the four known methods for living life in sobriety, sometimes consecutively, sometimes simultaneously, and none of them worked. Neither in isolation nor all taken together.

There are three ideas, or principles, that always seem to come up in counseling contexts or in twelve-step programs and I believed them. I don't anymore. I see them as myths.

Today I am finally free and I do not see a counselor anymore, nor do I attend twelve-step meetings of any kind, I do not take any medications or Polynesian herb-tranquilizers, nor do I search for and live an alternative lifestyle for the purpose of staying sober (I do swim, run, and work out regularly but for no reason other than I enjoy it).

The first myth that I believed is the idea that staying away from alcohol and drugs (or anything else to which you can become addicted) is the same thing as being free of them.

My pastor Forrest has been an older brother in Christ who has sat with me many times over many hours. I once prayed in desperation, right about the same time that I went to the conference in Delaware, that I needed godly men in my life or there is no way I could make it. It was the same moment that I rededicated my life to Christ and I didn't know any of the men I now know in this ministry.

Up until that time the brother that carried me, the brother who along with my sister (his wife) introduced me to Christ, was my only true spiritual help. My brother-in-law Tim and I have been closest friends for thirty years. He mentored and taught me; he poured his life into mine and showed me who Jesus is. I cannot imagine where I would be but for the years of his patience and loving discipleship. But when I got back from Delaware I lived in Phoenix and he lived in west Texas and was pastor of a church there. I very rarely saw him and though I thought about him all the time, he was off doing God's work where he had been called, in different pastures.

I asked God to send me godly men that I could have in my daily walk to help me where I was, where I lived, or I was scared that rededicating my life to faith and to Christ would be no more than dedicating my life to sobriety had turned out to be.

And with Forrest, He opened the floodgates on that one, buddy.

I can't tell you the number of times that Forrest and I sat alone together and he heard my pleas about how desperately I wanted to be free of alcohol. He kept responding, "John you ARE free, but you're not claiming it." He told me that so many times. I finally described it to him like this…I told him it was like being in a jail cell with two broken legs. It didn't matter that the door was open; I couldn't walk to it to go out.

I believe that a person who really wants free of addiction doesn't want to stop doing what it is that they're addicted to; they want to stop *wanting* to do it. I didn't want to stop drinking; I wanted to stop *wanting* to drink.

And every person who suffers under addiction that I have ever met, who truly wants to be free would tell you the same thing.

The second myth that I believed is that addiction/alcoholism is an incurable disease.

This and the next myth are the most insidious, in my opinion.

I'm not exactly sure where this idea came from. I think it came out of the early days of AA or maybe the early days of the formation of psychology as a study related to human health. I know that psychology seems to have long been involved in a struggle to make itself as scientific as possible, so it can be taken seriously. Evidence of this is in the fact that counselors sometimes even still refer (erroneously in my opinion) to the people they serve as "patients."

Maybe it has held on because with a lot of mental/emotional disturbances, the effects they have on people and their behaviors often do mirror the effects of actual biological diseases of the brain (conditions legitimately labeled "diseases"). But just because counselors in the field of psychology sometimes help folks who are clinically bipolar as well as they help folks who are depressed...does the one being considered a disease force the conclusion that the other is one too?

I think the other reason why it has come to be considered a disease is that in the early days there was such a social stigma attached to it (alcoholism). It was considered the depth of depravity, an absolute moral failure. And as long as it was considered that, no one would come forward for treatment. So calling it a disease meant that having it was no more your fault than catching the flu or coming down with cancer.

But because it doesn't have an identifiable agent, like an infection, or a discernable biological pathology, like a cancer, it must also be incurable. The idea that alcoholism is not only a disease but an *incurable* disease just makes me angry.

It's all semantics. You can call alcoholism or addiction a disease, a moral failure, or a Jumbo Slider with a side of slaw if you want to. The real question is this: What is accomplished by this vernacular? The only thing I can think of is that it helps to soften society's perception of people who struggle against it, and so, more people do actually seek help because they feel safer to do so.

This is a huge benefit to the idea, to be sure. But at what cost? Thinking of it as an incurable disease may have made it less embarrassing for me to be honest about it, but I had to consider a life where I would never be free of it.

The source of society's empathy with me was the life-long sentence of what amounts to a curse.

And the third myth is this: You are powerless against it.

Since it is a disease, and there is no known cure other than to stop drinking, which is not really a cure because you are never NOT an alcoholic, and because you could not stop drinking/drugging on your own, you are therefore compelled to conclude that you are powerless against it, and always have been.

I cannot imagine a more perfect set-up for despair. And what is even more tragic is that not a shred of it is true. At least it has proven not to be in my case. And because of the nature of this particular vernacular one exception is sufficient to negate the entirety of the myth.

What if we compare it not to a disease but to a trap?

What if we *are* responsible for doing things that seemed harmless at the time but incrementally and gradually began to ensnare us, even though we were completely unaware of it at the time?

I know for a fact that I was in a trap (a prison cell, as I described it to Forrest) and that I could not get myself out. But that in no way meant that I was powerless against it. It only means that the power I needed was not power that I had.

Now you may be thinking that the twelve-step program people are saying the same thing. That is why they depend on the concept of a higher power. But there is a critical difference here. The higher power in the twelve-step program is counted on to keep you from drinking again. Not to free you. In the twelve–step programs not even the higher power can make you a "recovered" alcoholic. You are always just recover*ing*. The power is not one that heals you because the disease is incurable.

I knew that there was a time when I could have stopped drinking without any assistance from anyone else. But that time was long ago and I was no longer in that situation because I kept drinking and taking drugs when I could have otherwise stopped. It went on and on until I was completely trapped. This is not an original idea; it is at least twenty-five-hundred years old (Proverbs 5: 22).

Why did anyone ever go searching for a disease metaphor when the real one was sitting there in scripture all along?

By switching to this comparison a lot of things became clear to me. By changing the way I thought about this affliction and abandoning the myths (first recognizing them as such) that seem to be so very pervasive, everything else changed too.

Now I have to make sure I don't mislead you. Changing the metaphor is not what set me free. It isn't what made me free. I'll get to what did that later.

But the new way of thinking about it provides a new set of ideas in a way that is much more useful. And, I believe, actually true.

First, it explains that even if you are not able to get yourself out of the trap, with help, you can be freed from it. You are not powerless at all; it's just that your power is not sufficient.

Second, it helps you to realize that once you are free, you are actually free. You do not swap an addiction to some mood-altering substance for one to a daily meeting where you get to check in.

Now there are things to consider with this freedom. All life in freedom requires vigilance. If I choose to go back to the very thing that entrapped me to begin with I will most surely get trapped again. Being free from alcohol does not render it harmless. I am free to go swim Shark's Cove on Oahu in the wintertime when there is no one in the water there. And if I do I am likely to get bashed against the lava rocks and cut to ribbons, too. Just because it is unwise for me to swim there at that time, and yet I still want to, does not mean that I am bound to it. My freedom is exercised by my decision.

My freedom is evidenced by the very decision it affords.

I am free do drink again, yes. If I do I will most probably get caught up in it again, but I am absolutely free to do it. What I key here is that I am also free of the desire to do it. And no meetings, counseling sessions, drugs or lifestyle is keeping me free. I am simply free. And that is what I desperately wanted all those years. Not to stop drinking, to stop wanting to.

There is great satisfaction in exercising that freedom. Sometimes I think the feeling of getting drunk would be more enjoyable than the satisfaction I get by exercising my choice not to, but I think back to another piece of scripture, "As a dog returns to his vomit, so a fool returns to his folly" (Proverbs 26: 11). Were I to go back to it, I would just be a fool.

This form of freedom shed light on the first myth I identified above for me: Staying away from drugs, alcohol, and prostitution is the same thing as being free of them. There's a huge difference.

Seeing addiction as a trap, which is a biblical concept, changed everything too.

For me, it opened the door to a deeper, more beautiful truth. And in me it began to stir once again a leaning toward that which these principles in their insidious falsity can sometimes quietly if compassionately destroy.

8. About Hope

When I started this I had planned to go from talking about addiction to talking about *despair*. But this morning as I was waking up and knowing that I was going to sit down to write this, I knew I had changed my mind and was going to write about hope instead. But I thought, *you've been so influenced by what you used to think, you saw the down side so much, that you were going to talk about the wrong thing.*

I was going to talk about despair because it is something I most certainly have known. Anyone who ever spends as much as a moment thinking to themselves that they (and maybe everyone else) would be better off if they were dead knows despair. And just to put a cap on it, let's agree that despair in its simplest meaning is just the absence of hope. Funny then, how you can't really talk about hope *without* first talking about despair, even if you don't want it to be your focus.

So it (despair) would seem to be the complete and utter absence of hope.

People do not kill themselves because their situation is so terrible or because they hate themselves. They kill themselves because they are convinced that it won't change. People kill themselves because they are convinced that there is no other way out.

In the mental health community we have a collection of platitudes we sometimes use, "Suicide is a permanent solution to a temporary problem," being maybe the most popular. If you look at it, this statement suggests one major thing, that the problem is not permanent. Don't kill yourself because there really IS hope, even if you don't feel it.

But the problem is deeper than that. It isn't just that they don't feel it. For me (I should say) it wasn't just that I didn't feel it; it wasn't even that I didn't believe it. It was beyond that, more messed up.

When I went through my first bout of suicidal depression I was actually only thirteen years old. I remember it vividly. I was standing in my bedroom and I am not even sure why I was there, but I think I had taken an egg out of the refrigerator and hid it in my closet and had a light shining on it because I wanted to hatch myself a chicken. This is another of those memories of which I have no doubt, as ridiculous as it might sound.

I can even remember the rough texture of the candy-striped carpet my folks had put throughout the upstairs, because it was virtually indestructible and there were six of us kids at that time.

While I was standing there, all of the sudden a thought hit me. *I am never going to be okay; I am never going to be like the other guys because my dad is dead and he is never coming back. Nothing can change this. It is never going to change.*

It was such a stray thought, but it gripped me so deeply that it seemed as if every muscle went into spasm. My head hurt I tried so desperately to think it away, but I couldn't stop it. It was a slow realization at first but then it flooded every corner of my mind and I just Could. Not. Stop it.

It hurt like a burning board that fell against you and you couldn't knock it away. I cried out aloud not so much for the pain but just as much for the panic and desperation that there was nothing I could do, but I couldn't stand it. I wish I could explain it better.

That was the very first time that I ever remember experiencing the fear that I would go insane and that I would not be able to do anything about it. It was the first time I experienced that sick feeling in the pit of your stomach that comes on you when you really do fear that you will lose your mind.

One time many years later I was at my parents' home in the mountains outside of Taos, New Mexico. Pretty much the whole family had gathered there for Christmas and it was the first Christmas that they had owned the house. There were a lot of us then, many of my sisters had married and were already having children.

One of my nieces and I took the sleds and headed out to the valley because there was about four feet of snow on the ground and the sledding promised to be pretty good. I knew the valley pretty well because I had been visiting it for about eight years before my folks bought their home there. I was going to show my niece a really good hill I knew about.

We got to the top of the hill, which was actually a road that went down along the edge of the hill a distance of maybe a hundred yards or so. It was a fairly gentle slope, but long, so I knew it would be a good ride. I decided to go first.

As I sat on the sled and took off with a good push my first realization was that the hill was steeper than I had remembered. At only about twenty feet into it or so I was already going faster than I really wanted to go and started thinking I probably need to do something to slow down. But I hesitated.

Then I hit what was a long stretch of black ice (on the road) only thinly covered by a dusting of snow. My speed doubled in about ten feet. By then I realized that the only way I could slow down was to either stick my leg out and risk breaking it, or roll. But the ice was too hard, and I figured that if I rolled, my head would take the impact and I could be really seriously injured.

I looked ahead and then saw it. It was not going to be a ride I could just hang on and wait out, sending me coasting into the distance perhaps a lot further off than I wanted but eventually stopped. No. The road itself was going to bank right, and the lip of that bank would serve just like a ramp. At the speed I was going I knew for a fact that I would be launched, high, much higher than I would survive without injury. It was about forty feet ahead of me and there was nothing I could do. I was going to go up that ramp and into the sky and nothing was going to stop me.

For the remaining three seconds or so there was a sick feeling in my stomach and my arms felt like they had turned to wet noodles. I was going to get hurt, and hurt bad. I ended up nine days in the hospital with a compression fracture to my thoracic twelve vertebra, lucky not to be permanently paralyzed.

The reason I tell this story is to suggest that the pain you get in the pit of your stomach, the sickness you feel, is the same. It's the same pain you get when you come to the cold realization that you are helpless against desperation. Something really bad is going to happen; you are going to get hurt and maybe seriously, and there is not a thing you or anyone else can do about it. It is hopelessness.

Sometimes I think that I have grown up and old to be conditioned to it. You know, the way a horse might always speed up when it turns back in the direction of the barn. I have experienced it so many times that I respond to little episodes of it as though they are bigger than they are. Like being hypersensitive to it.

Maybe that is why I couldn't stand AA. Maybe I was just hypersensitive to the idea that if I really was permanently and incurably sick, then I would never be free. There would never be hope. Maybe some people could handle that, accept it, and move on. But I couldn't.

Maybe if same sex attraction is an identity, then it can never be changed. I would never be different, and I would never stop having to face those feelings and choose to ignore them. And what about the deeper identity? What about the identity that I was vile and detestable? How was that ever going to change, and how could I stand that hopelessness? Maybe I just couldn't stand any more of it because I had already had my fill. So even a little bit was too much.

I used to tell my close friends that I could live without anything, except hope. I could not live without hope. And maybe that was because I knew too well what it felt like to be without it.

And how do you have hope when you don't have any hope? How do you go and get it?

We hear about being "given hope." "It fills our heart with hope when we see..." this or that. "Oh, he is completely without hope." "We lost all hope..."

But I have been wrong about that too.

I think the answer is in the vernacular. Look at those statements. In fact, ask yourself about pretty much *all* the old adages we hear and use when it comes to hope. They're all couched in terms of hope being a *thing* you have or don't have, something you are given, or you lose. In fact, I used to pray for hope. I have even begged God to give me hope.

But what if hope is not something you *have*; it's just and only something you *do?*

The idea occurred to me when I read Isaiah 40:31, "But those who hope in the Lord will renew their strength, they will soar on wings like eagles, they will run and not grow weary, they will walk and not be faint."

I noticed that the verse does not say "But those who are given hope in the Lord." It clearly uses the term "hope" as a verb. When it talks about those who renew their strength and rise up on wings, it is not talking about those folks who are *having* hope; it is talking about those who are *doing* it.

This idea had a big impact on me.

All of a sudden the notion of hopelessness was not yet another condition like alcoholism over which I am told that I am powerless. If hope is something you *do*, then I can either do it myself, or I can learn to.

And as it happened, I did need to be taught.

The lesson came first in the words of a sermon. I wish I could remember who first wrote and delivered this sermon, but when I heard it a visiting preacher delivered it to our congregation and even HE hadn't written it. He was recanting it from another preacher he had heard it from. He called it "The Three Forms of the Will of God."

I researched it and a document came up in which Buddy Dano, Anderson Bible Church pastor, discusses the three types of the will of God. But reading the document I see that Pastor Dano identifies the Directive, the Permissive, and the Overruling will of God as the three types. But the sermon I heard was different. In it there were three types: the Direct, the Permissive and the Divine. And the descriptions were different.

So I wonder if maybe it is such a good word that God prefers it not to be attributable to any single person. I assume it is, though, and if you ever find out who wrote the original sermon please let me know so I can make sure and give the credit where the credit is due when I talk about it because I often do (it is really good stuff). Since I heard it and began to ponder it, a lot of other things became clear to me too. But it kind of goes like this...

There are three forms of the will of God: the direct, the permissive, and the divine. The first, the direct will of God, refers to events that God brings about specifically. These are things He does intentionally (not like He does anything unintentionally) and there is no mistake possible but that it is God doing it, and usually people being on the receiving end. The flood and rainbow, the destruction of Sodom and Gomorrah, the parting of the Red Sea, and the manna from heaven are all examples.

When I started thinking about this I noticed that it seems that there is no single example of anything God ever did that caused anyone pain that He didn't warn people about. There is no instance in which He purposefully did anything to bring harm to anyone that He did not also provide ample warning and give folks a chance to change something and avoid it. When it comes to Sodom and Gomorrah he even *negotiated* with Abraham who was trying to get Him to change His mind altogether.

When I thought about it, it occurred to me that if His only purpose had been to wipe people out because He had lost favor with them, He would have no reason to warn them. No, He must have had a different purpose.

And another interesting thing, no such destructive acts in retaliation are ever mentioned as historic events in the New Testament. Apart from John's dream on Patmos (Revelation), there is no mention of God's wrath resulting in death and destruction. Hmmm...isn't that interesting...

The second form of His will is referred to as His "permissive" will. This is the classic case of when bad things happen to good people. It springs from the argument that if God really is omnipotent, then bad things happen only because God either causes them or permits them. But human beings have argued for millennia about whether God could be considered benevolent in light of the fact that bad things really do happen, and they even happen to good people. So either God is not purely benevolent, or he is not omnipotent, because we do know that bad things do happen to good people.

Still, it is difficult to reconcile God's omnipotence and His benevolence when we conclude that bad things happen because God permits them. It's almost as if we would prefer thinking of Him as omnipotent to thinking of Him as benevolent in every situation. Some theologians throw in the idea of "Justice." They suggest that above all, God is "just" and so things may appear to be random bad things but they are really a form of divine justice.

I don't think this idea lasts very long when you see a child suffer or die needlessly. But there is a way of thinking that does seem to reconcile all of it into a single idea and that is a combination of the third form of will, and the thing that all three forms of His will share: His purpose.

The third form of His will is labeled the "divine" will. Simply put, this is His will that we are reconciled to Him because He loves us and wants to be in a relationship with us. He wants us to come to Him.

Now there are many examples of things He did and does that are related to the first two forms of His will. The Old Testament is littered with stories of things God did, miracles He performed to take care of the people of Israel, acts of punishment when the people incurred His anger, and a variety of other things that He specifically did to make Himself known to the people of the Old Testament.

And we are all aware of the many things God has allowed to happen, too numerous to count, that fall under the umbrella of His permissive will.

But the Christians would argue that there is only one thing that He ever did or ever will do that is an example of His divine will; He sent His son to be a sacrifice for us so that our sins could have atonement (He is a just God) and we can be reunited with Him. It was His act of love.

One time I was thinking about it and it occurred to me that as humans we sometimes get into really terrible arguments with someone we love, and the argument doesn't end well, and we both go away angry. I know there have been times when someone I care deeply about turns their back on me and in my heart I don't want to lash back at them; I want them to know how much I love them. I think to myself, *if only they knew how much I love them, they wouldn't turn their back on me.* It occurred to me that it is the same way with God.

When we turn our back on Him He feels the same way. So He did something that would prove to us that He loves us, maybe even thinking that if we knew how much He loves us we wouldn't turn our back on *Him*. So He did the most significant thing He has ever asked anyone to do: sacrifice their own son. That is what He asked Abraham to do.

It accomplished both; it paid for the offenses, which require atonement and sacrifice, and it proved to us how much He loves us. It is almost as if He is saying, *Now do you see how much I love you? Can you still turn away from me when you know this now?*

If you look at all of the events related to all three forms of His will they all have the same purpose. They are all designed to give us the opportunity to go back to God.

His crashing anger episodes in the Old Testament were a chance He was giving to the folks back then who were messing up in terrible ways to change the direction they were headed, to turn back to Him.

In our lives today when bad things happen we have a choice. We can turn away from Him in anger or we can turn toward Him with our pain. I believe He permits them because our turning toward Him is that precious to Him.

I have believed this since I first heard this sermon, which was about eight years ago. One night four years ago in late February 2007, I was asked to say a few words on the back patio of a home in Austin where my family and I were gathered with my brother's friends and family to honor him because he had died a few days before. All I could think to say to those people was that I always wondered if it was really possible to turn to God when you were angry and in pain, but in that moment I finally knew you could. Abe Lincoln once said, "I am given to remember all the many times I have been driven to my knees, mindful of the fact that I had nowhere else to go."

For me, I learned that not only can you go there, but there is no better place to be. There is no *other* place to be.

And as far as the divine will, the advent of Jesus, well, that was the ultimate act of reconciliation. It accomplished his divine will and gave us the ultimate opportunity to turn back to Him.

Now, what does all this have to do with hope? What does this have to do with what I said about learning that hope is not something you have but something you do? What does any of this have to do with the idea that *if* hope is not something you have but something you do, what would it matter if you do not know <u>how</u> to hope? How does this relate to knowing, learning to, or becoming able to hope, when before you simply couldn't do it?

It's really simple after all.

Everything points to the chance that this omniscient, omnipotent God we have loves us. Everything suggests that He knows *exactly* what has happened to us, what we have done, even who we are in the deepest reaches of our soul. And no matter what we think, no matter how much we despise ourselves or each other…no matter how much we hate Him, He loves us. He…loves us.

The way we hope is to remember that.

One day back in 2005 I learned that the organization Promise Keepers © was having its very first conference outside of the United States. My brother Tim, who has been such an incredible support to me over the many years I have known him, has long been a strong supporter of the organization and I know he had attended many of the conferences. This one was going to be held in Nassau, the Bahamas. I was making pretty good money at the time so I decided, as a gift to him, that I would send us both to the conference. We would be there for a week.

The hotel was beautiful and right on the water. It was near the basin where the cruise ships go to turn around and also near the old part of town. My joint pain was pretty bad at that time and I was walking on a cane.

One of the funny things about the trip was that the entire time we were there, we kept missing things. They had a whole week of events planned for the attendees, and we seemed to always be ten minutes late or we never even knew they were happening.

I think it was the very first afternoon we were there we were standing out on the balcony of our hotel room and we heard a lot of music heading toward us from off in the distance down the main boulevard near the beach where the hotel was situated. We stood on the balcony (on about the third floor) realizing that it was some kind of parade or something and waited for it to pass to see exactly what it was. By the time it was passing beneath us it became apparent that it was a parade for the participants in the Promise Keeper's conference. We could have been IN the parade, but we never knew about it.

On another occasion we went to the hotel lobby where the conference events were all taking place to see if there was some sort of schedule of events we could get so that we didn't miss any more of them. While we were there we learned that they offered a guided tour of the town of Nassau and we could go on it. It was to leave about thirty minutes later. In order to kill a little time we went looking around the lobby of the hotel. Tim noticed a piano and asked if I would play a little for him. I told him I'd be happy to.

I don't think I played for more than ten minutes or so, and we decided to head back to the lobby because the tour bus would most likely be leaving in about five to ten minutes. When we got back to the lobby – right across from where we were – we learned that the bus had already left, fifteen minutes earlier than we had thought.

But it was a great trip and we had a nice time exploring Nassau. One time in particular we went to the market in the old part of town near the cruise ship turn-around basin. I wanted to buy a cane. We encountered this old lady selling canes and she struck up a conversation with us. She sensed that Tim was a pastor, or maybe she guessed it with all the pastors in town for the conference, and she spoke openly to us about the love of God and the joy of life in Christ. It was really uplifting.

The actual conference itself occurred in a field down the street from the hotel where we were staying. It was a large field overlooking the bay, and they had set up a huge bandstand area with these giant speakers and folding chairs for about seven hundred people.

We met some local pastors and they explained that the Bahamas had invited Promise Keepers to come to Nassau to have the conference because the local churches believed that there was a crisis in the community of men there. They explained that there was an astonishing fifty percent of the young men of the island that were either in jail there or had left the islands. And they explained that men were just gone from the church, otherwise. They described what they thought of as a crisis in the men standing up to their responsibilities as husbands and fathers, too.

The local Bishop of the Anglican Church opened the conference by welcoming the men who had come to encourage the people of Nassau and possibly to spiritually reinvigorate the men of the Bahamas. Of the seven hundred or so chairs, only about two hundred had anyone in them.

One morning early, Tim and I walked down to the field and joined with some other men in the center of the field before the chairs had been unfolded and set up and prayed.

But something happened later that afternoon. Something that changed my life. I will never forget it, and there are not many days that go by that I don't thank God for it. I had asked God for a blessing on that trip, and I surely received one. Truly I did.

That afternoon we left the hotel and walked down to the field about an hour before the day's conference events were to start. We passed by the booths along the edge of the bandstand where the sound equipment and microphones and all were set up. We each bought a ball cap and wandered around a little. All seven hundred chairs were set up and we had our pick of any we wanted.

We made our way to the edge of the main corridor left open between groups of chairs and sat down, me on the end and Tim to my right. Just as we sat down another guy walked up and introduced himself to both of us and struck up a conversation. He turned out to be a pastor (from Dallas I think) and he and Tim had a lot to talk about. Because he was on the other side of Tim from me I couldn't really hear what they were saying, but I'm not a pastor anyway and they seemed to be talking about pastor things, so I very contentedly sat back to watch them set up the stage...the Caribbean Sea off in the background. I had my ball cap on my head, my legs draped over the chair in front of me, the sky was clear, sun bright, and the palm trees gently swayed with the ocean breezes coming up off the sea. It was beautiful.

I am finding it a little difficult to find the words to describe what happened next. I can't tell you when it started or how. But I felt so much at peace. I was a little boy again. I had this all-encompassing sense that everything was perfect; everything was absolutely perfect. Nothing was wrong, anywhere or with anyone. And it was like I was six years old again.

Everything had the same curiosity for me; nothing was dangerous or dirty; no one had ever done anything bad, and I had never done anything bad. In the distant background I heard Tim and the other guy talking on about church things, and I felt somehow safe because of that. I felt completely safe and cared for very well. Very well cared for. All was new and fresh, and good. I noticed myself swinging my feet like a six year old, unintentionally. I was pure; I was happy. I was innocent.

After a time, maybe five minutes, maybe fifteen, I don't know, my thoughts sort of lifted out of it, or above it, and I was aware that I was experiencing the innocence again, which changed it. I was noticing it rather than being *in* it. And then the thought came into my head. It was worded exactly, "This is how **I** see you."

I never asked God to comment on how I saw myself. I never questioned how I saw myself because I always saw myself the same way. I had completely forgotten what it was like to have the mind of a six year old. I had utterly forgotten the experience of innocence. I could not in the farthest reaches of my imagination come up with how God could possibly love me, because I could not remember a time when that was possible. My memory did not reach that far back.

So God put me there. He gave me a few minutes to experience what I lost when I was seven, and what I could no longer even imagine let alone remember, for the purpose of giving me the sense that He *could* love me, because He saw me differently than I saw myself. He gave me the ability to imagine how He saw me, so that I could imagine how He loves me. So that I could believe that He does.

Later that night there was a point at which all the men were invited to come forward (an altar call) to pray and be prayed over. At least a hundred men all huddled at the front of the stage, some standing, others kneeling, all praying. I had the sense that each and every man in that group carried with them some weighty burden that they had been carrying a long time, but I would have no idea what it was. I would have no idea what any of them were. I knew that each man there was both the twisted and corrupted version of what God had made, and the six-year-old boy. Each and every one of them were both, just like I was. And God loved us, because he never stopped seeing the child.

I left that field that night a different person.

You see, first He gave me the sermon that explained intellectually how to understand that God does love us in every situation. Then He gave me an experience to allow me to *feel* it.

We can't really know something if we only know the thoughts about it. Some things we have to feel, we have to sense on some deeper level, in some corridor of our soul. And when that something is the truth that God loves us desperately, deeply, without any reservation, with all abandon and absolute searching care…what else can matter? How can we do anything other than hope?

He had understood that I did not know how to, so He taught me.

Now that was five years before I actually got free of the alcohol and the self-hatred. The work He was bringing about in me had not been finished; it had just taken a big step forward.

At that time I started praying for deliverance from all of it. That is when I got serious. And interestingly, my joint pain got worse and worse. My drinking got worse and worse (as I already described), and my life was coursing for a lot more catastrophe, and I was completely unaware of it.

I believe that had I not known those moments in that field in the Bahamas, I never could have survived what was to happen in the years that followed.

I believe now that hope is not something you have, or something that is given to you, or something that you lose. Hope is the process of realizing that we have a God who loves us too much to leave us where we are. He loves us too much to spare us the burden of our own sins, or the consequences of our own actions. And when we suffer from the consequences of someone else's actions it is because He loves us too much to take our free will away from us – and that means the free will of those that hurt us. Because if we had no free will, as they say, of what good would our decision be to love Him in return?

But He also loves us enough to be waiting for us when we hurt. If we consider that He knows our tears because He sees them through His own, there is no label that can stick to us, no depth to which we can descend that can drown us. No cell can imprison us. And there is no trap from which we cannot escape.

And to know that <u>IS</u> to hope.

The stage was set; five years more and I would finally be brought to what would lead me to the healing I sought.

9. About Forgiveness

WHEN I WAS TELLING YOU ABOUT mental illnesses and emotional problems I stopped at the point where I said that there was something during all those years that I didn't know. All those years there was always a way out and I never saw it. There was always a door opened to me that led out of all the mess I had made and I never knew to go through it.

Forgiveness.

I know that you're probably thinking, *I bet he starts by saying that he was wrong about forgiveness.*

Well, it's true that I was wrong about it (of course) but what I planned to say was more that I never really thought about it at all. If someone asked me if I was a "forgiving" person I would most likely have said that of course I was, without giving it a second thought. Because I never gave forgiveness a first thought to begin with.

In Catholic school we were taught that Jesus suffered the agony of the cross so that we would be forgiven, but that didn't really make sense. I would look up at the statue of Jesus nailed to the cross, mostly naked, and bloody all over the place, and I'd think to myself, *he did THAT for ME? What an idiot.* (Can you imagine what the nuns would have done to me if they knew I was thinking that? Come Sunday Mass the good folks might see some real blood on that cross with me tacked up there in my tighty whiteys.)

It just never made any sense.

So I grew up like most of my friends not really having a grasp on forgiveness, how to do it, or when. And I remained completely ignorant as to why. Now I knew, just like the rest of us did, that we were *supposed* to forgive…but it fell in the same pile as being *supposed* to eat fish on Friday and *supposed* to genuflect as we filed into the pews and cross ourselves at the same time. Stuff that also made no sense.

But we did it because we knew we were supposed to and because we were sorry that Jesus got himself into such a mess trying to help us and he ended up looking like *that*.

By the time I was in high school I doubt the concept of forgiveness flashed across my mind even a single time. And into adulthood I only ever thought about it when I was watching a murder show and the family of the victim tearfully told the narrator of the documentary that they forgave the murderer. *Yeah,* I thought. *Sure you do.*

Like most people, I had come to believe that we were supposed to forgive folks, but that some things were so serious that we didn't really have to forgive them: the gravity exemption. I can forgive you for missing your driveway and accidentally driving on my grass, but leaving your garden hose running when you KNEW it would freeze last night, and turning MY driveway into an ice slick…well, that's just stupid. I can't forgive stupidity.

And there is a variation to that theme. It's when we hear about some crazy guy who shot and killed an innocent person while robbing a bank and then was convicted and sentenced to die. I could forgive him because I already knew he was going to be punished by being forced to just lie there and have folks very ceremoniously inject poison into him in front of a bunch of witnesses and then would end up spending eternity in the basement of hell on slow bake.

Yep, won't be shooting folks down there, you selfish S.O.B. I call it the paid back deduction. It's easy to forgive when you know the suffering they will endure for their crime at least approximates what they inflicted on others. Like the gravity exemption, which excuses us from the requirement to forgive because the crime is just too severe, the "paid back" deduction lowers the price of forgiveness (the difficulty) because they have already paid at least part of their share.

And I also think that I have always thought of forgiveness as a form of exchange.

I will give you my forgiveness as long as certain conditions are met:
1. You're sorry for what you did.
2. You paid back something…in some cases if you are so sorry that you just cannot contain your grief and it is obvious that you will live the rest of your life tormented by what you did…and that is acceptable payment if you suffer enough.

3. You have to fall all over yourself gushing gratitude for my forgiveness.

And this model of forgiveness seemed to satisfy me. You have to note that at this point I still had not come up with an understanding of what forgiveness actually IS; I just figured that it was a form of thinking that things were *even* now so we can move on and forget it. Forgiveness, for me, was the act of being willing to stop thinking about an injustice because the score had been settled.

But in the scale of seriousness, even if the score had been settled and things were even, sometimes you did not have to forget. You just had to move on. You were allowed to hold on to the thought that the S.O.B. was a jerk who would most likely spend eternity in the basement of hell on slow bake, but you *had* forgiven him for coating your driveway with ice. I call it the seriousness-scale adjustment. You had to forgive, but you were allowed to remember.

But in my latter years when I began to really try to live the faith I had been professing for some twenty-five years and I started taking the notion of forgiveness seriously, the whole model began to break down. It didn't take long before I realized that I couldn't do it. I wouldn't do it. So I dismissed it, but this time not because I never thought about it, but because it wasn't really possible.

Going back to the three conditions I mentioned earlier, what if they weren't sorry? What if they hadn't paid anything back and maybe didn't even know what they had done to me? What if they would NEVER fall all over themselves begging me to forgive them and grateful when I did? What if the offender cannot meet the conditions and earn my forgiveness? What if they're dead?

Forgiveness as an exchange is not always possible. Is there an impossibility exclusion?

But as a Christian I know that, in fact, He did do that for me, when I had not been sorry for what I had done, before I was even born, before I would someday hate him. He did that for everyone, even the person who thinks him an idiot.

So, no. No impossibility exclusion.

In fact, no gravity exemptions, paid-back deductions, or seriousness-scale adjustments either.

The more I read in scripture about forgiveness and the more I heard sermons and read the writings of great and godly men on the subject, the clearer it came to me that we are compelled to forgive, so much so that we are told that if we withhold forgiveness, it will be withheld from us. That is some pretty serious reality for someone like me who carried around with him a lifetime of things to be forgiven. No basement in hell would be deep enough for what I deserve.

So my first motivation to forgive came in the form of selfishness; I wanted to make sure MY slate was wiped clean. Looking back I realize that God used my own selfishness to lead me into something that would bless me beyond what I had any ability to predict, or even imagine. Had I known what He was going to do, my selfishness would have lit a fire under my butt so hot I'd be out there forgiving people I didn't even know for things they didn't even do.

But I didn't know. So I just sort of looked into it cautiously and reluctantly. In fact, the first time that Pastor Ron ordered me to say the words "I forgive..." I refused to do it. I refused even to say the words.

And besides, I did not know how. So I prayed that I was willing to forgive, if He would help me understand how.

Then I read Matthew 18:22 when Jesus answered the disciples that they were not to forgive seven times, but seventy-seven times. And I learned later that the number seventy-seven in Hebrew is a metaphor for an endless number. Then I learned that Jesus was saying that they had to forgive that many times in a single day.

I felt like the guy who shows up to lend someone a hammer and then gets asked to build the house.

For a period of time, I think about two months, every morning when I would spend some time in prayer I would think about someone I needed to forgive (I had made a list) and then I would close my eyes and think about forgiving them. I never got anywhere. Every time I closed my eyes, I just ended up thinking of people I needed to add to the list. I was getting nowhere.

I have to mention again that at that time – this was before I went to Mexico and met Pastor Ron and he prayed for me – I had no idea about the connection between forgiveness and healing. It never crossed my mind. It never occurred to me. I wasn't trying to forgive people because I thought it would heal me of anything. I had never heard that forgiveness heals. I mean, after all, Jesus said, "Your <u>faith</u> has healed you." So I had no reason to make the connection. I was trying to do it because I thought if I didn't, I would go to hell for everything I had done...and for no other reason.

Even when I went to Florida for the Ellel Deliverance retreat, I went begging God for healing from same sex attraction, alcoholism, and depression, and I never once gave forgiveness a thought. Not once. I went there convinced that my faith would heal me if it was strong enough. And when I wasn't healed I concluded that my faith had been too weak. I was grateful for the experience I had had, witnessing the love of God pour forth from those folks in the room that night. And that alone was worth it. I would have crawled on my hands and knees to Florida for that alone. But no healing. My faith just wasn't enough.

You know, I have said many times before that sometimes God puts thoughts in my head. I don't hear Him out loud or anything, but sometimes thoughts come to me that I am certain are not my own. They always have three characteristics: they're brief; they are never something I would think of myself – they always surprise and sometimes shock me – and they are always loving no matter how stern they may also be. I am reminded of Lily Tomlin's quote, it goes something like this, "When people talk to God it's called prayer. Why is it then that when God talks to people it's called schizophrenia?"

But I have already copped to being crazy, so I'll just move on ahead with this.

It has happened to me a number of times; a few of them I have already told you about. Now I have another.

One night a little over two years ago I woke up in the middle of the night. This was a few months before things in my life came to a pretty major crash: just before I lost my house to foreclosure, broke up with my girlfriend, had some friends ditch me, and damn nearly overdosed on Zanax and Chardonnay.

I woke up pretty suddenly from a dream. It wasn't a nightmare because it wasn't fear or panic that woke me up. But it was a dream filled with disappointment and discouragement. In the dream it was as if a list of subjects, or things that I had held dear to me – things that I thought I couldn't live without – were addressed with me one at a time. For each and every thing, and each and every person that was considered, I became aware that I was completely mistaken about them. All the things that I thought I had, that I thought I could count on, were not safe. This was before I started truly losing all of it. But it wasn't a warning. It was the beginning of loss, sort of.

Somewhere in the back of my head I must have known I was going to lose it all. I must have known that the people were going to turn their backs on me who did, and in the dream I just realized it in the front of my head.

At that time I had developed a strong interest in spiritual warfare and I made the mistake of thinking of everything in terms of oppression and the actions of the enemy.

I sat upright and prayed as I was crying. I said out loud, "Father, I can't do this anymore. I can't fight this fight. I'm losing this battle." Almost as if in the background I was also saying "Can't you SEE that? Why are you not stopping this?"

I remember putting my face in my hands and just letting myself cry about it. Then the thought came to me, *I'm not asking you to fight; I'm asking you to die.*

What!?

I jumped out of bed the way you do when you feel a giant roach crawling on you.

WHAT !!

My first thought was that Satan himself had entered my head and was now telling me to kill myself, right there, right then. God would <u>never</u> tell me He wanted me to die. God would just <u>never</u> tell me to do that. I was pacing in the room thinking there were demons everywhere. It was three o'clock in the morning; I couldn't call anyone, and there was nowhere I could go. So I went back over to what I call my prayer chair and started hunting in the bible. I wasn't sure what I was hunting for, but I figured that if it was God who put that thought in my head, He would explain it.

Within a minute I came across Colossians 3:2-3, "Set your minds on things above, not on earthly things. For you died, and your life is now hidden with Christ in God."

He was telling me that I was suffering not because of demons attacking me, not in some battle, but because of my own choices to hold onto what was not of Him. Somehow I knew He was about to take things away. I even had a sense of who and what they were going to be (although I never thought I would end up having to give up my piano – that one surprised me). I remember sort of surrendering to it. I then asked Him that if He had to do this, to please make it as painless as possible. But I knew then it was going to hurt anyway.

The reason I wanted to tell you this story as I am talking to you about forgiveness is because this is how I came to think of forgiveness, too. I started to understand what I think is the truth. Forgiveness is the process of letting God take something from you that He does not want you to have. And it helps me to remember that He loves me, so He would only take it from me because to keep it causes some other problem, of which I may not be aware.

I realized that for me to truly forgive, He had to be in the equation. In fact, He had to be in the center of it. So I tried something.

I went back to the process of taking each person on the list one at a time. With each person in my mind I went back to the scene where they did whatever it is that they had done to me, and I replayed the events. In my memory I started before the bad things happened, and before they started I imagined Jesus walking into the room, or place. Then when the person was doing what they did, Jesus just sort of tapped them on the shoulder. After they looked up at Him, He quietly asked, "What are you doing?"

The effect on me was amazing. Not at first; I had to practice it. But the more I did it the easier it became.

It introduced a whole new dynamic. I could imagine the surprise and even the FEAR that the person committing the offense against me would feel when they looked up and saw Jesus asking them that question.

"What are you doing to my child?"

But what is more surprising is that in my imagination, Jesus was not angry. He was hurt.

Something in the way Jesus asked them the question, or the way He stopped them and put his hand on their shoulder, not in judgment so much as in a strange kind of love for *both* of us, caused them to collapse. In my imagination I could see them completely fall apart. They were disassembled. But not as a result of punishment or some kind of retribution, condemnation to that basement, but because they then knew His love, too. And knowing His love for them destroyed them for what they were doing. Experiencing His love blew them away, and blew away the decision they had made to hurt me.

In that vision in my imagination, it was no longer mine. In the scenario as I imagined it, the offense was no longer against me.

I later learned that this is a known technique for bringing yourself to forgiveness and I can understand why. As a method, it helped me immensely. I have also heard criticism against it. People have called it a form of "guided imagery" and argue that it is misleading and ultimately a false process. They say that imagining that events happened differently does not change the way that they actually did happen.

But this is not on point. It is empty criticism.

I am not so easy to fool as to think that when I was molested it didn't happen as I remember, but that Jesus showed up. I am not so easily deluded as to think that all the times folks did things to me that seemed to be born of nothing other than a sick need to satisfy some twisted desire or some selfish disinterest in the wreckage they are causing, they didn't actually happen the way I remember. But Jesus walked into the room and they dissolved into a blob on the floor.

The point is that it enables us to see a dimension of the truth that our memories often don't accommodate. Sometimes we remember things so fully, or the feelings that we remember things with are themselves so strong that they let nothing else in.

Going through a process like this does not change events. It doesn't even change our memory of them. It adds to it a realization that God IS asking that question. It points our focus in a new direction, away from the offense, away from the offender, and on to the loving God who grieves the act more deeply than we can imagine, and a Messiah who gave His own life to pay for it. Because both of the people in that room are loved, no matter what happened there.

I am not saying it's easy; I am saying it's true.

But up until this point I've only been talking about when the person who needs to be forgiven is someone else. What happens when the person who needs to be forgiven is you, yourself? That is another story altogether. Changing the scene and imagining something new isn't so easy when you are the other guy in the room. Because you have to bear hearing the question directed at you this time. You don't get to be the one sitting off to the side being rescued.

As difficult as it might be to forgive someone else for doing something, it is much harder to forgive yourself. I envy the person who doesn't know that.

I think the only way out of the situation when you are the one who had done wrong, when you are the one who should be cast away, is to do yet another thing I always found so impossible to do: trust. It's all you can do.

For me it became a matter of nothing other than deciding whether or not I was going to trust. Here's what I mean.

My faith tells me that God loves me so much that He sent His Son to even the score, pay for my crimes, and wipe my rap sheet clean. He did that because He is a just God, because offenses have always required atonement in His law, and that because, as it says, vengeance is His. But so is forgiveness. He gets to choose.

All I have to do is believe that, have faith in it. What is before me to do is to approach the throne of grace and ask for His forgiveness, accepting the truth of Jesus' sacrifice on the cross. Because He has already chosen, and He chose to forgive. They say that we are to ask Jesus into our lives...but I think that is backwards. I think we are to ask permission to come into His. And we are already told that when we ask, the door will be open to us.

To forgive ourselves, we have to trust that.

The problem for me was that I have always hated myself so much, I have always been so deeply discouraged even to the point of being disgusted with myself and the things that I have done, that I was solidly convinced that no one, not even God, could forgive me.

But the fallacy in that is that it has always been about me. My belief that God cannot forgive me is actually a disguised belief that I cannot forgive myself. And that is true – I couldn't. But it doesn't happen to be true about God.

I once heard a sermon that basically described God as a God whose heart can be broken. Do you remember when we walked along the golf course across from the Norton House and I told you about this? You did not agree. I always love it when you do not agree, because I know you know your stuff, buddy. You always disagree in a way that means you have thought about it. You always have a reason to disagree.

Your reasoning went kind of along the lines like this (as I recall): if God is a God whose heart can be broken, that means He is vulnerable. That means we can hurt Him. How can an omnipotent God be vulnerable? How can we have the power to hurt an omnipotent God?

I am not sure but I suspect a reason. I am no bible scholar or theologian, but I think the answer has to do with His *choice*. I think He *chooses* vulnerability because He *prefers* to love us.

What I do know is found in Matthew 23:37. It reads "…how often I have longed to gather your children together, as a hen gathers together her chicks under her wings, but you were not willing."

I repeat, "How often I have <u>longed</u>…" A God who longs for us sounds vulnerable to me. To me, that describes a God who is pained for us, who loves us so much that separation from us creates a longing. That is a God who wants to forgive.

Now I say that cautiously because it carries with it two truths. One of them is comforting; the other not so comforting. The first truth is that His desire to forgive is based on HIS nature, not OURS. It is NOT the result of the fact that we *deserve* to be forgiven. It's based exclusively on the fact that He is a loving God. The second truth is that His willingness to forgive does not create an ability in us to continue to offend Him. He gets to choose. He's a loving God, yes. But He is no doormat.

But the bottom line is that when I get to feeling like there is no hope for me, I cannot be forgiven, so I should just give up, the thought always comes back to me, *It's not about you. It's about Him.* I am at a point where I can go in one of two directions: I can turn toward Him or away from Him. I can focus on my own feeling miserable and sorry for myself, or beat myself up over things I can't change…or I can turn toward Him and <u>trust</u> that He is who He says He is, and He did what He says He did. He forgave me.

And if He forgives me, who am I not to?

One other thing has helped me. I find myself often needing to say to Him that I am sorry I disappoint Him. But I don't need to ask Him to forgive me after I have confessed a specific sin anymore. I can mourn over the nature in me to naturally mess up and do things, or want to anyway. I can tell Him that I want to be more pleasing to Him and I am sorry that I am not. But that is not the same thing as to believe that He has refused to forgive me. Because everything suggests that He only ever refuses forgiveness when we do. And that, by the way, includes forgiveness for our self.

But there is another form of forgiveness that I had to learn, and it may be the hardest of them all for me. I had to forgive *Him*.

I think that when I sometimes find myself completely uninterested in prayer, when I notice that I really just want distance and don't want to be in contact with or connected to God, it's often because I am mad at Him. I'm like a child who pouts and refuses to come out of my room.

But sometimes I get into these funks that take that state of mind much, much deeper. Sometimes I am not like a child who pouts; I am like an adult who has been egregiously wronged, and that injustice is real. And my anger with God is not the passing whim of an immature child. It is far more serious than that.

My anger follows a line of reasoning that is very difficult to refute: If a person (or God) was in a position to prevent a crime, and had the ability to prevent it, and did nothing, then they share in the guilt of it.

Earlier on I talked about the sermon of the three forms of the will of God, the second one being the permissive will. I talked about how all three forms of the will of God have the same purpose, being to give us the option to turn toward God or to turn away from Him.

Well, in this case, what do you do when you are willing to turn toward God, but you're not turning to him with hurt or pain, you're turning toward Him with anger? Your anger really compels you to turn away from Him and want nothing more to ever do with Him. After all, He shares in the guilt of what happened to you. He is not safe. God Himself is not safe. What do you do in a situation like that?

For me there has been only one thing I have ever been able to do. Sometimes, I realized, all we can do is dig for a deeper level of honesty with God. I realized that He can handle my anger, but not my silence.

So I went to Him and told Him how angry I have been. I accused Him of failing me and told Him that I was furious about it. And as I was doing that my anger sort of melted. I'm not sure why. I wish I did know why so I could tell you, but I don't know.

I once saw a young girl yelling something at her father. I think it was at the rides on the island in Encanto Park but I'm not really sure. He was standing there patiently, and she sort of spun out her anger and ended up crying in his arms. It's kind of like that. Whatever it was she wanted, I didn't see him give her, so it wasn't that she moved in toward him because he had relented on something. She just did, because that is what children do, I guess.

It helps me to also remember that I don't ever have the full picture. I don't ever really know what all is going on, what is happening in other peoples' lives, and what God may be up to that doesn't involve me. After all as they say, "He's God and I'm not."

So again, it gets back to me trusting Him and heading back to those arms that I always find waiting for me no matter what. And there is nothing else like being there.

One last thing that occurred to me about forgiveness. Remember when I said that hearing that we are not only supposed to forgive for one sin or for seven, but for seventy-seven sins all in the same day? Remember when I mentioned that it felt like we are being asked to do way too much?

Well, something else occurred to me. Sometimes we have to forgive the same sin that many times. Forgiveness, it seems to me, is not a single event, sometimes even for the same sin. It isn't always for us the way it is for Him. When He forgives sin it is as far away from us as the east is from the west. I once heard someone talk about that metaphor. They pointed out that when you are traveling east, if you don't stop or turn around, you will always be traveling east. But if you travel north you will eventually be traveling south. The "east" could not possibly be further from the "west" because it is opposite of it. That scripture (Psalm 103:12) turns out to be more perfect than I ever realized. Scripture usually is.

Because we are not always capable of forgiving sin once and forgetting it forever (like He is) we have to be willing to forgive the same sin over and over again, no matter how many times it takes. We have to become willing to forgive, always. We have to become forgiving beings.

Forgiveness has to be more than an event; it has to become a lifestyle.

I've already mentioned how Ron led me through a forgiveness exercise and my joint pain went away. Then a year later Ron and Daniel prayed with me for four hours when I just couldn't stand my situation and all the drinking anymore, and in that four hours we went through the process of me forgiving everyone since I was five years old, myself, and even God. That was a Tuesday. On Friday the bike accident happened and I have been free from alcohol ever since that day.

I have come to know that among the things I have to do to remain healthy is to be vigilant. Not to keep myself from drinking or sleeping with prostitutes. I don't have the desire to do that anymore. The occasional thought, but not the desire.

I have to remain vigilant that I am always willing to forgive, even if not at first. I still find myself purposefully and concertedly forgiving someone for things that I have forgiven already ten, twenty times or more. I do that privately with God, because my nature is selfish and I hold on to things. They don't need to know it; only God and I have to deal with it. Because again, it's not about them; this one is about me.

And I really do not know exactly how forgiveness heals.

I am not sure if it is something like the idea that when we give up our anger and right to vengeance, when we hand that back to God, something else gets taken off of us at the same time. I don't know. Or maybe it is that when we truly forgive and we no longer bear the darkness, it opens us up to a deeper intimacy with God that is impossible otherwise. And whatever ails us, body or soul, cannot withstand such purity and melts away like ice in the warming sun.

I do know that it is a very important thing. I know that it is the important thing. His forgiveness healed my spirit and restored me to Him; my soul is to be healed by my own forgiveness, as surely as I sit here writing this.

I know that my story is a witness to the fact that a person's entire life can be lived in wreckage for lack of a single thing, forgiveness. That events can bring you to it (forgiveness) when you had no idea that's where you were headed, and that when you get there you will find healing despite all your expectations that you never would.

And that all of it, everything, boils down to one thing.

10. Grace

You know how I started this by telling you that there is something in the stories that I wanted you to know? Well, this is where I try to explain it.

My undergraduate degree, although a degree in Philosophy, is actually in the subject of the philosophy of theoretical mathematics, and logic. The structure of reason. So it shouldn't come as much of a surprise to you when I launch into a subject as divine and even elusive as this by talking about something as mundane as a theory of mathematics. Even one that gave birth to a whole new form of geometry.

After the summer of 2009 when the worst of the worst had happened, I went to Taos to spend the summer with family (as you know). I was recuperating in a way, convalescing. It's when I started working on this letter for you. And by fall I think I had leveled out quite a bit. The summer had been very good for me, and it was purely restorative to spend time high in the mountains with family. I got to know my mom better, and what a gift that has been. I have months of good memories now that I wouldn't have had otherwise.

I began to be able to see things differently.

When I came back to Phoenix for a visit after that, some friends from church with whom I visited were understandably concerned and wanted to know how I was doing. They wanted reassurance that the dangers were over and I would be okay. I told them that they were, and that I would. I told them something that seemed even strange to me as I said it. I said, "It's all grace. I can look back and see that it's all grace."

There is a mathematician that you may have heard of (somewhere among your readings of <u>Critique of Pure Reason</u> and other contemplate-your-navel related stuff) named Mandelbrot. You might recall that he created a structure that has been called the Mandelbrot Set, and from it the field of "Fractal Geometry" came onto the stage, which enables us to measure odd shapes and dimensions with much better accuracy. It is particularly useful in the development of maps and coastline measurements because they don't adhere to any regular dimensions, typically. But his work has spawned a lot of thought and ideas, in many different directions.

Even an art form. I think you may have seen the computer-generated video clips of paisleys swirling around at you, each new one blooming out of the edge of a larger one, first really small then really big and spawning a whole bunch of new little swirling paisleys of its own. The clips usually have the appearance as though you are "zooming in" or "zooming out" and that is how you see the new paisleys form.

I could be wrong, but I believe that one of the *philosophical* ideas that has come out of Mandelbrot's work has to do with the perception of order, or symmetry.

As you zoom in, the little paisleys do not look like they are ordered in any way; they look totally random. But then the more you zoom in, all of a sudden they look ordered and perfectly symmetrical. Then when you zoom out they look disordered until you zoom out some more and they look ordered and symmetrical again.

It leads you to the conclusion that everything in the set you are looking at actually IS ordered and symmetrical, but you can't tell that when you are at different levels of zooming in or out. That the *perception* of order and symmetry is dependent on the point of reference, but the truth of order and symmetry is that it is all there, all of the time.

A corollary can be found when we observe nature.

If you are looking at the tiniest components of a cell, it looks like they are all behaving randomly, with no order or relationship. The movements are all perfectly unpredictable because they follow no set patterns. But if you zoom out you see that, in fact, they form a cell. A perfectly describable structure.

Then you zoom out to a group of cells that seem to have no definition until you zoom out again and discover that they form a bone and a hand. The purpose of the bone and hand seem random until you see the whole body. And then you zoom out to masses of people behaving like ants, in a sort of collective disorder. Until you zoom out and see a planet, peacefully rotating in space in a perfectly predictable and orderly way. Then a solar system, then a galaxy, then a universe.

I probably didn't do a good job of describing this, and it may have its own name (this idea) that I don't know about, but I am hoping you get the idea because I need to use it to describe something else.

That good friend of mine I mentioned earlier, named Geoff, was telling me about how he used to teach folks in high school. I don't remember the course specifically but I think it probably had to do with literature. In this story specifically, he was teaching the class about grace. And he gave them a test.

I guess from what Geoff told me the test was particularly difficult and he designed it that way on purpose. When he collected all the tests he graded them in front of the students, and almost every one of them failed. Those that didn't had very low scores as well. No one did well.

He handed back all the tests and let everyone see their grades. There was quite a bit of dismay in the crowd because the test made up a high percentage of the course grade, and it would be difficult for any of them to pass the course itself, given their performance on that test. Weeping and gnashing of teeth.

Geoff had them pass their tests back up to him so he could record their grades, but as they were leaving he told them to come up and get their test. For each one, as he handed them back the test, he marked through their grade and gave them an "A."

Incredulous, they asked, "Is this some kind of joke?" And he answered that it wasn't. It was a demonstration of grace.

I have been thinking a lot about this story (It is a true story).

But I think that grace is actually much bigger.

It isn't the event of being given an "A" when you deserve an "F," even if you really did deserve an "F" and the teacher knows that and isn't giving you the better grade out of ignorance. That is the event that shows you grace, but it isn't grace itself. The real grace is in being in *that* classroom to begin with. You have to zoom out. Sometimes, being able to perceive grace means having to change the point of perspective.

The better part of grace is being able to see it in its earliest moment and most obscure dressing, when you realize that is isn't distant, and never was.

My niece once asked me on Facebook what my favorite word in any language is. I answered that it is the word "misericordias" in Spanish. It looks and even kind of sounds like it means "miseries" in English. But it means "mercies."

To bring it back to my stories and the things that transpired in my life that I've just told you about, there was never a point in time when anything happened to me or when I did any of the things that I would so deeply come to regret that did not lead to this moment sitting here writing this to you.

Had I never hated God as much as I did, I would never know how sweet it is to love Him now. And there was grace...even then.

I've also changed what I think about happiness. I don't believe that we are designed to pursue happiness, after all is said and done. And I don't think that God always heals, even though I know He always can. There are wounds I have that may never heal, at least not completely, and I know a lot of others who have wounds deeper and much more traumatic than mine. Some wounds just don't heal; that's really all there is to it.

But I don't think that in our life here on earth we are intended to be perfect, maybe not even whole, after the world has ripped into us.

We are intended to experience grace; to live in it and have it fill us and spill over to others around us. We fail, we make mistakes, we get hurt, and we hurt others and ourselves. We regret.

And we receive grace when we don't expect and least deserve it. Because it is always there, and always was.

I guess that's about it. One last thing. You know how I started this by mentioning about wounded dogs and werewolves, how they look and act alike, both dangerous and all. Well, there is one thing they don't have in common.

Werewolves don't exist. They're all wounded dogs.

ybic,

John